JOE FRANKLIN'S ENCYCLOPEDIA OF COMEDIANS

JOE FRANKLIN'S

ENCYCLOPEDIA
OF COMEDIANS

THE CITADEL PRESS   SECAUCUS, N.J.

First edition
Copyright © 1979 by Joe Franklin
All rights reserved

Published by Citadel Press
A division of Lyle Stuart Inc.
120 Enterprise Ave., Secaucus, N.J. 07094

Manufactured in the United States of America by
The Book Press, Brattleboro, Vt.

Designed by A. Christopher Simon

Library of Congress Cataloging in Publication Data

Franklin, Joe.
  Joe Franklin's Encyclopedia of comedians.

  1. Comedians—United States—Biography—
Dictionaries. I. Title. II. Title: Encyclopedia
of comedians.
PN2285.F7 791'.092'2 [B] 79-13952
ISBN 0-8065-0566-4

I acknowledge a debt
to the comedians who made America laugh
from the turn of the century
to the present.
Without them, of course,
there would be no book

J O E   F R A N K L I N

To the memory of
my childhood idol,

E D D I E   C A N T O R

Contents

Introduction

Comedy wears many faces, and as is the case in any compilation, there is the problem of selection. It is obviously impossible to cover everyone who has ever uttered a funny line; on the other hand, a work of this type should offer a cross-section wide enough to at least suggest the breadth and width of the subject. To strike the right balance between too much and too little is not easy.

But if you will accept a good try, this volume represents an effort to cover most of the bases of comedy. Naturally, the emphasis is on the comedian who delivers funny lines: someone who entertains you directly, without the benefit of a script placing him into an artificial situation or into a character. This is your typical standup comic, or monologist, in front of a microphone in a nightclub or on a variety show on TV. This definition covers Bob Hope but not, for example, The Fonz.

Already, there is room for argument. While it may be said that someone like Bob Hope entertains you purely by his funny lines, how about someone like Jack Benny, who was every bit as funny, but only because he played an entirely artificial character—stingy, vain, and mean—who was funny through our thorough knowledge of these attributes? What is intrinsically funny about lines like "Well!" or "I'm thirty-nine"? Clearly, the reason such lines could create long laughs was that they were uttered by the carefully created character known as "Jack Benny." We must stretch our definition to accommodate him.

While we are at it, then, let us also include comic characters created by actors in special situations. Every once in a

9

while, an actor given a certain role would do such an extraordinarily good job, limn the desired character with such a definite special touch, that a major comedy milestone was achieved. There are many examples of this. What we have done here is to use a few representative samples in cases where the character, as created by a single performer, took on the dimension of a real person, and often overshadowed the performer to such an extent that the character became predominant, the actor subordinate. Such a situation was rather commonplace in radio: everyone knew The Mad Russian, Senator Claghorn and Lum and Abner, but 99 percent of the listeners did not have the vaguest image of the actors whose voices had created them.

This is a familiar situation in more recent years. While Art Carney, for example, is not a standup comedian as such, the character of Norton that he created for *The Honeymooners* was such a masterful portrayal that it would be unfair to omit him simply to satisfy "the letter of the law."

And who remembers Lucille Ball or Carol Channing when they were mere all-purpose actresses, before they were firmly incarnated in their marvelously funny characters? Again, the guiding criterion was whether, in our admittedly subjective opinion, a definitive comic creation had taken place, above and beyond an actor reading someone else's funny lines. When our judgment was that this happened, we included the guilty party in our collection.

It should also be remembered that there are many more ways of creating comedy than firing off funny lines, in or out of character. Charlie Chaplin never told jokes, and without a doubt he is one of the funniest comedy artists the world has ever known. Since film brought us so many great comic moments, we have included a representative selection of the funny people of the silver screen. Again, the criterion was that they had to be active creators and originators of comedy, whether pure pantomime, as in the case of Buster Keaton, or a combination of funny business and funny lines, as in the case of Laurel and Hardy.

We have also been entertained by those who can sing in a specially funny way—such as Fanny Brice or Sophie Tucker—or play humorous music—such as Spike Jones or the Hoosier Hot Shots. So help us, it is even possible to dance funny (Ben Blue has managed it), sneeze funny (Billy Gilbert), or sound like a funny automobile (Mel Blanc).

Neither dare we forget the humorist, the genuine author of humor—provided, of course, that he performs his material at least some of the time. In this category, we find Robert Benchley, Will Rogers, and Bill Mauldin. Somewhat related to this is the raconteur, the teller of rambling anecdotes rather than one-liners—such as Myron Cohen.

Now it's beginning to be clear, we hope, that comedy is basically anything that's funny, and trying to refine the definition beyond this point would be not only foolish but also singularly unfunny. Should we say that Rube Goldberg was not funny with his inventions, merely because no one readily thinks of inventors when trying to define comedy? And what of Roger Price, who does funny doodles, or Anna Russell, who sings funny opera, and Theodore the funny ghoul?

How do you create comedy? No one really knows. Obviously, to be consistently funny over a long period requires a lot of hard work: Chaplin spent as much as four years shooting one film. On the other hand, some people seem to have a natural knack for making people laugh simply by their appearance—like Ed Wynn.

But great comedy can also spring up spontaneously, without the originator even being aware of it. Every time I see someone wear a Betty Boop shirt, I am reminded of Helen Kane. She was an obscure musical comedy starlet performing an entirely undistinguished song. True, she was a cute little flapper, but in the late 1920s these were a dime a dozen. Miss Kane sang the lyrics, in her little-girl style, and then for some reason—perhaps seeing that the music did not finish when she did—improvised a timid little afterthought: "Boop-boop-a-doop."

Who could have predicted what would happen next? All of a sudden, everyone was buying the record. A cartoon strip named *Betty Boop* appeared, and then an animated movie character of the same name. Even imitators appeared, such as Mae Questel, doing caricatures of Miss Kane; child actress Mitzi Green got a lot of mileage from it.

Incredibly, a half century later, that little one-shot characterization of an otherwise long forgotten starlet was still with us, being printed on posters, T-shirts, and jean patches. I'm sure Miss Kane could not have felt in her wildest dreams that she was boop-boop-a-dooping her way to immortality.

That's comedy for you.

JOE FRANKLIN

Eddie Anderson, Jack Benny's Rochester, strikes a pose.

In the Beginning There Was Laughter

Back in the mists of antiquity, a hairy primate one day decided to walk on his two hind legs instead of lumbering along on all fours. His attempt was at first so clumsy that his friends, looking at him, fell all over themselves making strange sounds like "ha-ha." Thereby they invented laughter and the human race.

To this day, laughter is the only characteristic that we share with no other animal, and the history of comedy is as old as our species. And so are most of the jokes. Hence, to attempt an accurate tracing of the development of humor is beyond the scope of not only this book but probably of any book.

Perhaps a rough beginning of a formalized approach to comedy can be found in the Greek civilization. The old Greeks differed from all other cultures of their time in that they had wondrously unruly, lusty, joyful gods—quite unlike the stern deities everyone else worshipped. They even invented a special god of all that was capricious and strange, calling him Pan—a word that also means "everything," and thus already a joke in itself.

Pan combines in one package virtually all the elements of humor. Basically a peasant's god, dwelling in fields and woods, he has an aura of earthiness about him; he is the god of sensuality and license, not to say licentiousness, and this is one of the oldest foundations of humor. It is the vulgarity that we detect in some of Shakespeare's puns and Swift's satire, and in the slapstick of early films.

Pan was physically grotesque, having goat's feet and horns, shaggy legs, and a propensity to jump and cavort in a startling way, which was apt to throw unprepared spectators into a state of uproar (in his honor called "panic"). Again, physical oddities have for a long time provided

13

an easy source of humor to the uncivilized savages, such as the kings and courtiers who kept dwarfs, hunchbacks, or otherwise unfortunates as court jesters. Freak shows were always popular in the preradio and pretelevision days in all rural areas, and every self-respecting circus had a sideshow of fat bearded ladies and two-headed monstrosities.

But Pan also had in him the elements of higher humor. In time, he became combined with, or merged into, another deity named Hermes, whose attributes were mercurial wit, nimble movement, and spiritual enlightenment. It may seem a paradox that the one god who was firmly rooted—or, shall we say, "rutted"—in the pursuit of earthbound pleasures should also aspire for the unattainable heights of spiritual uplift. Yet it is really quite fitting and proper for Pan to have these contradictory traits, since humor thrives on paradoxes and inconsistencies, and on the awareness that all our strivings are marred by our feet of clay. A bottomless wellspring of humor may be tapped by anyone exploring the vast difference between the lofty dignity we desire to attain and the ludicrous pratfalls we are prone to along the way.

The beginning of clowning on stage can also be traced to the Greeks. They had presentations consisting of a dialogue between a pretender or impostor and a straight man who used his cunning to expose the crook. The cunning man was called "*eirōn*," and the technique he used to draw out the villain was therefore called "irony." A third person was also on stage, explaining to the uninitiated what the whole thing was all about. He acted as a sort of referee and interlocutor (today an emcee), and since he did this in a humorous vein, he was the buffoon. Eventually, the role of the buffoon was enlarged and he became the predecessor of the later clown.

The Romans, being martially oriented, had little appreciation of comedy; apparently, the military mind and a sense of humor have been mutually exclusive since the beginning. (Please don't write me about the richness of GI humor or M*A*S*H: remember that soldiers laugh *at* the army, never WITH it.) Nevertheless, there is mention of a third-century (B.C.) clown named Maccus, who apparently succeeded in establishing a reputation for impertinence, wit, and irony in a theatrical setting.

He was such a trend-setter that he became a model for the impudent character who thereafter remained a feature of Italian theater. By the sixteenth century, this character was fully developed, complete with a set of other standard players in standard situations, and bearing the name of Pulcinella. The plays centering on the conflicts between him and the others were performed by itinerant companies that spread this tradition throughout Europe, and went by the name of *commedia dell'arte*.

Whether the keepers of this comedy tradition were conscious of the basic dichotomy in Pan is not known, but it is a fact that they were also struck by some of the inconsistencies in Pulcinella, and in time they split him in two. The lower, base half of him was incarnated in the harlequin, and later in the medieval court jester and Punch; the upper, spiritual portion came to be known as Pedrolino and later Pierrot, the white-faced patron of pantomime.

As the comedy tradition spread throughout medieval Europe, the split between the two facets of Pan became even more marked, and became combined with national traits of the major

14

countries to produce two totally different approaches to stage humor. In essence, the Romance race took the high road, the Anglo-Saxon race the low road.

Thus, in France, it was Pierrot who dominated comedy, with all the fragility, wistfulness, and expressive gestures of pantomime. The tradition was perhaps most strongly personified in Jean-Gaspard Debureau (1796–1846), who established standards of excellence that all French comedians since have tried to emulate, and to which unwittingly they owe a debt. There is a relatively straight line from Debureau to Paul Legrand, Louis Rouffe, Severin, Max Linder, Jean-Louis Barrault, and Marcel Marceau.

The English chose the cruder aspects of humor as their characteristic approach. Their models were the grotesque Falstaff of Shakespeare, the deformed jester of the Court, and the repulsively masked mummer. No wonder that the embodiment of Anglo-Saxon humor is Punch—who is hook-nosed, hunchbacked, and mean, and has a shrewish wife to boot. When pantomime did make it across the Channel, it was mostly relegated to a single annual appearance at Christmas.

The British equivalent of Debureau was Joseph Grimaldi (1779–1836), who made a specialty of portraying a character known as Robin Goodfellow. His origins are not too hard to spot since he was goat-footed, horned, and shaggy. He was also anything but a good fellow, as the following lines attributed to him will demonstrate:

Father heard the children scream,
So he threw them in the stream
Saying, as he drowned the third:
"Children should be seen, not heard."

This robust vein of humor was evident in Grimaldi's followers, such as Harry Payne (died 1895) and Don Leno (died 1904). Theirs was a comedy of exaggeration: faced with a cream pie, Debureau might have managed to smear a couple of fingers and then have an embarrassing time trying to lick them without being observed, while Grimaldi would simply thrust both hands in and try for laughs by getting himself as dirty as possible.

Meanwhile, what began as a minor trend in eighteenth-century England was gaining momentum as a secondary outlet for comedy, and eventually it gained major importance. At first it was called "penny gaff"—for a penny, customers could see brief pantomime bits and humorous sketches performed by otherwise unemployed actors. In 1837, in London's East End, a theater was opened especially for the presentaiton of such acts, to the accompaniment of music—thus, the music hall came into being. The acts were usually introduced by the comedian, continuing the Greek tradition of the funny emcee.

The music hall brought forth the flowering of British comedy, and virtually all the great theatrical personalities of the late nineteenth and early twentieth centuries were directly or indirectly involved with it. The music hall sent to America such distinguished graduates as Sir Harry Lauder, Gracie Fields, Stan Laurel, and Charlie Chaplin.

Comedy in America

American comedy is an amalgam of imported and indigenous strains. The circus clown and the stage comedian were brought over from the Old Country; but here they became transformed, because of the different geographical factors and political atmosphere. They also became seasoned by the addition of purely American elements, such as the minstrel show, traveling medicine shows, Mississippi riverboats, ragtime and jazz, and eventually vaudeville and the movies.

Comedy got off to a slow start in the United States, primarily because the majority of the original settlers had a puritanical aversion to any public display of gaiety and fun. In 1774, the Continental Congress actually decreed the closing of all places of public amusement.

Fortunately, insanity prevailed, and by 1787 the first indigenous comedy was written and performed on stage by Tom Wignell. It was named *The Contrast,* and featured the character of Jonathan the servant, who became a prototype for many similar comedy personae in the early days of the Union.

Wignell was followed by James H. Hackett, George H. Hill, Joshua Silsbee, Dan Marble, and John E. Owens. It was Owens who created another durable type, the shrewd Yankee farmer, whom he named Solon Shingle. Traces of him have survived through the years, and were still alive and kicking in Fred Allen's Titus Moody.

Early U.S. clowns included Dan Rice, a friend of Abraham Lincoln who was probably the source for most of the anecdotes for which Honest Abe was famous; George L. Fox, who performed in the traditional white Pierrot makeup and introduced burlesque; and Thomas D. Rice, who was the first important performer to appear in blackface, thus opening the door to minstrels.

Fox's burlesque was the original burlesque, essentially a caricature: he would perform a whole *Hamlet,* with the plot basically intact, but with his own embellishments—his Hamlet wore earmuffs for protection against the cold wind around the castle, was frightened at sight of the ghost, and so on. The degeneration of burlesque into a flesh show did not come until a century later.

Michael B. Leavitt took burlesque a step closer to the brink of vulgarity. A former child actor and later minstrel show manager, he took a troupe of female minstrels around the country, realized that good profits could be had by displaying feminine charms in the guise of entertainment, and by 1879 put into operation two burlesque booking routes, known as the Eastern and Western Wheels. Since burlesque customers relished fun of a rather coarse type, Leavitt was not too particular about the qualifications of the comics he hired, and for a long time burlesque was a good proving ground for low-grade comic talents who wanted to break through to the higher ranks of comedy—namely, vaudeville, musical comedy, and the Follies.

The minstrel show was a genuine innovation. The combination of African tribal customs brought by the slaves, the Christian tradition of church hymns that they subtly changed into spirituals, and their need to find an entertainment outlet since they were unable to attend white theaters had produced, among the Southern blacks, a new hybrid form of musical presentation that stressed banjo playing, joyous singing in stark contrast to the then prevalent church music, and plenty of spirit and movement. To this was later added ragtime and jazz, which were urban rather than rural, attesting to the Negro's further cultural and spiritual development, still apart from, but now coming closer to, the American mainstream. Minstrel troupes usually used comic interlocutors, and kept native humor alive during the period that the races were otherwise kept culturally apart.

Because of the enormous dimensions of America, as compared to the tightly knit and much traveled Europe, the vehicles through which all entertainment, including comedy, were spread were of paramount importance in the New World. Thus, the showboats plying the Mississippi River, the medicine shows that were the forerunners of commercials, and the various circuits and wheels that familiarized the whole country with the latest trends played a big role in the formation of the national character.

After the minstrels, burlesque, and snake oil purveyors, the maturing country's show business finally came into its own with the variety show, also known as "vaudeville." One of the pioneers of this form of entertainment was Tony Pastor, a walking compendium of all the elements that were jelling in his time. He had been a circus clown and tumbler, minstrel, burlesque comic and vocalist, and by 1860 made it to the Broadway stage. However, the rather rigid form of the Broadway stage comedy made him yearn for the greater freedom of the rural show. He decided to combine the best of two worlds, and in 1881 opened his own place, where entertainment was provided in an informal atmosphere, without the restrictions of a play format. Pastor called his programs "variety shows." They were so successful that imitators came on the scene with alacrity, and also with a new name: vaudeville.

The first to call variety "vaudeville" was Benjamin F. Keith, who started his career in a dime museum where they exhibited freaks and trained fleas. In 1883 he bought the Bijou Theater in Boston and presented shows that he called vaudeville. The name was supposed to have been derived from Val de Vire, the valley of the Vire River in France where they had a tradition of singing bawdy ballads, but this story may well be apocryphal. Whatever its origin, the word was first brought into general use by John W. Ransone, who assembled his own troupe and toured the country with it, himself playing a "Dutch" (German dialect) comic. This probably took place in the late 1870s and early 1880s. Keith simply borrowed the word, and it stuck.

Keith, later joined by Edward F. Albee, recognized the value of controlling a chain of theaters, thereby making out-of-town bookings automatic, rather than having to rely on individual theater managers in many towns. He acquired a string of theaters all over the country, and started the business of "circuits." An act booked by Keith anywhere would complete a circuit of all his theaters before being released—an invaluable boon to struggling actors, and a gold mine for the originator of this deceptively simple system.

Other circuits springing into existence in short order were run by Alexander Pantages, Gus Sun, Sullivan and Considine, and a number of smaller operators. The biggest Western circuit was named after the Orpheum Theater in San Francisco, which was the home base.

This practice of controlling the exhibiting end of the business survived in America, and was a major force in shaping the future film empires. In fact, the names of some of these individuals have carried over into the film era, such as in the Radio–Keith–Orpheum organization, better known as RKO.

Vaudeville, of course, was the major breeding ground for comedians. Legendary names like Eddie Foy, Frank Tinney, Frank Fay, Lew Dockstader, Joe

Cook, and hundreds of others came into national prominence, thanks to exposure on vaudeville circuits. They, in turn, paved the way for Al Jolson, Eddie Cantor, W. C. Fields, and others who came into prominence during the transition period, training in vaudeville but coming into their own in the new media of film, records, radio, and television.

On the distaff side, the first generation had comediennes like Lotta Crabtree, May Irwin, Eva Tanguay, Nora Bayes, and Marie Dressler. They, in turn, were succeeded by Fanny Brice, Sophie Tucker, Mae West, Irene Bordoni, and others made famous in the modern media.

Vaudeville also produced legendary teams. In the 1800s among the best known were Harrigan and Hart, McIntyre and Heath, and Collins and Harlan. The ones who followed them were lucky enough to be immortalized on film or in shellac, and they include Smith and Dale, Weber and Fields, and Clark and McCullough.

The high point of vaudeville was the great Broadway period of the revue, which combined the best of vaudeville, musical comedy, and legitimate theater in an opulent setting, enhanced by beautifully clad, gorgeous girls. Although the shows sometimes went on tour, they were almost exclusively a New York phenomenon, building on and enhancing Tony Pastor's pioneering concept.

The Broadway revue period started around the turn of the century with the presentations of Weber and Fields. Charles Dillingham stepped into the business in 1914 with shows presented at the New York Hippodrome. The Shubert brothers branched from regular theater into the revue business with their *Passing Shows,* given at the Winter Garden Theater regularly from 1912. Then there were

George White's Scandals, starting in 1919, *Greenwich Village Follies,* also starting that year, *Earl Carroll Vanities,* commencing in 1923, and a number of other miniseries and one-shots.

The king of Broadway during this period was Florenz Ziegfeld, whose *Follies* were considered the classiest of these spectacles. They ran from 1907 uninterruptedly until 1925, and later had a few spasmodic revivals. All of the revues demanded the very best comedy talent available, to hold its own with the glittering spectacle.

Where the early *Follies* and other revues were mostly talent oriented, the later editions became largely costume extravaganzas, and the quality of comedy began to deteriorate.

In 1912, there was a minor ripple in the world of comedy, and it was the first nail in the coffin of vaudeville. A man named Mack Sennett opened a studio in Hollywood under the Keystone banner and started hiring comic talent. At first, of course, all his comedians were experienced vaudeville hands, but in time film produced its own crop of talent, such as Harold Lloyd and Buster Keaton, who developed their craft entirely in the film medium.

Next came radio, which entered the scene in 1921. By the mid-1920s, radio also had its own stars, some from vaudeville, but others entirely the children of the airwaves. Finally, the competition of film and radio combined with the collapse of Wall Street, and by 1932 vaudeville, for all intents and purposes, was dead.

Probably the next most important breeding ground for young comedy talent was the nightclub and the resort. A special type of comedy school was the "Borscht Belt"—the chain of resort hotels in the Catskill Mountains that catered primarily to the Jewish trade from New York. Comedians Joey Adams, Danny Kaye, Red Buttons, Milton Berle, Jerry Lewis, Jan Murray, and many others started out as "social directors" or "toomlers" (from "tumult makers," or people capable of stirring up the guests) in these hotels, which came into their own in the 1930s, just as vaudeville as a potential place of employment was dying.

By the end of the 1930s, burlesque was also dying, but its place was slowly taken over by the nightclub. It became fashionable for nightclubs to feature comedians. At roughly the same time, bohemian quarters like Greenwich Village in New York and similar sections in other large cities began opening small intimate coffeehouses and niteries where budding comics could learn their trade in front of live audiences. To this day, these remain the best workshops for comedy talent.

Today, a young comedian wishing to break into show business usually starts out in local nightclubs, perhaps in a locally sponsored TV variety show. Then he tries to get booked in one of the bigger hotels and maybe he can hit some of the national TV talk shows that from time to time display new talents.

Finally, the pinnacle: bookings in Miami or Las Vegas, or featured spots on network comedy specials. Heaven? That is being hired for a successful situation comedy, or featured in a film by Mel Brooks or Woody Allen. The media change, but the Pan-demonium goes on.

JOE FRANKLIN'S ENCYCLOPEDIA OF COMEDIANS

ABBOTT and COSTELLO The callous con man/straight man could manipulate his short, chubby patsy into anything— even the belief that he was not actually present: "Are you in St. Louis?" "No." "Are you in Chicago?" "Of course not!" "Well, if you're not in St. Louis and you're not in Chicago, you must be somewhere else." "Ye-es." "Well then, if you're somewhere else, you're not *here!*" Bud Abbott and Lou Costello did not change their on-stage characters or even their jokes, but audiences through the decades, from vaudeville to radio to television to movies, did not tire of them. As comedians, they were inferior to Laurel and Hardy and The Marx Brothers, but for pure nonartistic hilarity they were second to none, and that is the explanation of their success. Not masters of filmic form, they put across some of

the zaniest moments ever captured on celluloid.

Louis Francis Cristillo (Lou Costello) was born in 1906, probably in Paterson, New Jersey, the locale for most of his comedy routines. As an athletic and considerably slimmer young man he ventured to Hollywood, where he worked his way up from lugging around fake buildings as a prop man, to jumping off them as a stunt man. He abandoned this role as one of Hollywood's early daredevils to explore the life of the vaudeville comedian. This delivered him to the man of his destiny.

William (Bud) Abbott was born in Asbury Park, New Jersey, in 1895. His mother was a wild horseback rider for the Ringling Brothers Circus, and as a youth he divided his time between lion taming and race-car driving. When a chain of

Abbott and Costello

theaters he built up failed, Abbott teamed up with Costello in 1930 for an engagement in a Brooklyn grindhouse.

Years of touring burlesque theaters landed the duo a regular spot on Kate Smith's radio program in 1938. The national hookup propelled them from burlesque to Broadway: they were in *Streets of Paris* in 1939. Abbott and Costello's first important film came in 1941: it was *Buck Privates,* in which they are involuntarily volunteered for the army—with sidesplitting consequences. But whatever the setting, whatever the medium, their unequal comic relationship remained constant.

In all, they made 38 films together, some poor, some good. They include *Hold That Ghost* (1941), *Who Done It?* (1942), the very funny *Abbott and Costello Meet Frankenstein* (1948), and follow-ups like *Abbott and Costello Meet Dr. Jekyll and Mr. Hyde* (1953).

Greatest of all their routines is their classic cornucopia of confusion, the "Who's on First?" bit. It opens with Abbott delineating the lineup for their baseball team. Who's on first base, What's on second, and I Don't Know's on third. But, as usual, Costello is bewildered by his partner's swift patter:

ABBOTT: I say Who's on first, What's on second, I Don't Know's on third . . .
COSTELLO: Yeah, do you know the fellow's name?
ABBOTT: Yes.
COSTELLO: Well, who's on first?
ABBOTT: Yes.
COSTELLO: I mean the guy playing first.
ABBOTT: Who.
COSTELLO: The fellow playing first.
ABBOTT: Who.
COSTELLO: The first baseman.
ABBOTT: *Who!*
COSTELLO: The guy playing first.
ABBOTT: Who is on first!

COSTELLO: Well, what are you asking *me* for?

In the end, the exasperated Costello gives up, shouting, "I don't give a damn!" Abbott counters, "He's our shortstop."

They had a reputedly amicable break-up in 1956, but two years later Abbott sued Costello, claiming his former partner had rooked him out of his share ($222,655) of the proceeds from their television series. Was it life's perfect irony—the sucker apparently conning the con man? But specific guilt or treachery is a matter of speculation. Suffice it to say that a memorable partnership ended on a sour note. Lou Costello died the next year (1959), Bud Abbott succumbed in 1974 after enjoying a nationwide television revival of their work.

GOODMAN ACE Goodman Ace was the brains and costar of *Easy Aces,* a radio program that was a national landmark of entertainment during the 1930s and 1940s. A brilliant writer of comedy, he has turned out scripts for Perry Como, Sid Caesar, Milton Berle, Danny Kaye, Tallulah Bankhead, and others.

When he was television's highest priced ($10,000 a week) writer, he was also its most vehement critic. "Television spends the greater part of its regular season mired in the muck of mediocrity. Everybody knows it. Why not say it? What's wrong? Not enough courage. Too much slavish imitation of the shows that get the ratings."

Ace was born in Kansas City, Missouri, on January 15, 1899. He began his broadcasting career in 1927. Unlike most comedy writers, then and now, he never used gag files, believing them to be a crutch. "If you get used to leaning on them," he said, "you begin losing your natural sense of humor. In the time it takes to look up an old joke and switch it around to fit Perry [Como], I can make up five new ones."

The *Easy Aces* radio show featured Ace and his wife Jane in the traditional smart husband–dumb wife formula. Jane was a mistress of malapropisms and whirlwind confusion, to the dismay of her husband. On one broadcast she burst into his office to announce, "Dear, I just did the most terrible thing I've ever done in all the years we've been married and ten months!" During the buildup she pleads for forgiveness: "I didn't do it of my own violation. I was talked into it, by somebody I should have *known* better. . . . And you know me when somebody talks me into something. When I get the urge to do it, I'm completely uninhabited." The crime alluded to? Ordering a mink coat.

Although being Jane's straight man afforded him little opportunity for jokes of his own, Ace is really a conversationalist of George S. Kaufman–Dorothy Parker caliber. Once a bettor on horse races, he remarked, "Now I have the horses right where they want me."

Jane and Goodman Ace

26

In the *Easy Aces* routines, Goodman would act as straight man, and Jane would deliver the puns:

JANE: I'd like to go on stage. You know, the thrill of getting behind the footnotes, the smell of the goosegrease, seeing my name up in tights. . . .
GOODMAN: But I don't want you to work, in the theater or anywhere.
JANE: But please! You're giving me an interior complex. And here I've desecrated my life to you, worked my head to the bone for you.

DON ADAMS After an apprenticeship as a nightclub monologist, Don Adams hit it big in television with his definitive portrayal of the nitwit agent in the spy spoof, *Get Smart,* which came on in 1965 and stayed for several seasons.

Adams smartly played the agent with a deadpan seriousness that served to underline the dumb-cluck capers. A favorite catch phrase was "Sorry about that, Chief," quite an understatement after perpetrating some ruinous idiocy. There was also a running gag of "Would you believe—" bits, such as:

DON ADAMS: It's no use threatening me, I've got the place surrounded by a dozen agents with machine guns.
HEAVY: I doubt that!
ADAMS: Well, would you believe a Girl Scout with a box of hard cookies?

The series made a star out of the comely Barbara Feldon, playing the patient, long-suffering coagent number 99, and of the late Edward Platt in the supporting role of Chief.

Don Adams, after the show's demise, went on to more club and casino appearances, another TV series *(Don Adams Screen Test,* in which old-time movie scenes were reenacted with one real actor and a contestant), and appearances on variety shows.

JOEY ADAMS With nearly twenty books, many of them big sellers, Joey Adams has proven himself no mere flash in the pen, and he donates the proceeds of his writings to charity. He is a rare specimen of the dying breed of the show business "trouper."

His books include *The Joey Adams Encyclopedia of Humor,* the *Joey Adams Joke Book,* and *You Could Die Laughing.* He has acted in several films, including *Ringside* (1949) and *Singing in the Dark* (1956), besides guesting on the big television talk/variety programs. His syndicated daily radio broadcast over WEVD featured such comedians as Bob Hope, Jack Benny, and George Jessel. His international nightclub tours are legend, and his innumerable acts of public philanthropy have won Adams honors from New York City's Mayor Beame, police forces, and the March of Dimes.

But it's hard to believe that Joey Adams is such a nice guy if you've ever been the target of his sarcastic retorts. Those who tangle with him face a barrage of masterly insults: "His idea of an exciting night is to turn up his electric blanket. . . . Stay with me, I want to be alone."

Born Joe Abramowitz on January 6, 1911, in Brooklyn, he developed his act in the Borscht Belt, and graduated that course to enter the big time. An affable, jolly, laugh-a-minute character, Joey has hosted many television programs, and participated in feats of one-upsmanship on several panel shows, such as *Make Me Laugh* (1958), where comedians were trying to top each other in ad lib quips.

27

Joey Adams

He has an inexhaustible supply of jokes on all subjects, as he has proven in his books.

A typical Joey Adams joke is a put-down. He will put down anything, including himself, or his hometown of Brooklyn:

Peter Minuit has just bought Manhattan Island. As he's getting ready to sign the check, he looks across the river and asks: "Say, isn't that Brooklyn over there?" "So what?" replies the Indian chief. "For twenty-four bucks, you expect the place to be perfect?"

When Cincinnati pitcher Waite Hoyt was injured in a ball game at Ebbets Field one day, all the papers in the country carried it under the headline: HOYT HURT. The only exception was *The Brooklyn Eagle,* which captioned it: HURT HOIT.

FRED ALLEN Fred Allen was radio at its best. He was the most caustic com-

mentator on the passing scene the medium ever knew—and radio's top-echelon executives were his pet peeve.

"A radio executive," Allen would say, "is a guy who comes into his office at nine and finds a molehill on his desk. He has until five P.M. to make it into a mountain."

He was well educated, and for years wrote all of his own material. Even when he finally had to hire writers, they did the guest-star routines and prepared raw materials for the boss, but Allen put his inimitable finishing touch on them.

He used similes and metaphors with an offhand ease and cleverness that few could equal. "As quiet as a Boy Scout

banging two pussywillows in a vacuum" is a fair example.

When he met a fellow performer with the unlikely name of Portland Hoffa, he tried to give her punchlines. When he found that her voice registered through microphones "like two slate pencils mating," he gave her nitwit lines to suit the image conjured up by her voice. He also married the girl.

His most cherished contribution to the folklore of radio was "Allen's Alley"—populated by a series of characters he regularly interviewed as a door-to-door opinion pollster. This segment became so popular that each character assumed the dimensions of a real person, and received mail as if he (or she) was an ethnic archetype that touched a responsive chord in the nation's collective conscience: the garrulous Irishman Ajax Cassidy, Jewish mama Mrs. Nussbaum, demagogic Southern senator Claghorn, and taciturn New Englander Titus Moody.

Moody was not only a type rarely portrayed in show business, but Allen's personal favorite, as he himself was a dyed-in-the-wool Down Easterner. Born John F. Sullivan in Boston on May 31, 1894, Allen started along the road to fame as "Freddy James, the world's worst juggler," traveling the vaudeville circuits.

As he added patter to his routines, he gained a reputation for being far more clever at juggling words, and the Shuberts offered him work as performer and writer for *The Passing Show of 1922.* He also contributed material to *Artists and Models, Lee Shubert's Vogues,* and *The Greenwich Village Follies.*

But he did not find his niche until the fall of 1932 when he broke into radio with a comedy program sponsored by a starch company, *The Linit Bath Club Review.*

Quickly, he developed the basic format that was to remain fairly uniform over the years, although the name of the program changed as the sponsors changed: *Best Foods Salad Bowl Show, Ipana and Sal Hepatica Hour of Smiles,* and *Bristol-Myers Town Hall Tonight.* There was a monologue in which he commented on a current topic, sketches with guests, and then Allen's Alley.

The program was broadcast live, with a studio audience, and ran into timing trouble whenever the audience laughed more than anticipated—which was often. If a program ran overtime, the network had to cut it off at the hour or half-hour, since the succeeding time slot had been sold to another sponsor.

Allen would retaliate against his favorite target:

PORTLAND: What does the network do with all the time it saves cutting off the ends of programs?
ALLEN: Well, there is a big executive here at the network. He is the vice president in charge of "Ah! Ah! You've run too long." He sits in a little glass closet with his mother-of-pearl gong. When your program runs overtime he thumps his gong with a marshmallow he has tied to the end of a xylophone stick. Bong! *You're off the air!* Then he marks down how much time he's saved.
PORTLAND: What does he do with all the time?
ALLEN: He adds it all up—ten seconds here, twenty seconds there—and when he has saved up enough seconds, minutes, and hours to make two weeks, the network lets the vice president use the two weeks of *your* time for *his* vacation!
PORTLAND: He's living on borrowed time.
ALLEN: And enjoying every minute of it.

Fred Allen appeared in a few films (such as *Love Thy Neighbor* [1940] and *We're Not Married* [1952]) and on early

TV (as emcee for *Judge for Yourself*), but with nothing like the success he enjoyed on radio. He died on St. Patrick's Day, 1956.

GRACIE ALLEN

see GEORGE BURNS *and* GRACIE ALLEN

STEVE ALLEN The mind of Steve Allen penetrates to the heart of what is funny—the anatomy of humor—with unmatched acumen. The word "versatility" is employed too frequently in show business writing, but the word was probably coined to *understate* Steve Allen's career. Not only a scholar of comedy and a comedian, he is an accomplished dramatic actor, director, singer, songwriter (he once composed 350 songs in one week on a bet with Frankie Laine), sculptor, orchestra leader, pianist, poet, political activist, critic, columnist, biographer, novelist, television personality, and man-about-causes.

Steven Valentine Patrick William Allen was born on December 26, 1921, into a family of vadeville comedians. A childhood of class-clowning his way through eighteen different schools was "frequently unhappy." He recalls having been "a pampered, sickly beanpole."

Allen worked as a disc jockey early in his show business career, and on radio he first explored the potentialities of the ad lib, of which he was to become a master. The vehicle was a late-night radio program in L.A., from 1948 to 1950, and Allen twisted the sayings of people selected from the studio audience into clever witticisms. This talent for spontaneous, off-the-cuff humor was enjoyed by the entire nation when Allen hosted NBC-TV's *Tonight Show* from 1948 to 1950. This innovative program set the style for all subsequent talk shows, including those of Jack Paar, Johnny Carson, Merv Griffin, David Frost, Dick Cavett, and Mike Douglas.

During Steve Allen's tenure at the helm of the *Tonight Show*, he introduced to television a host of other comedy talents who could never have gotten such instant nationwide exposure any other way. They include Louis Nye, Don Knotts, Tom Poston, Bill Dana, Pat Harrington, Gabe Dell of The Bowery Boys fame, and Dayton Allen (no relation).

Allen's credits include a starring role in *The Benny Goodman Story* (1956), among other films in which he appeared. Television-wise, he was a panelist on *What's My Line?* and emcee of *I've Got a Secret*. And he has written over a dozen published books. Like we said, the man is versatile.

WOODY ALLEN "The difference between sex and death is, with death you can do it alone and nobody's going to make fun of you," says Woody Allen. His is the comedy of sexual failure, incompetence, and feelings of inferiority and paranoia—and at least some of it is autobiographical. When he was breaking into small Greenwich Village nightclubs, his manager had to forcibly propel the cowering comic on stage.

Woody was born Allen Stewart Konigsberg on December 1, 1935, in Brooklyn. While studying at Brooklyn's Midwood High, he was already writing gags for newspaper columnists. Soon press agents were purchasing his material for prestigious clients, and Allen's material was finding its way into top TV programs, in the routines of Pat Boone and Sid Caesar, among others.

Steve Allen

Woody Allen

In an interview, Allen summarized one of his pet formulas: "Sex and food are always good for laughs." His sex jokes ("Bisexuality instantaneously doubles your chances for a date on Saturday night") number into the hundreds, and the visual things he does with food on film are not far behind. Thus, one thousand grilled cheese sandwiches are ordered by Mr. Mellish in *Bananas* (1971), pork chops are served in their cellophane wrappers in *Take the Money and Run,* and vegetables that grow larger than people are terrific impromptu weapons in *Sleeper* (1973).

In *Everything You Always Wanted to Know About Sex (But Were Afraid to Ask),* Gene Wilder is a doctor who has fallen in love with a sheep. In the same film Allen undergoes transformations to such things as a spider, a sperm cell, and a court jester who successfully slips a love potion to the queen, but whose progress is abruptly arrested by her chastity belt, and by the king catching him in the queen's embrace.

In *Sleeper* he disguised himself as, and impersonated, a futuristic robot butler in formal dress.

Among his other films are *What's New, Pussycat?* (1965), *Casino Royale* (1967), *What's Up Tiger Lily?* (1966), *Love and Death* (1975), and his first serious dramatic effort, *The Front* (1976). *Annie Hall* (1977) won critical acclaim and earned Allen an Academy Award. Allen usually takes care of all the basic artistic processes in his films, especially writing the screenplays.

His books (*Getting Even* and *Without Feathers*) contain some of the dour 1970s most refreshing wit. Among Allen's most inspired comic techniques is the juggling of the profound and the prosaic in a parodying understatement, with results that range from the ridiculous to the thought provoking. Witness these words of wisdom in the Random House book, *Without Feathers:* "Whosoever shall not fall by the sword or by famine, shall fall by pestilence, so why bother shaving?", and "The wicked at heart probably know something."

AMOS 'n' ANDY Thousands of comedians mined the vein of ethnic humor, but Amos 'n' Andy struck the mother lode. It was estimated that fully one third of the nation, coast to coast, dropped everything they were doing every week night from seven to seven-fifteen and listened to them during their peak years, the early 1930s.

This phenomenon was never equaled in any medium, although Milton Berle's Tuesday evening TV comedy hour in the late 1940s came close. It was done not by particularly brilliant lines or sparkling situations, but by creating characters so vivid and distinctive that the audience could easily visualize and love them.

Black historians and critics of limited vision have complained that the hustling Amos, the slow-witted Andy, and the scheming Kingfish were demeaning caricatures, stereotypes not reflecting reality. To say that is to disclose a lack of understanding of the American psyche: it was precisely this acceptance of the safely fictional blacks on radio that slowly prepared the ground for the acceptance of real blacks in the American cultural mainstream.

Amos 'n' Andy—as well as all the other characters on the beloved radio and later TV show—were the creation of two white employees of a Chicago firm that specialized in staging amateur theatricals.

Charles Correll (born February 3, 1890, in Peoria, Illinois) and Freeman Gosden (born May 5, 1899, in Richmond,

Amos (seated) and Andy

Virginia) met in Durham, North Carolina in 1919, sent there by their employer to stage a show for the Elks Club. They liked working together, and by 1925 worked out a routine that they tried out on a Chicago radio station.

Surprised at the favorable response, they had decided to ask for $10 a week and were flabbergasted to be offered $250 if they quit their jobs to remain on radio. At first their characters were called Sam 'n' Henry, but in 1928, when they switched to another station, they had to rename them, and Amos 'n' Andy were born over WMAQ, Chicago, on March 19, 1928. Sponsorship by a prominent company (Pepsodent) and network radio (NBC) followed starting on August 19, 1929.

The show lasted on radio until 1951, then switched to televison, using black actors for the first time (Alvin Childress as Amos, Spencer Williams as Andy, Tim Moore as Kingfish, and Johnny Lee as Calhoun). It was dropped after insistent harangues by rabid, self-appointed extremists in 1970, by which time it was being marketed as a syndicated program by CBS.

In 1930 Hollywood made *Check and Double Check,* using Gosden and Correll in blackface plus the Duke Ellington Orchestra, but with the studio's heavy-handed touch it was not a funny film.

Amos lost his long time partner when Charles Correl (Andy) died in 1972.

The radio show contributed a number of catch phrases: "I'se regusted," "Ain't dat sumpin'?", "'Splain it to me," and the durable "Holy mackerel!"

As the years went by, the mild-mannered Amos was usually relegated to a subordinate role, and the lion's share of the action went to the devious doings of Kingfish:

ANDY: Hey, who dat snorin'? Who dis in my bed wid me? Git them covers off yo' head. Hmm—ain't no head—it's feets—an' if I ain't wrong dey is de Kingfish's. Kingfish, whut yo' doin' in my bed?

KINGFISH: Er—Andy, whut is yo' doin' in my bed?

ANDY: Your bed? Kingfish, one of us is crazy an' I ain't sayin' which one it is, but it ain't me. Whut yo' doin' here in my room?

KINGFISH: Oh, yeah, now I 'member.

ANDY: 'Member what?

KINGFISH: Oh, Andy, me an' de Battle-ax done had a fight, an' to tell yo' de truth, she done throwed me out on my ear. 'Course all my frien's coaxin' me to stay wid' em. But I figgered dat yo' is my best friend an' if I went any other place to sleep yo' would be mad.

ANDY: Well, I don't git mad dat easy.

KINGFISH: Yo' door was unlocked so I done snook in. I hope it's okay if I stays here till this blows over.

ANDY: Well—

KINGFISH: Good, den it's settled. I knew you'd be overjoyed.

MOREY AMSTERDAM Many personalities witnessed the birth of television comedy, but Morey Amsterdam practically delivered the baby. He preceded Jerry Lester as the master of ceremonies on *Broadway Open House* back in 1950 when it was still locally televised in New York. He is a respected veteran of many comedy skills, including gag writing, acting and the art of being a superior monologist.

Amsterdam was born in Chicago on December 14, 1914. A precocious fourteen year old college student, he dropped out to drop into vaudeville. "TV," he aptly explains, "stands for tired vaudeville." Long before the advent of TV, as a radio star in his early twenties, Amsterdam was paid the supreme compliment when his older peers began bootlegging his best witticisms. In the radio days Morey was for years a featured regular on *Al Pearce and his Gang.*

One of Morey Amsterdam's most fondly remembered roles is the steady spot he enjoyed on the *Dick Van Dyke Show,* beginning in 1961. During the show's run, his creation of the word "yukapuck" offered a popular contribution to the current lexicography. His appearances on the *Ed Sullivan Show,* complete with his comic prop, a cello, made him one of America's "in" comedians for a time. By way of congratulations, his father, a cellist who had wanted his son to follow in his footsteps, wired Morey the message: "Your cello is out of tune."

Morey Amsterdam has one-liners on any subject under the sun. Since his private hobby is history, he likes them best if they relate to historic figures.

The battle of Bunker Hill wasn't on the level. Washington had a lot of trouble trying to throw a dollar across the Rappahannock River. At first he tried it with paper money.

My father was a liver and brain specialist: a butcher. That way he could make both ends meat.

Freud was the first psychiatrist to lie on the couch with a patient—that's how he invented socialized medicine.

In my youth I was a buffalo hunter. I collected nickels on a merry-go-round.

In 1898, Little Egypt danced at the Chicago World's Fair the first belly dance seen in America. That's how they started Navel Observatory Time.

She was so fat, she needed a bookmark to find her pearls among all her chins.

EDDIE ANDERSON

see ROCHESTER

Morey Amsterdam

FATTY ARBUCKLE This baby-faced, roly-poly clown had an overflowing reservoir of comic talent. In an obscure film, *The Cook* (1918), he spears two buns with forks and makes little dancers out of them—a routine that everyone credits to Charlie Chaplin as one of the most original bits in *The Gold Rush,* made in 1925.

In another of his shorts, *Backstage* (1919), the facade of a building falls in such a way that an upstairs window comes down precisely where a man is standing, sparing his life by an inch or two. Anyone for Buster Keaton's *Steamboat Bill, Jr.* (1928)?

Arbuckle accomplished something far more difficult: in a series with Buster Keaton, whom he taught the rudiments of film comedy, he makes Keaton *smile*—on camera!

And yet, Arbuckle, if he is remembered, at all, is usually recalled only for his tragic downfall. In 1921 a girl died at a party in his hotel suite. He was exonerated three times from any direct involvement with her death, yet the stigma finished him personally, and, beyond his own tragedy, the affair had a profound impact on American public morality, causing Hollywood to be branded as a sinful, wicked place, and putting its denizens under a pressure culminating in the appointment of a supercensor whose reign lasted three and a half decades.

Roscoe Arbuckle was born in 1887 in Smith Center, Kansas, and was on stage by the age of eight. In 1909 he became acquainted with the new industry of motion pictures when he joined the Selig Polyscope Company, one of the earliest film producers. He soon became disenchanted, leaving to join a touring vaudeville group as tenor and funnyman. There he met and married fellow trouper Minta Durfee—later, leading lady in most of his pictures.

In 1913 he joined Mack Sennett's Keystone, then in its second year of existence. From the first film (*The Gangsters,* made in April, 1913), he became an important figure around Keystone, performing, devising story lines (though nothing was written down at Keystone) and directing.

A year later, when an English newcomer named Charlie Chaplin joined up, Arbuckle came through when the new man needed a funny costume: he gave him his own pants, which were a few dozen sizes too big for him, and shoes. He also appeared in a number of shorts with Chaplin making him feel at home by playing pranks on him—Fatty was a notorious practical joker.

In 1917 Arbuckle formed his own producing unit, Comique Film Company, making two-reel shorts as director and star. As second lead, he took along Al St. John (a close relative), an acrobat who could cover up a lack of talent with agility and silly antics. Then Fate sent Buster Keaton, who came in as third banana but soon eclipsed not only St. John but his mentor too. Arbuckle not only recognized Keaton's talent, but was willing to let him get the lion's share of the laughs, even in Arbuckle vehicles.

In 1920 Arbuckle joined Famous Players/Lasky Productions (later, Paramount) to star in full-length features. He made nine, but only seven were released; by the time the last two were ready for release, the unfortunate episode had taken place in Arbuckle's hotel in San Francisco, and the distributor halted further showing of his films. (The withheld films, *Fast Freight* and *Leap Year,* scheduled for the fall of 1921, were first seen publicly at a Museum of Modern Art screening in 1976.)

Fatty Arbuckle (with Mabel Normand)

Suddenly, Arbuckle was poison. After months of hysterical houndings, though given a clean bill of health, he was still condemned by the public. In 1923 director James Cruze bravely gave him a walkon part in his film *Hollywood,* where Fatty poignantly plays the part of a hapless extra who cannot get a job. Even this was criticized—mostly by the Hearst press, which crucified him.

After that, Arbuckle could only work for friends who would let him direct— under an assumed name, so as not to arouse public indignation. He got work through none other than Mr. William Randolph Heart himself. Convinced by show business friends that his papers had been unfair to Arbuckle, Hearst consent- ed to let Fatty direct his film, *The Red Mill,* starring Hearst's protégé, Marion Davies—provided that Arbuckle use an- other name.

Buster Keaton suggested the name Will B. Good as an implied public apolo- gy; Arbuckle thought it would be too transparent, and chose William Goodrich—close, but not too close. He also directed, under this pseudonym, *Special Delivery* (also a 1927 release), with Eddie Cantor, who was never afraid to take up an unpopular cause.

Finally, Vitaphone let Arbuckle ap- pear in six sound shorts made in 1932 and 1933. It was too little and too late. On June 29, 1933, Arbuckle died of a heart attack.

EVE ARDEN Approaching spinsterhood made her a bit vinegary; she had her cap set for a biology teacher who was more interested in his frog McDougal than in amorous peccadillos; she had a cat named Minerva; and she was in charge of assort- ed dimwits as the English teacher of a typical subnormal high school, with the inimitable Gale Gordon at his stern best as the principal.

This was the format that made a top- rated radio star out of experienced actress-comedienne Eve Arden (born Eunice Quedens, April 30, 1912, in Mill Valley, California) in the show *Our Miss Brooks.* Her cynical comments on life were always devastatingly illusion- shattering, but delivered with a saving grace of humor: bitter Miss Brooks may have been, but she never lost her sense of proportion.

The acclaimed show was transferred virtually intact to TV and lasted a few seasons. Later, Miss Arden went on to other things, such as a similar wisecrack- ing role on a less well-written series, *The Mothers-in-Law.* She appeared in more than fifty films, starting with *Song of Love* (1929). Her most recent one is *The Strongest Man in the World* (1975). On Broadway, she started with *Very Warm for May* in 1939, did two more shows in rapid succession, and then returned to films. She did the road versions of two very popular hits, *Auntie Mame* (1958) and *Hello Dolly* (1967).

CLIFF ARQUETTE

STRAIGHT MAN: What do you hear from Mt. Idy, Charley?

CHARLEY WEAVER: Well, Mama writes she just bought 300 pounds of steel wool. She wants to knit a new stove.

Charley Weaver's letters from Mama were gems of rural humor that delighted millions of viewers of Jack Paar's *Tonight Show.* Later, he became a permanent fixture on *Hollywood Squares,* using more of the same.

Weaver was Cliff Arquette, born De- cember 28, 1905, in Toledo, Ohio. His

Cliff Arquette (with Cathy Rigby)

parents, of French–Irish extraction, were in vaudeville with an act called Arquette and Clark. When they retired, they opened a barbershop in Toledo.

Cliff organized a band of school kids to play at an amusement park when he was fourteen, and joined Henry Halstead's band at seventeen. He toured vaudeville with a partner under the name Cliff and Lolly, the Nuts of Harmony; later, adding another member, they named it Three Public Enemies. After disbanding the group in 1936, Cliff went on radio; even then, he liked corny "hick" humor, and one of his shows on radio was *The Oldtimer* (originally a guest character on *Fibber McGee and Molly*)—he was about thirty-two at the time.

In 1950 he switched to TV, and with partner Dave Willock started a show called *Dave 'n' Charley*. It lasted three years, and there he developed his Charley Weaver character to full bloom. He was married and divorced twice, and had one son. As a sideline, he was interested in American history, and in 1959 he opened a Civil War museum in Gettysburg, Pennsylvania. He died on September 23, 1974.

GEORGE K. ARTHUR and KARL DANE Theirs was goofball comedy, pure

and simple-minded. Since they capitalized on a physical disparity (Dane was tall and thin, Arthur small and silly), and since they were teamed up in the same year in which Laurel and Hardy clicked as a team, it may be inferred that they were meant to take advantage of a comedy trend. They made a dozen or so films in quick succession, from 1927 to 1932, but lacking the Laurel and Hardy imagination, they never quite caught on.

Karl Dane was born in Denmark on October 12, 1886. He was a very fine actor, having been around theatrical people all his life, and having served in many capacities on stage. He came to this country at the conclusion of World War I, making a name for himself in the movies, where his portrayal of a soldier in a key supporting role in *The Big Parade* (1925) was appreciated by audiences.

George K. Arthur, born in 1899, was a diminutive small-time comic when the two were teamed up in 1927. Karl Dane's career was cut short when he died on April 13, 1934.

AVON COMEDY FOUR

see SMITH *and* DALE

JIM BACKUS He's known to millions of kids as the voice of Mr. Magoo. However, the older generations may remember him as the creator of one of radio's most original characters, Hubert Updyke, the ultrarich snob on the *Alan Young Show:*

HUBERT UPDYKE: I have to get a new Cadillac.

ALAN YOUNG: But you just got one last week.

UPDYKE: I know, but the ashtrays are full already.

UPDYKE: I had to go to a hospital. I sprained my back trying to lift my wallet. Oh, yes, Alan, please remind me I have to get a new cigarette lighter.

YOUNG: Ronson?

UPDYKE: I don't care what his name is, the last one's was Smith, I think, but he didn't work out.

UPDYKE: For Christmas, Dad gave me two golf clubs.

YOUNG: Only two?

UPDYKE: Well, one has a swimming pool, and the other one has thirty-six holes and a hotel.

Born in Cleveland in 1913, Backus is a versatile actor who has done radio, films (starting with *One Last Fling,* 1949), and television—where his best remembered roles were those of husband to the slightly nutty Joan Davis in *I Married Joan,* which had a three-year run starting in 1952, and the wealthy stockbroker on *Gilligan's Island* (1964). He wrote his hilarious memoirs, *Only When I Laugh,* in 1965. His wife Henny (they're married since 1943) is an actress and writer.

Backus has played minor roles in dozens of memorable films, from *Pat and*

Jim Backus

Mike (1952), *Rebel Without a Cause* (1955), and *The Great Man* (1956) to *Boys' Night Out* (1962), *It's a Mad, Mad, Mad, Mad, World* (1963), and *Pete's Dragon* (1977).

BELLE BAKER One of the premier entertainers of the 1920s, character comedienne and song stylist Belle Baker was born in New York City in 1895. She commenced her career in vaudeville around 1909 and became one of the top attractions on the Keith-Albee circuit. In 1924 Miss Baker headlined the vaudeville bill at the Palace Theatre and remained one of its major drawing cards until the demise of vaudeville in the late 30s. Her renditions of *Little Man, You've Had A Busy Day, Dirty Hands, Dirty Face* and *My Yiddishe Mama* were guaranteed show stoppers.

Miss Baker made her Broadway musical comedy debut in *Vera Violetta* in 1911 and was starred by Ziegfeld in a Rodgers and Hart show, *Betsy*, in 1926. Very little of her talent has been preserved on film as she appeared in only two talkies, *The Song of Love* (1929) and *Atlantic City* (1944). During the peak of her career she recorded extensively and successfully for Victor and Brunswick.

Belle Baker died in Los Angeles on April 28, 1957.

PHIL BAKER Like several other comedians—notably Henny Youngman, Jack Benny, and Victor Borge—Phil started out with a music act, but gradually added humor—until in the end the instrument disappeared, or remained only as a prop. In his case, it was the accordion.

Born in Philadelphia in 1898, Phil Baker first learned how to play the piano. After moving to New York, Phil found his first job while in his teens, as office boy for film producer Carl Laemmle. But he soon tired of the dull routine and took a job playing piano in a movie house.

Before long, he had a music act with violinist Ed Janis, and obtained bookings in vaudeville. When Janis left the act, Phil found a violin player named Ben Bernie, who was soon to become a major band leader.

After an interruption in 1917–18, when he served in the navy during World War I, Phil returned to vaudeville, using as a sidekick at first a burlesque graduate known only as Jo-Jo, later veteran comedian Sid Silvers. The act, a kaleidoscope of bright jokes and breezy sketches, was booked in the prestigious *Ziegfeld Midnight Frolics* and the *Greenwich Village Follies*. For six years, Baker stayed with the Shuberts in several editions of *The Passing Shows* and other presentations.

He came into his own in radio. After an appearance on Rudy Vallee's *Fleishmann Hour,* he was offered his own show, which lasted from 1933 to 1940, and rivaled in popularity even such stalwarts as Jack Benny and Fibber McGee and Molly. His stooges were Bottle, a veddy British butler, and Beetle, the voice of his conscience, a typical radio gimmick.

In 1942 Phil took over as master of ceremonies for a new quiz show, *Take It or Leave It,* which left its imprint on the American scene by popularizing the term "$64 question." This was the highest prize a contestant could win. Despite the puniness of the prize compared to later counterparts, the show was immensely popular and remained on radio for more than ten years. (Among its later emcees were Garry Moore and, in 1950, Eddie Cantor.)

Phil Baker died in 1963 at the age of 65.

An example of his material:

BOTTLE: Sir, I have brought the circulars on resorts so that you can plan your vacation.

BAKER: Okay, let's see if we can find a nice spot. Let's see—The Hodge Podge Lodge. Get beautiful views of Yellowstone Park, the Statue of Liberty and Lake Michigan—only five cents a postcard.

BOTTLE: It says "Very low rats."

BAKER: That's "Very low rates." Ah, here's another. Termite in the Woods. Only twenty minutes from New York—by telephone. Elegant tables with chairs to match.

BOTTLE: What does it mean, "Lunch served twelve to two"?

BAKER: That's the odds you'll live. Maybe this one would be nice: Petty Coat Inn on the outskirts. Dance to the music of our three-piece orchestra. They are now learning another piece.

BOTTLE: Yes, that would be nice. It says "Fifty-foot pool, water supplied on request." And formal dress is required on all occasions. Guests must wear riding habits when pitching horseshoes.

LUCILLE BALL In 1951 a pretty but not very distinguished actress starred in a television comedy, *I Love Lucy,* supported by her Cuban husband Desi Arnaz, and a neighbor couple played by Vivian Vance and William Frawley. The response was so overwhelming that the obscure film contract player became the hottest single property on television. Her format became *the* format for situation comedy. The show ran for nine straight years, incorporating even Lucy's real pregnancy and the birth of her son into the story. When it finally went off the air in 1960 (the year that Lucy and Desi were divorced), it was immediately revived in syndication and became the most frequently rerun show in dozens of countries and on thousands of TV stations. It may run forever; its popularity does not seem to diminish with time.

Lucille Ball was born on August 6,

1911, in Jamestown, New York, and was hit by stage fever at the age of fifteen. She came to New York and worked as model and chorus girl, since drama school coaches rejected her as being too shy for the theater. In 1932 she was spotted on a cigarette ad by an MGM talent scout who was supplying the chorus line for Eddie Cantor's film *Roman Scandals.* Dance director Busby Berkeley wanted to use her in more films, and she started on a movie career in which she was often a dancer or featured actress but never quite the star. You might remember her from *Room Service* (1938), a Marx Brothers vehicle, in which she had no real chance to display her comic talent, and from *The Dark Corner* (1946), in which she plays a nameless, agreeable girl Friday to a private eye.

Even after Lucy's success on television, the movies, at last giving her star billing, still somehow could not make a stellar film attraction out of her—although she was teamed up with such top stars as Bob Hope in *The Facts of Life* (1960) and Henry Fonda and Van Johnson in *Yours, Mine and Ours* (1968). She was often funny, but not quite up to the inspired zaniness that made her a perfect TV sitcom personality.

KAYE BALLARD She is a daffy pantomimist, one of the few women who appeared in burlesque as comedy partner rather than stripper, and a girl with a definite bent toward the ludicrous—who else would feature, for her "big" number, a song called "I Just Kissed My Nose Goodnight"?

But Catherine Gloria Balotta (born in Cleveland on November 20, 1926) is also an ardent student of comedy: she started out doing an impression of the durable Sophie Tucker, was instrumental in cre-

Lucille Ball

47

ating, for the prestigious Blue Angel nightclub in New York, a *Tribute to Fanny Brice,* and served an apprenticeship with the zaniest band in the business, Spike Jones and His City Slickers.

She made her TV debut in 1952 on Mel Torme's show, was a weekly guest with Perry Como for nearly two years, and visited Johnny Carson and Merv Griffin at least fifty times each. She was on Broadway several times and was featured in the touring company of the 1957 *Ziegfeld Follies,* where she replaced Beatrice Lillie; she was the highlight of an off-Broadway show, *The Decline and Fall of the Entire World as Seen Through the Eyes of Cole Porter, Revisited* (she was the only one who could remember the title).

BELLE BARTH One of the first entertainers to tell X-rated jokes and "blue" stories in nightclubs and plush hotels, Belle Salzman was born in New York City on April 27, 1911. She quit highschool before graduation to make her vaudeville debut—and her career, which continued until her death, was under way.

Belle Barth's early material consisted primarily of impressions of such stars as Al Jolson, Harry Richman, Sophie Tucker and George Jessel. She later included devastatingly funny take-offs on such strippers as Gypsy Rose Lee and Lili St. Cyr. From there, it was a brief journey to the nightclub circuit, where her bawdy tales and ribald songs met with an enthusiastic reception. She became well known in Miami and Las Vegas—"thirteen years on the beach without an arrest," she boasted—and put some of her routines on best selling recordings.

Belle Barth married three times, using the last name of her first husband as her stage name.

She died on February 14, 1971.

Here is a sample of her material:

When the world war broke out, I joined the WACS. Right away, they sent me to the worst spot, Guadalcanal. The doctor who gave me the physical took one look and said, "What a canal." So then I figured, what the hell, at least I'll see a lot of action, and I felt as happy as the girl who got raped on Essex Street and thought it was Grand. But I had my disappointments in the service; I discovered that a 21-inch Admiral was only a television set.

A priest and a rabbi were enjoying the fights at Madison Square Garden. One of the fighters crossed himself before the opening gong sounded. "What does that mean?" the rabbi asked. "Not a damn thing if he can't fight," replied the Father.

ORSON BEAN An erudite and versatile man, Orson Bean is equally adept at standup comedy, acting in theater and films, and taking up various causes: he has been alternately fascinated with political extremes, diet fads, Far East philosophy, environmental issues, social problems, and ESP.

Born Dallas F. Burrows on July 22, 1928, in Vermont, he started to get attracted to show business by sending in for a magician's kit and training himself in sleight-of-hand skills. At college, he became a campus humorist, then took his magic-cum-humor act to nightclubs. He adopted the name Orson in tribute to a fellow magician he admired, Orson Welles, but he wanted to follow that ponderous first name with something silly, to offset its pomposity—hence, Bean.

He first attracted attention in 1952 at the Blue Angel in New York, with his impressions of Ivy League types, and with his fresh New England insights: "My Vermont grandfather hated Southerners; he told me to stay away from Hartford."

His nightclub act led to an offer to appear in two productions in 1953, *John Murray Anderson's Almanac* and *Man of Distinction,* and to appearances on television variety shows, including the prestigious *Tonight Show.* In 1956 he married Jacqueline de Sibour, an actress known professionaly as Rain Winslow. In 1962 they divorced, and he married Carolyn Maxwell in 1965.

Onstage, here's Orson:

An old lady is dying and calls her husband to her bedside. "Walter, promise me that when I go, you'll find some other woman."

"Okay, dear, I'll try."

"You can give her all my jewelry . . ."

"Okay, dear."

". . . and all my dresses."

"I can't do that, dear, she's size 9 and you're size 14!"

A lady comes to the cemetery with some flowers. A new gateman stops her and asks which grave she's going to see.

"That's all right, I always come here, I know where it is."

"Sorry, Madam, I'm new and I don't know you yet, but I must ask. You know, we've had vandals here."

"Well, if you must know, it's my dear husband."

"What's the name?"

"Rappaport."

"Well, I'm sorry, but there's no such man here."

"What do you mean? Look again!"

"I did. There's only one Rappaport, and it can't be your husband. Here, see for yourself: Rose Rappaport."

"That's right. Everything's in my name!"

ROBERT BENCHLEY Robert Benchley turned to acting in films after a long and distinguished career as a writer. He turned in brilliant performances as a caricaturist of the upper middle class.

He was born on September 15, 1889, in Worcester, Massachusetts. Despite poor grades, he managed to graduate from Harvard in 1912. From there he went through a number of odd jobs in newspaper writing, advertising, and public relations. During 1919 and 1920 Benchley was the managing editor of *Vanity Fair,* which at the time counted among its editors and contributors Dorothy Parker, Robert E. Sherwood, Stephen Leacock, and Frank Moore Colby. After several other jobs, Benchley became the drama editor of *The New Yorker* in 1929, and remained there through 1940.

In 1921 the first of his fifteen humorous books was published. Through his books and magazine pieces, Benchley became one of America's favorite humorists.

Benchley deflated American history and heroes, among other things, in his writings. After Paul Revere's ride, Benchley related, a man "seemed pretty sore and said that some crazy coot had just ridden by and knocked at his door and yelled something that he couldn't understand and that if he caught him he'd break his back. . . . A lot of people . . . were up and standing in front of their houses, cursing like the one I had just seen. . . . 'Some god-damn drunk,' said one . . . and they all went back to bed" (From *Paul Revere's Ride).*

Benchley's theatrical and film career was unpremeditated. In 1923 Irving Berlin heard him at a party giving a monologue, which has since become a classic, "The Treasurer's Report," later made into a film short. He invited the humorist to join the cast of his *Music Box Review* and recite it there. By 1927, it became one of the first shorts of the all-talking era; it was made at Fox within days of the premiere of *The Jazz Singer.*

The film short became Benchley's favorite vehicle. It allows him to do what he does best: deliver mock lectures on various subjects and foibles of mankind. Benchley always appears at either a desk or a lectern and seems serious about his subject, using a somber-faced delivery. It takes careful listening to discern the many jibes and satirical barbs hidden in the verbiage; they are invariably subtle, based on accurate observations of human behavior in its more absurd aspects. For this reason, he has always enjoyed a vogue among intellectuals as a connoisseur's humorist. His dozens of film shorts include a number of "how tos." Like *How to Break 90 at Croquet* (1935), *How to Train a Dog* (1936), *How to Raise a Baby* (1938), and *How to Take a Vacation* (1941). He won an Academy Award for the best comedy short of 1935, *How to Sleep.*

He always portrays a docile middle-class gentleman for whom everyday chores become a series of embarrassments and frustrations (*How to Start the Day,* 1937), or who lectures on an offbeat subject that allows him to make observations seemingly about something else but really aimed at society (*The Courtship of the Newt,* 1938). His humor is never bitter or sarcastic. Like Benchley himself, it is urbane, polite, gentle, and self-deprecatory.

Robert Benchley suffered a cerebral hemorrhage at the age of fifty-six and died on November 21, 1945.

JACK BENNY Everyone in show business agreed—most of all Jack himself—that without a script prepared by his writers, Jack Benny was not very funny. He was better at laughing at other people's jokes—like those of his best friend, George Burns—than at producing his own.

Robert Benchley

51

How, then, could this man be one of the acknowledged giants of comedy, the most celebrated comedian ever to appear on radio, and the generator of the longest spontaneous laughter by any studio audience?

It was done by trial and error. Not naturally gifted as a laugh-getter, Benny had to work at it harder than most. But that forced him to become an innovator, and therein lies his secret. He found, by trying every possible approach, that he could get bigger laughs by allowing himself to be ridiculed than by ridiculing his stooges, as other comedians did; therefore, he became possibly the first to use successfully the comedy of self-depreciation.

Benny had no preconceived notions about the character that he should portray so that it could be ridiculed, except of course that it would have to be a preposterous figure. So he and his writers tried everything, and found that they were getting big laughs out of stinginess: that they could get mileage out of a running feud with another comedian (Fred Allen); and that they were winning with references to Benny's age (he insisted he was "thirty-nine" for decades), his toupees, his bluer-than-blue eyes, and so on.

Whatever worked was left in, everything else was abandoned. By this simple stratagem, Jack Benny created a genuine comedy character that became far bigger than the real man inside; instantly recognized by millions of radio listeners, this character could get a whopping two-minute laugh with the least possible exertion. When a holdup man said to him, "Your money or your life," he said nothing at all for the next two minutes, and the audience went into paroxysms of laughter, realizing that for *their* Jack Benny, it was an impossible choice.

The real Jack Benny was Benny Kubelsky, born in Waukegan, Illinois, on February 14, 1894. He took violin lessons as a child, and became quite a proficient violinist. He gave music recitals but they did not earn him much recognition. When he added lines to his fiddling, he went into vaudeville and tasted the sweet reward of laughter.

In the early 1930s, after a brief career in Broadway musical shows, he tried a few sound shorts, and then, in 1932, took to radio like a duck to water. In 1935 his new brand of comedy made him the top-rated radio personality, and he stayed on top for as long as radio lasted—and repeated his success on television for as long as he lived.

Among his contributions to comedy was the systematic development, over the years, of supporting comedians who became every bit as popular as the master himself: including his real wife, the long-suffering Mary Livingston; bandleader Phil Harris, ridiculed for his fondness for booze and broads; addlepated singer Dennis Day, whose job was to exasperate Benny; the world's foremost goofball larynx, belonging to Mel Blanc, who could imitate any sound produced by man or beast and who created the wheezy Maxwell car Benny allegedly used (being a methodical man, Benny *owned* such a car, but it could never sound half as funny as Mel Blanc); Eddie Anderson playing Rochester, the most impudent valet/chauffeur in the business; and a gallery of lesser lights.

Having studied his craft so intensely, Benny developed a sense of timing that approached perfection; in television he could get laughs out of virtually nothing, by folding his arms and saying, after a brief pause, "Well!" It is instructive to watch him in films, nearly all of which were resounding flops, written by Holly-

Jack Benny (with Mary Livingston)

wood writers, not his own crew; the scribes did not know what made the man funny, and gave him lines that may have been brilliant but that were simply not Jack Benny. In movies such as *Artists and Models* (1937), *Man About Town* (1939), and *George Washington Slept Here* (1942), he didn't set the world on fire, and the Academy Awards people also overlooked *The Horn Blows at Midnight* (1945).

The best lines in any Jack Benny show were always *about* Jack Benny, not *by* him:

MARY: You say you just got into town, Rochester? How come? Were the trains late?

ROCHESTER: What trains? I was out on Highway 99, free-lancing.

MARY: You mean you hitchhiked? Why didn't you come by train with the rest of the cast?

ROCHESTER: Well, instead of a train ticket, Mr. Benny gave me a road map.

MARY: No!

ROCHESTER: And a short talk on the generosity of the average American motorist.

MARY: Is that all he gave you?

ROCHESTER: Well, no. He also gave me a white glove for night operations.

In his later years, Benny gave a number of one-man performances (often for charitable causes) as either a comedian or a violinist. He died in 1974.

GERTRUDE BERG Gertrude Berg was both the creator and the voice of the beloved Jewish mother, radio's Molly Goldberg. Later, she excelled as an actress on Broadway, and on television.

Gertrude Edelstein Berg was born in the fashionable Harlem of 1899, on October 3. As a little girl, her strongest desire was to write radio scripts. She enrolled in university-level writing and acting courses. When Miss Berg submitted her first effort to a radio station, an executive rejected it, but was impressed with her voice and gave her a $5 assignment, translating a gasoline commercial into Yiddish. This was her debut as a professional radio author.

Her next attempt at writing for radio was a proposed series revolving around two department store salesgirls: she titled it *Effie and Laurie*. The show was canceled after the first airing when it became apparent that its notions of love and matrimony were too progressive.

Undeterred, she began to write a script depicting life in a Jewish family, featuring a dominant, though sprightly and quick-witted, mother whose quaintly jumbled English and warm empathy would soon charm millions of listeners.

Miss Berg presented the script, in an illegible handwriting, to a group of radio executives. Naturally, they were unable to read it, which was her intention. She plunged into a reading for them, using all the subtleties of voice modulation that made the Goldbergs come vividly to life. She was signed for $75 a week, which was "big money" during the Depression.

On November 20, 1929, *The Rise of the Goldbergs* hit the airwaves. Miss Berg wrote every script for the program, which ran uninterrupted for a total of 4,500 broadcasts, ending in 1946 when she left radio to write a Broadway show, *Me and Molly* (also the title of her autobiography), and a film, *Molly*. The Goldbergs soon became the subject of a popular television series; it ran for five years, with Miss Berg again starring.

Gertrude Berg died of a heart attack on September 14, 1966, at the age of sixty-six.

Gertrude Berg

EDGAR BERGEN and CHARLIE McCARTHY One day ventriloquist Edgar Bergen (a high school student) hit on the idea of a dummy. He hired a craftsman to fashion his vision out of basswood, springs, string, and paint for $35, and Charlie McCarthy was born. In years to come, he would become such a national favorite that the public would have trouble remembering he was just a dummy.

Bergen was born on February 16, 1903, in Chicago, where he grew up and developed his trick voice. He hit the vaudeville circuits and beyond (London, Sweden, and so on) after studying at Northwestern University. Making a smooth transition to nightclubs when vaudeville died out, Bergen was spotted in one club by Rudy Vallee, who invited the comedian and his dummy to appear on his radio show. They were elevated to "regular" status on the Vallee show in 1937, and later that year acquired a show of their own, sharing the microphone with such regulars as Dorothy Lamour, Don Ameche, and later W. C. Fields. Charlie commented, "Radio is just what a lousy ventriloquist like Bergen needs. The big stiff moves his lips!"

If Charlie didn't appreciate the man who breathed life into him, he did appreciate the charms of a woman. On one occasion beautiful Zsa Zsa Gabor guested on their radio program, and she was pleased to meet "Sharlie." "You must excuse my accent," Ms. Gabor explained, "but I am very short in this country." Charlie inquired, "Short of what?—Heh-heh—Oh, Zsa Zsa, my little lily cup, let me drink from the fountain of your beauty. . . . Hic. . . . Strong stuff!"

Edgar Bergen and Charlie McCarthy also became popular movie stars. They worked with the Ritz Brothers and Bobby Clark in *The Goldwyn Follies* (1938), with W. C. Fields in *You Can't Cheat an Honest Man* (1939), and with Lucille Ball and Fibber McGee and Molly in *Look Who's Laughing* (1941). The dummy became such hot box office that in 1939 he was the title star of *Charlie McCarthy, Detective*.

Charlie had become the star, and Bergen was seldom recognized on the street without his dummy. Perhaps to demonstrate that he was the brains and master, Bergen added two more wooden friends to his repertoire, country boy Mortimer ("Duhhh") Snerd, and spinster Effie Klinker.

Bergen and McCarthy worked sporadically on television and in nightclubs in the 1950s, and Bergen attempted a solo career as a dramatic actor, appearing in one production with his famous daughter Candice. It was not a major success, and he returned to what he knew best. Finally, after 56 years in show business, Edgar Bergen announced his retirement in the fall of 1978. Two weeks later—on September 30, 1978—he died.

Here are Edgar Bergen and Charlie McCarthy in action:

CHARLIE McCARTHY: I can't take this schoolwork any more, it's driving me crazy.

EDGAR BERGEN: Well, Charlie, I'm sorry, but hard work never killed anybody.

CHARLIE: Still, there's no use taking chances.

EDGAR: You have a test tomorrow, am I right?

CHARLIE: Well, yes, in a way.

EDGAR: All right, now, I see what brought this on. You're scared you won't pass. Suppose you tell me what you know about the brain.

CHARLIE: It's made from cereal, the silly-belly, and the muddled alligator.

EDGAR: No, no, that's the cerebrum, the

*Edgar Bergen
and Charlie McCarthy*

cerebellum, and the medulla oblongata! Didn't you read books on the subject?

CHARLIE: To tell you the truth, I didn't read all the books on the subject. Perhaps one book. Well, maybe it was just a pamphlet.

EDGAR: Charlie!

CHARLIE: All right, so it was the label on an iodine bottle!

MILTON BERLE Uncle Miltie was Mr. Television, the medium's first superstar, and Tuesday night in America was *his* night. On that night those rare homes with televisions became the point of rendezvous for entire neighborhoods.

After enjoying watching Berle, thousands of people would go out and buy TV sets of their own. The television industry credits him with singlehandedly popularizing the then infant medium, and selling more sets than all of the salesmen combined.

His TV programs were a mélange of brash slapstick decorated by hordes of bizarrely garbed stooges screaming one-liners. Subtlety and intelligence was not Berle's game. He would implore his gag writers (including the great Goodman Ace) to "make it lappy," that is, to minimize the comedy's subtlety and drop it right in the audience's *lap*. He rarely credited his audience with being sophisticated or intelligent. But Berle kept the nation laughing.

"I have to tell you," he once told his audience, "the Republicans are in bad trouble. They're searching for somebody to run for President, and if they'll listen to me, I have a perfect candidate—Marilyn Monroe. She'll get plenty of votes up north, and she's got a solid south, and what Marilyn could do with the UN! The Russians would sit still and watch *her* walk out!"

By the middle 1950s Berle's popularity was declining, as attested to by headlines like the one in the *Sunday Mirror Magazine:* "Mr. Television's Slip is Showing"—referring both to his decline in popularity and to his frequent appearances in women's dresses, which were becoming hokey. By 1956 Phil Silvers lured away his viewers, and the show went off the air. He continued to appear—in desperation even on a bowling show—but never regained his preeminent position of the early fifties.

He was born Milton Berlinger on July 12, 1908, in New York. As a youngster, he played child parts at Biograph; by the age of eleven, he toured with the Keith–Albee vaudeville circuit. For the 1920 revival of *Floradora,* he developed a gag routine at the insistence of his mother: it got him the notice of J. J. Shubert, and he gratefully referred to his mother for many years in his act.

In 1925 he was the interlocutor (later called master of ceremonies) at Loew's State Theater. Here he firmed up his smart-aleck comedy style, with masterly putdowns of hecklers and the habit of editing other comedians' material to his style. This got him a reputation for stealing jokes; when other comedians made a big hit somewhere, they would say, "Boy, was I funny tonight! Milton

Berle laughed so hard he dropped his pencil and pad."

In 1941 he married showgirl Joyce Mathews; they divorced in 1947 and remarried later, but it didn't take the second time, either; in 1955 he married Ruth Cosgrave.

Berle has been in around twenty films, with nothing approaching the impact he made in television. They included *Always Leave Them Laughing* (1949) and *It's a Mad, Mad, Mad, Mad World* (1963); in the latter, he was swallowed up in a cast that reads like a "Who's Who of Comedy."

When he appeared in a theatrical flop that closed out of town, he remarked, "The show was such a hit we sent the whole audience home in a taxi. The doorman was arrested for loitering."

Most of Berle's stuff goes something like this:

I made more than four hundred live shows for NBC back when there was no such thing as video tape. And I never missed a single performance because of illness: no matter how sick the NBC brass got of me, I showed up.

Who says we didn't have controversial subjects on TV then? Remember *Bonanza?* It was about three guys in high heels living together.

Of course, today, they are much more daring. I saw a show the other night about a surgeon who became intimate with his patient. But he was a tree surgeon!

SHELLEY BERMAN Only after a decade of attempting to make it in legitimate theater did Shelley Berman resign himself to becoming one of the world's top nightclub and recording comedians.

His monologues are seasoned with anguish, frustration, rage, and satire. One of his many pet peeves is the com-

Milton Berle

Shelley Berman

mercial airline: "Airlines are constantly bragging about their safety records: 'Flying is the safest way to travel.' I don't know how much consideration they have given to walking." Even the comedian himself is not exempt from a bit of his own friendly satire: "I may have neuroses, but at least I'm not unhappy."

Sheldon Leonard Berman was born on February 3, 1924, in Chicago. In the midst of Chicago's brutal South Side, he grew up creating sensitive wood sculptures and writing short stories. In the mid-fifties, he became a member of an improvisational trio with two other unknowns, Mike Nichols and Elaine May. He went solo in 1957. "I've been working steadily ever since," he says.

To his credit are several million-selling record albums, including *Inside Shelley Berman, Outside Shelley Berman,* and *The Edge of Shelley Berman.* He has written a book, *Shelly Berman's Cleans and Dirtys.* He has also appeared in such films as *Divorce, American Style* and *The Best Man,* and traveled the talk show circuit.

JOE BESSER

see THE THREE STOOGES

JOEY BISHOP A perennial sourpuss, Joey Bishop dispenses his punchlines almost belligerently, daring you to laugh. But the gags do not attack anyone: in fact, most of them are inwardly directed and self-deprecating. "In kindergarten, I flunked sandpile" is a typical Joey Bishop statement.

He comments bitterly on the passing scene. "Today you go to a gas station and you find that the cash register is open but the toilets are locked. They must think toilet paper is worth more than money."

Or: "My wife will buy anything that is marked 'Down.' Yesterday she tried to buy an escalator."

He refers often to his poor childhood. "We had so little to eat one year that I forgot how to swallow."

He was born Joseph A. Gottlieb, the last of five children of an immigrant couple in the Bronx, New York City, on February 3, 1919. He broke into show business in 1936, winning $3 in an amateur show for his imitations of Joe Penner and Jimmy Durante.

In 1938, Joey teamed up with two friends in a comedy act that played nightclubs around Philadelphia, where the family had moved. When the others were drafted, Joey continued the routine alone. In these clubs he developed the offhand, throwaway approach that later made him a TV hit. Eventually, he also wound up in the Service during World War II.

After the war, he continued the nightclub routine, and worked it up to the top spots at $1,000 a week. But he might have remained strictly a local celebrity if Frank Sinatra hadn't caught his act in 1952 and asked him to join the Sinatra entourage on a cross-country tour. He wound up in a couple of Sinatra films, on the *Jack Paar Show,* and finally, in 1958, on the ad-lib show *Keep Talking* on CBS-TV, which brought him national exposure.

In 1967 Bishop got his own talk show, and although he did not get as high ratings as competitors Johnny Carson, Merv Griffin, and Dick Cavett, he has remained one of the reigning TV wits, either as emcee or guest, on many shows over many years.

Joey has appeared in a number of films, including *The Naked and the Dead* (1958), *Sergeants Three* (1961), and *Valley of the Dolls* (1967), but as a sideline, really—television's his big thing.

He has been married since 1941 and has a son, Larry.

MEL BLANC Most artists supplying voices for cartoon characters remain unknown to the general public, but Mel Blanc is the exception. The creator of Bugs Bunny, Woody Woodpecker, Tweety-Pie ("I Tawt I Taw a Puddy Tat"), and four hundred others, Mel has earned recognition for his unbelievable versatility over a period of more than four decades.

His zenith was the long tenure on the *Jack Benny Show,* where his tasks included wheezing for Benny's Maxwell automobile, droning out the irritating monotone of a railroad announcer who made the Los Angeles suburbs of "Anaheim, Azusa and Cuc——amonga" famous, and playing the monosyllabic Mexican whose exchanges with Benny went something like this:

JACK BENNY: Do you have any relatives?
MEL BLANC: Sí (*pronounced "seee"*).
JACK: Well, who?
MEL: Seees.
JACK: Oh, you mean you have a sister?
MEL: Seee.
JACK: What's her name?
MEL: Sue.
JACK: Sue?
MEL: Seee.

Born on May 30, 1908, in San Francisco, Blanc started creating funny voices for the amusement of school buddies, but his first job was as a musician—string bass, violin, and sousaphone—in a radio studio orchestra ("Sou?" "Seee."). In the mid-1930s he joined Leon Schlesinger Productions, a cartoon workshop that became the source of Warner Brothers' Looney Tunes and Merrie Melodies series. In 1938 he came up with Bugs

Bunny, and since then his inspiration has never deserted him.

In addition to his chores on the *Jack Benny Show* on both radio and TV, Mel did various voices on a dozen other radio shows, and during the 1946–47 season had his own show on CBS. On television, he created voices for dozens of Hanna-Barbera characters, working for *The Flintstones, Huckleberry Hound, Yogi Bear,* and so on.

He is one of the few artists who has had two million-selling records in the category of children's songs: "I Tawt I Taw a Puddy Tat" and "Woody Woodpecker's Song."

Blanc had minor roles in several films, including *Neptune's Daughter* (1949) and *Kiss Me, Stupid* (1964), and in 1976 he appeared in a stage production, *Bugs Bunny Follies.* From the early 1960s he ran his own company, giving lessons to budding voice animators and producing commercials for TV.

Married since 1933, he has a son, Noel.

BEN BLUE With his slender figure, nimble feet, and rubber face, Ben Blue was a natural for comic dancing, and became one of the most adept and most durable practitioners of this rather rare type of comedy.

Both his dancing ability and his talent for pantomime came as gifts: he never took a dancing or acting lesson in his life. Born Ben Bernstein in Montreal in 1902, the son of an antique dealer, he was raised mostly in Baltimore where the family moved. At thirteen, he accompanied his family to New York, where he found his first job as a shill for a movie house: it was his duty to imitate Charlie Chaplin on the sidewalk in front of the theater to attract passersby.

Eventually, someone was impressed by his mimicry and sent him to try out for a

Ben Blue (right) with Burns and Allen

job in a musical comedy chorus. He made his Broadway debut dancing in *Irene* (1919), followed by *Mary* (1920).

Two years later, he opened a dancing school with a partner; it developed into a chain covering many cities. But Ben was always restless; we find him next in Los Angeles with the Milt Britton dance band, and in the vaudeville circuit, where his most famous routine was "Death of a Swan."

He convulsed audiences in nearly two hundred films with bits of clever pantomime and terpsichorean agility; few of his appearances in feature movies involved much dialogue, which may be just as well. When the Hal Roach Studio teamed him up for a series of shorts with Billy Gilbert, with the pair starred as "The Taxi Boys," the series flopped because neither man was allowed to do what he knew best, but had to suffer through stale lines and contrived visual gags.

Ben saved and invested his money, and by the forties was the owner-operator of three nightclubs. During the fifties, he was doing his best pantomime bits on many TV shows, and was a regular on the *Colgate Comedy Hour* and on *Saturday Night Revue*. He had minor roles in a number of films, with a memorable bit in the 1966 hit, *The Russians Are Coming, The Russians Are Coming.*

He married showgirl Axie Dunlap, who appeared in the 1939 edition of the *Ziegfeld Follies.* He died on March 7, 1975.

ED BLUESTONE

ED BLUESTONE A newcomer to comedy, seen on the *Merv Griffin Show* and such in addition to nightclubs, Ed has a wild imaginative streak. He is very witty, and many of his punchlines are deeply Freudian; most audiences take a few extra seconds before the absurdity of the situation really hits them. This is especially true because his face is permanently wreathed in an innocent smile, which contrasts with the pungency of his imagery:

"My parents didn't like me. They felt that if sex were meant to be fun, God wouldn't have included kids as a punishment. I first realized how they felt when in our home movies, they hired an actor to play me. When I had measles, they went to court and fought for my right to die."

Ed was born in 1949. He played some New York spots, and was a big hit in Las Vegas in the 1976–77 season. He was given a permanent berth in the 1977 revival of TV's *Laugh-In,* with this kind of material:

In Las Vegas they have funny religions. I met a girl who invited me to a combination human sacrifice and Tupperware party.

I checked into a California motel. They warned me to use the pool in the morning, so that if I drowned the body would be out by checkout time.

To contrast that with New York, in a New York hotel I called for a reservation, and the clerk asked me if I would need a clean spoon.

I believe in capital punishment as an alternative to birth control. If you're going to punish a guy, do something he'll never forget.

BOB and RAY Bob Elliott and Ray Goulding have much in common with Jean Shepherd; they are also humorists who poke fun at life's trivia, and they are products of radio. They also can make a little material go a long way, without reaching for gross effects: they deflate pomposity and reduce serious matters to shambles without the listener being aware how precisely it was done.

When a popular tear-jerking daytime soap opera was on radio entitled *Mary Noble, Backstage Wife,* Bob and Ray came up with the satire *Mary Backstayge, Noble Wife,* which was silly but enjoyed a long run on their show. The real series, *Mr. Keen, Tracer of Lost Persons,* became in their nimble hands *Mr. Trace, Keener than Most Persons.*

Perhaps the best testimonial to the essential gentleness of their satire is that they made national commerical advertisers aware of the potential of humor as an approach to sales, and in 1956 they broke through the stodginess of Madison Avenue with their series of TV commercials for Piel Brothers' beer.

Robert B. Elliott was born in Boston on March 26, 1923, became interested in radio, and after high school enrolled in the Feagin School of Drama and Radio in New York. He earned his tuition by working as an usher, and his first radio job was, appropriately, *A Page Boy's Impression of Radio,* done weekly over WINS in 1941.

Raymond W. Goulding was born on March 20, 1922, in Lowell, Massachusetts, and he also went into radio announcing after high school. After a year in Lowell, he auditioned for Boston's WEFI and got the job.

Both men joined the armed forces during World War II, and after discharge in 1946 drifted back to radio; both were hired by Boston's WHDH, Bob as a morning disc jockey, and Ray as newscaster. They began exchanging pleasantries on the air, and soon were in demand as a regular team. Given their own program, they started out mixing real news and records with comedy, but soon the humor got the upper hand, and it has been that way ever since.

They are still busy in radio, their preferred medium, but also appear in humorous commercials on TV.

MERWYN BOGUE

see ISH KABIBBLE

BETTY BOOP

see HELEN KANE

IRENE BORDONI For a couple of decades, from her first appearance in America in 1912 to the mid-thirties, Irene Bordoni typified the "naughty but nice" Parisienne to a generation of vaudeville and musical comedy patrons. Vivacious and charming, petite and chic, and with an accent to match, she sang her way into many a man's heart with her little-girl voice, rendering such numbers as "Let's Misbehave" and "Don't Look at Me That Way."

Born on Corsica in 1894 but brought up in Paris, she became a popular juvenile artist in the *varietés* (French vaudeville) in 1907. In 1912 she came to America to appear in the musical comedies *Broadway to Paris* and *The First Affair*. Vaudeville followed, and then a trip to London to act in *L'Impressario* in 1914. Back in New York the next year, she was in *Miss Information* and a string of other shows.

She was a huge hit in *Little Miss Bluebeard* (1923), and an even bigger one in the film *Paris* during the twenties.

Her exhausting schedule in vaudeville between Broadway shows is attested by the fact that she went through eight piano accompanists. She also appeared in a few shorts for Paramount and Vitaphone, in four features, and in touring companies of various shows; as late as 1952, she played Bloody Mary in a revival of *South Pacific* on tour. She passed away in 1953.

VICTOR BORGE Victor Borge, like Jack Benny, used his musical instrument as a launching pad for his comedy. His *Comedy in Music* set a record for one-man Broadway shows by running for three years and 849 performances; the late Brooks Atkinson, *New York Times* critic, attended the opening night, and his verdict was that Borge is "the funniest man who ever lived."

Victor was born Borge Rosenbaum in Copenhagen, on January 3, 1909. Musical studies dominated his childhood, and by the age of twelve he was a concert pianist. He diversified into comedy, writing, composing, directing, and acting, becoming Denmark's highest grossing performer of the 1930s. On tour in Finland in 1940 at the time of the Nazi takeover of Denmark, having satirized Hitler 1,001 times too often, Borge prudently elected to journey to America instead of going home. In 1942 he was a regular on Bing Crosby's *Kraft Music Hall;* later, he had his own program.

Borge's intelligent brand of comedy makes use of audience participation. He plays snatches of the masters' greatest compositions on his piano, and interweaves his comic remarks, tying it all into a neatly unified format. Apart from his spontaneous, fun-loving interaction with

Victor Borge

the audience, his comedy falls into two basic categories. The first exploits Borge's genius for music, in such imaginative routines as demonstrating how composers like Bach and Brahms would have composed the popular jingle, "Happy Birthday to You." The other category is his music-related quips: "This concerto was written in four flats, because Rachmaninoff had to move four times while he wrote it. And of course I play excerpts. . . . I don't know the whole thing. . . . The Steinway people have asked me to announce that this is a Baldwin piano."

A few typical Borgecisms:

What did you say—something by Bach? Which one—Johann Sebastian, or Jacques Offen——?

I hate to play "Clair de Lune." It's a coughing number. People who never coughed in their life will cough while it's played.

I have played all over the world. Piano, of course.

I remember my grandfather. He was Danish after his mother, and Swedish after a friend of his father's.

To be honest with you, I only know two numbers. One is "Clair de Lune," and the other one isn't.

I usually don't do requests, unless of course I am asked to do one. This one is from a lady—I sincerely hope. We haven't seen each other for years. Neither have I.

I will now play Rachmaninoff's *Second Piano Concerto*. Number Two. It is by Rachmaninoff, who also wrote the music. It's for a piano and a concerto.

THE BOWERY BOYS

see LEO GORCEY

BILLY BRAVER A newcomer to the ranks, Billy looks like a timid young kid, and derives much humor from exaggerating typical family rejection situations. He has been making the rounds of the *Merv Griffin Show* and similar talkshow tryouts, with material like this:

My parents had no patience with me: I was toilet trained at gunpoint.

My father was a transit employee—he drove a subway. One day he took me with him, put me down on the tracks, and gave me a five-minute head start.

My brother is a religious fanatic: he beats up nuns.

The way I met my wife—she was a cheerleader for the chess team at college.

EL BRENDEL Alfred (El) Brendel is remembered for little else than giving show business the expression "Yumping yiminy," which afterwards became an easy instant identification of any Scandinavian comic, but actually he was an experienced vaudeville old-timer of great talent and versatility. He specialized in simple-minded hicks with a Swedish accent because they gave him a trade mark.

He was a native of Philadelphia, where he was born in 1891. He attended the University of Pennsylvania. In 1913, he entered vaudeville with a partner, Sadie Burt; they were the first team to base an act on lip synchronization with a phonograph record, in 1920. Solo, he went on to featured roles in several Shubert musicals.

Between 1926 and 1949, El Brendel appeared in more than 100 films, beginning with *You Never Know Women* (1926), but nearly always in supporting roles. One of his best roles was in *Just Imagine* (1930), but he is also remembered for a marvelously nonsensical "Blah-blah-blah" song in *Delicious*

El Brendel in a scene from Olsen's Big Moment *(1934)*

(1931), and for his inspired work with Victor McLaglen in the Sgt. Flagg-Sgt. Quirt film *The Cock Eyed World* (1929). His last role in a feature film was in *The Beautiful Blonde from Bashful Bend* (1949).

He did better in shorts, which he started making for Warners in the late 1930s. At Columbia, to which he switched soon after, he got a series of two-reelers in which at last he had starring credit. At first, he was teamed up with Tom Kennedy; in 1944 for a period he worked with Harry Langdon, then already near the end of his sad decline from earlier prominence but still giving able support, and finally with Monty Collins. Unfortunately, although these vehicles gave him top billing, the studio insisted on making him too much of a simpleton, and the shorts viewed today appear weak and ineffective.

El Brendel died in 1964.

DAVID BRENNER David Brenner is a true student of the media, and his comic performances show a real awareness of how to exploit the camera's eye or the microphone's ear for all it's worth. In college he majored in radio and television journalism, and later produced and directed TV documentaries. He gave up that lucrative and promising career for comedy in 1969.

As a comedian, Brenner got nowhere for a year or two, going through his savings while trying to market comedy material. The breaks started coming in 1972 when network talk shows picked him up. Brenner's first appearance was with Johnny Carson, and he was a hit with such material as a scheme to commit the perfect murder and then get rid of the dead body in New York City. "You just shove him into the crowd," he claimed, "and he'll keep moving indefinitely. He'll be carried along through Macy's."

Through over fifty appearances on Johnny Carson's program and scores of top Las Vegas engagements, Brenner has retained his big city sense of humor (he is one of many show business winners to emerge from the legendary slums of Philadelphia). He tells of riding the subway, sitting on a newspaper. Someone asks, "Are you reading that newspaper?" Brenner replies, "Yes, I'm reading it." He stands up, turns the page significantly, and sits down again.

FANNY BRICE In the days when the *Ziegfeld Follies* were the standard by which female pulchritude was measured, a girl of ordinary looks had no hope of getting anywhere near the great Mr. Ziegfeld. And yet Fanny Brice, who was practically homely, was one of his biggest attractions between 1910 and 1923. There could be no better testimony to her talent and stage presence.

She had a natural flair for humorous pantomime, and with a mere gesture, grin, and lift of the eyebrow could make audiences laugh. In a song like "Cooking Breakfast for the One I Love," she treated the audience to a perfect picture of a rather overeager and undertalented young bride; in "Secondhand Rose," she made them see the problems imposed by approaching spinsterhood on a rather dowdy and poor turn-of-the-century girl "from Second Avenue"—a locale Miss Brice could sing about with authority, having been born on the Lower East Side of New York on October 29, 1891.

But, although one of the biggest headliners of vaudeville, Fanny was destined to be remembered most vividly for what grew out of a baby-talk characterization of a typical brat that she did at a party. A writer present at the party made her repeat it in the *Follies*—and the audience's response doomed her to remain "Baby Snooks" for the rest of her life. It became one of the top radio shows between 1938 and 1949, and gave her millions of fans who had never seen her on stage.

Her real family name was Borach, and she worked her way up from amateur nights at Keeney's Theater in Brooklyn. By 1910 she was in vaudeville, singing dialect songs written for her by a budding newcomer named Irving Berlin. Mr. Ziegfeld saw her do one of these in the Columbia Burlesque Theater, and hired her straightaway for the *Follies*.

She also tried nonmusical humorous roles in the theater (*Fanny*, 1926) and in a few films; however, these forays were not as successful as the musicals, in which she could frolic and mug to her heart's content. She appeared in the *Ziegfeld Follies of 1911* after her *Follies* debut in 1910, in the *Ziegfeld Follies of 1916,* ditto for 1917, in a number during the roaring twenties, and was still going strong in the *Ziegfeld Follies of 1936.*

Fanny was married three times but was not lucky in her choice of mates; her second husband was an underworld figure, Nicky Arnstein, and her third was

Fanny Brice (with Hanley Stafford)

the oft-married producer Billy Rose.

She suffered a heart attack and died in 1951 at the age of sixty.

But how's this for a little nostalgia?

FATHER: Today we'll have a grammar lesson, Snooks. Correct this sentence: "It was *me* who broke the window."

BABY SNOOKS: "It *wasn't* me who broke the window."

FATHER: No, no. The answer is: "It was *I* who broke the window."

BABY SNOOKS: It was you?

FATHER: No, it was you, but you must say, "It was I."

BABY SNOOKS: You mean I gotta say you broke it?

FATHER: No, you broke it.

BABY SNOOKS: Boo hoo (*cries*).

FATHER: What's the matter now?

BABY SNOOKS: I didn't break any windows.

MARTY BRILL A comparative newcomer, Brill was a singer at first, but during an appearance on the *Ed Sullivan Show,* a string in his guitar broke, and the laughter he got encouraged him to go for comedy on a full-time basis. Among his legitimate credits is playing in the show *Lenny* in England. He likes political material. Like this:

Idi Amin's government fell. The branch broke.

I hear Poland just won javelin catching in the Olympics.

A German soldier in Paris, 1940. Takes the first girl he sees to a hotel room, has his way with her, and says arrogantly, "In nine months, you'll have a baby. Call him Adolf." She replies sweetly, "In two weeks, you'll have a rash. Call it what you like."

Inflation has hit everything. Pillow down is up, Macy's basement is now on the fourth floor, and pumpernickel is pumperdime.

FOSTER BROOKS

I'm soo-s-superstitious. All-always knock on wood. It d-doesn't bring me any goo-good luck but it gets the bartender's attention!

An ex-boozehound can usually do the most devastating parody of his former besotted ways, and Foster Brooks proves this point with a flourish. He came to prominence rather suddenly and unexpectedly in the mid-1970s on Dean Martin's celebrity roasts on television, where he was introduced as a fictional former associate of the star being roasted.

To watch him swaying slightly, vainly attempting to suppress strange rumblings in his esophagus, tripping over his tongue, and maintaining the stiff dignity of the habitual inebriate is to watch a precision performance. He has repeated the bit on dozens of talk and variety shows since then.

MEL BROOKS A major comic force in television for over two decades, Mel Brooks has emerged, in the past decade, as one of the very finest (and, stylistically, one of the most maniacal) practitioners of film comedy, as a character actor, director, and screenplay writer. All this from a Borscht Circuit boy!

He was born in 1926 in the Williamsburg section of Brooklyn; his real name was Melvyn Kaminsky. After abortive attempts at becoming (or dreaming of becoming) a pilot, a chemist, and a drummer, Brooks joined the army, which had its hands full with World War II. His commanding officers sent him to pave the way for infantry advances by deactivating supersensitive land mines.

A stint on the Borscht Belt as a drummer, before switching to standup comedy, provided the formative years for Brooks' distinctive brand of madcap comedy. He left the circuit behind to write. His television writing began in the service of Sid Caesar, for whom Brooks contributed gags to *Your Show of Shows* and *Caesar's Hour.* The *Get Smart* TV series was a Mel Brooks creation/collaboration.

In 1960, along with another Sid Caesar teammate, Carl Reiner, Brooks recorded the first of a highly successful series of *2,000-Year-Old Man* albums. The 2,000-Year-Old Man was embarrassed about dying because he might bump into Jesus Christ whom he had once paid a measly "four bucks for a cabinet."

Mel's first major film effort was *The Critic,* a 1963 cartoon he conceived, wrote, and narrated, for which he shared an Academy Award with animator Ernest Pintoff.

Mel Brooks

72

Rejecting offers to do his own TV series, Brooks went to work on an idea called *Springtime for Hitler.* He wrote it three times; as a novel, a play, and finally as a screenplay. The film, released in 1968 as *The Producers,* concerns Max Bialystock (Zero Mostel), a washed-up producer of Broadway plays who gets backing for his productions by flirting with rich little old ladies. He convinces an infantile, hysterical tax accountant (masterfully portrayed by Gene Wilder) to help implement the scheme of selling the impossible and illegal total of several thousand percent interest in his play, *Springtime for Hitler,* to his elderly women, raising several times the cash needed to produce it, and embezzling the remainder. The play is meticulously designed as a flop destined to close on opening night (so that the backers will consider their investments total losses and expect no share of any profits); a freaked-out flower child (Dick Shawn) is cast as Hitler and an incompetent transvestite is hired as director. Unfortunately, the play becomes a smash hit, and the pair wind up in jail. All was not lost, however, for Mel Brooks was handed an Academy Award for Best Original Screenplay.

Brooks' next film was *The Twelve Chairs* (1970), about three postrevolutionary Russians racing to find a jewel-laden chair. Then came *Blazing Saddles* (1974), a satire of Westerns and a brilliant exercise in bad taste. His next effort, in collaboration with Gene Wilder, was *Young Frankenstein* (1975); then, in 1976, he produced and directed *Silent Movie*—a film with sound effects, music, and titles where lines would normally be spoken—except, of course, for one single word ("No!")—uttered, logically, by Marcel Marceau.

SHELTON BROOKS In 1910 Sophie Tucker, by then a headliner, agreed to listen to a young black composer who insisted on demonstrating his new song for her. A bit of show business history was made that day, for the song was "Some of These Days." But while everyone remembers the song, few know the name of the composer, Shelton Brooks —or the fact that he was also an able comedian and impressionist (specialty: Bert Williams imitation), accompanist to numerous vaudeville artists, and even lyricist.

Born May 4, 1886, to Indian–black parents in Amesburg, Ontario, he grew up mostly in Detroit, and started his career as piano player in local cafés, in the then prevalent ragtime style. Around 1909 he started composing and performing his own songs in vaudeville in the United States, Canada, and Britain. Among his better known originals is the immortal "Darktown Strutters' Ball." On Broadway, his credits include *Plantation Revue* (1922) and *Blackbirds of 1923.*

JOE E. BROWN Jimmy Durante had his prominent proboscis, Eddie Cantor had his banjo eyes, and Joe E. Brown had his mammoth mouth, which emitted an alarm-like shriek that automatically elicited peals of laughter from his audience—year after year. Brown was a consistently commercial, competent film comedian, from the late twenties into the forties. He remained active into the seventies, during a career that crossed six decades.

Brown was born on July 28, 1892, in Holgate, Ohio. The classic American clown biography was his—he ran away from home at the age of nine, got a job with the circus, and became an adroit

Joe E. Brown (with June Haver)

acrobat; this ability was to help immeasurably in the slapstick films to come.

After a period in burlesque, and rising to prominence in legitimate theater on Broadway, Brown made his movie debut in 1928, in *Crooks Can't Win.* Over the next twenty years he starred in almost fifty films, including *Wide Open Faces, Pin Up Girl, Going Wild, The Gladiator,* and *You Said a Mouthful.* The 1959 Marilyn Monroe picture, *Some Like It Hot,* featured Brown as a lascivious old millionaire. He performed well, despite the severe limitations of his part.

Perhaps his most memorable effort is *Elmer the Great,* which benefited from his excellence in sports. It was often said that had he not been so well suited for comedy, he could easily have played major league baseball.

In 1952 Brown replaced Milton Berle on television for a month, calling his segment *Circus Hour,* but it was not well received.

When not displaying his Grand Canyon mouth in films, Brown was engaging in traditional slapstick. More perfectly than any other sound comedian of his era, Brown duplicated the formula of his silent-film predecessors—that of the bungling, ingenuous, victimized buffoon.

After a protracted illness, Joe E. Brown died of heart failure on July 6, 1973, at the age of eighty. Even in his death throes, he remained the clown: newspapers ran photos of him manipulating large teddy bears from his hospital bed, and performing mayhem. Two years before he had enacted his final performance, at Las Vegas.

LENNY BRUCE Lenny Bruce used censored words but never told off-color jokes: his profanity was directed at the hypocrisy in our social system. He ranted and raved about religion, morality, the police, and the judicial system in thousands of performances that were essentially intimate talks with the audience; he had few regular routines, all used just to get things started, and from then on everything he said was improvised.

He was called a brilliant social satirist by some, a foul-mouthed punk by others. Like no other comedy performer, he was hounded by self-appointed guardians of public morals, and repeatedly arrested for obscenity and for possession of narcotics; after a prolonged exposure to this, he started venting his wrath against the judiciary, and his shows took on the aspect of a holy crusade. Certainly his followers formed more of a cult than a fan club. He said so many things that hit close to where people live that a great majority either loved him or hated him, but very few who heard him could remain indifferent.

Any time some schmuck tells me he wouldn't want his daughter to marry one of *them,* I ask him, "Which one do you mean? Suppose she had to choose between Hitler and, say, Harry Belafonte. Would you make your decision along racial lines?"

If you really believe God made your body, then how can anything that you do with it be dirty or obscene? The only way you can be obscene is by hurting it. A nude chick showing her nay-nays can be obscene only in a sick society. She's not obscene to me, but the war in Vietnam is the ultimate obscenity.

Show me the average sex maniac, the one who takes your eight-year-old, shtupps her in the parking lot and then kills her, and I'll show you a guy who's had a good religious background and strict moralistic upbringing. But you see, he saw his father or mother always telling his sister to cover up her body, when she was only six years old, and so he figured, one day I'm gonna find out what it is she's

Lenny Bruce

covering, and if it's so dirty as my father says I'll kill it.

You know why we're so hot after the Commies? It's the frigging Pope, you see, the Catholics have this giant monopoly going on, this church, and what the Pope is really doing he's selling franchises, like Howard Johnson. He sits there in the Vatican and says, "Okay, so you want Venezuela? That'll be twenty percent off the top, and I'll make you a cardinal." But the Commies, they're screwing it up, because they would take the customers away, and that's why we've got the cold war and all these things.

He was born Alfred Schneider in Mineola, New York, probably in 1924. He studied acting under the GI Bill after getting out of the navy following World War II. Soon he began doing comedy routines in nightclubs; he first attracted national attention on the Arthur Godfrey TV show. But he really came into his own in Greenwich Village, where fans regarded him as their messiah; there the blue language he habitually used got him into trouble with the law at last, making him an instant martyr. He even went on the *Johnny Carson Show* just to prove he could get along without four-letter words, but by then he was typecast and the persecution gathered momentum.

On August 6, 1966, Lenny Bruce was found dead in Los Angeles, apparently of an overdose of narcotics. Swiftly, a posthumous legend sprang up: he was done in by a conspiracy of the CIA, FBI, and other assorted villains, who rigged it up to look like he was a dope fiend to discredit him. His routines were published in book and record forms, a couple of films were made about him, biographies were written, and memorabilia were sold. Since most of the furor was created by either crass opportunists or rabid worshippers, it is nearly impossible to get an accurate, impartial picture of the angry young man who tilted against sacred windmills.

JOHN BUNNY John Bunny popularized film comedy in America. He was *the* pioneer. He was born in New York City on September 21, 1863, the son of an English government representative.

Bunny quit the legitimate theater and a stable $150 a week to seek uncertain employment in motion pictures. In 1910 he approached the Vitagraph Company which responded coldly and signed him for $40 a week. Playfully explaining why he left artistic and financial success behind for relative poverty and obscurity, and a debatably "lower" form of art, Bunny said, "I didn't aim to be a comedian, but nature was agin' me. How could I

John Bunny

77

hope to play Romeo with a figure like mine? It was many years before I learned to yield gracefully to the fate for which nature had endowed me." His decision was most justified, for a year later he was a star and Vitagraph was handing Bunny $1,000 every Friday.

In the next few years (up to his death in 1915), Bunny made over one hundred fifty films, most of which are irrevocably lost. He was second only to *Broncho Billy* in popularity among American filmgoers.

Bunny's film character was the complete hedonist—an inveterate drinker and gambler whose eye wandered as prodigiously as his belly protruded. Comic conflict arose between him and his wife, Flora Finch, a singularly nasty woman who sought nothing but to impose virtue and restraint upon Bunny.

Although today his films would be labeled as chauvinism because masculine behavior and vices are glorified, and feminine traits depicted as ridiculous, John Bunny does have a singular distinction in the development of the cinema. He was the first movie star whose name became a generic term for a short film comedy: during his heyday, people went to see their weekly "bunnygraph," and when Miss Finch joined him, the "bunny-finch."

He was a jolly-looking figure, always up to marital mischief and inebriated. His lampooning of society's ludicrous affectations and pomposities became a dominant theme in American film comedy. A favorite line of his was: "Here's to our wives and sweethearts—may they never meet!"

He died on April 26, 1915.

CAROL BURNETT Now that Carol Burnett is one of the most accomplished comediennes on television, few recall her humble beginnings. For instance, the fact that in 1955 she won the dubious distinction of being wooden dummy Jerry Mahoney's girlfriend for 13 weeks of ventriloquist Paul Winchell's television program, or that she had to work as a hatcheck girl when she couldn't open show business doors, or that her 1964 Broadway show and her TV series *The Entertainers* were simultaneously beset by lawsuits, injuries, breach-of-contract allegations, and then, to top it off, her own pregnancy. Such predicaments are, however, very much a part of the Carol Burnett comedy persona.

Born in San Antonio, California, on April 16, 1933, Ms. Burnett studied theater arts at UCLA. Her big break came when she and her boyfriend were spotted entertaining at a society party by a wealthy gentleman who staked them each to $1,000 to go to New York and seek the bigtime. After the semicompulsory period of struggling, her career ignited, and the $1,000 debt was gratefully repaid.

Once upon a Mattress, in 1959, was Ms. Burnett's first Broadway play. That year she became a regular comedienne on the *Garry Moore Show,* and dealt the show a fatal blow by leaving it in 1962, when she was lured away by CBS and their 10-year, million-dollar contract. Going solo gave her the opportunity to develop more fully her comic technique, and to exploit her talent under her own spotlight. In addition to her perennially successful television show, Ms. Burnett has appeared in such plays as *Plaza Suite* and *I Do I Do;* such films as *Pete 'n Tillie* (1972) and *The Front Page* (1974); and her nightclub engagements have included several major Las Vegas pleasure palaces.

Her comic identity is designed to evoke pathos and sympathy; she is the kindly klutz, the underdog you love to laugh at

Carol Burnett

and root for, the girl you would love to protect and comfort. Her handsome male date promises, "You're never going to forget tonight." With intense longing, she blurts, "I'm not?", revealing her pure innocence and desolate soul.

A mobile face that magnifies every expression enabled Carol to create a gallery of beautifully absurd characters for her TV series. There is Nora Desmond, the ex-movie queen tottering languidly about her ghastly mansion; an obnoxious bespectacled Girl Scout selling cookies by subtle blackmail; Mrs. Wiggins, a slow-motion, slow-witted secretary to Boss Tudball (Tim Conway); and Eunice, slovenly housewife of the bickering family whose members are perpetually at each other's throats. The series was discontinued in 1977 but is certain of a long life in reruns.

GEORGE BURNS and GRACIE ALLEN

Both were in show biz at a tender age, but neither made a big name until they teamed up in vaudeville one fateful day in 1923. At first they tried the standard routine, in which Gracie asked the straight lines and George delivered the boffo replies. To George's surprise, Gracie was getting laughs even while asking the straight questions, while he had trouble getting snickers with his best zingers.

A showman, George made the sound decision that kept the team a smash success through three and a half decades in all media: he reversed their roles, contented himself with an occasional "Who was that?" and "What did he do?" and relinquished the laughs to Gracie.

Which is not to minimize his contribution: the exasperated patience with which he bore Gracie's accounts of her bizarre relatives and weird experiences was a perfect background against which Gracie did her scatterbrain bits. Jack Benny considered George's dry comments the funniest in show business, and was known to break up when George played a practical joke on him.

George Burns was born Nathan Birnbaum in New York City on January 20, 1896, one of a family of twelve. Leaving school at thirteen to help support the family (his father had died), he sang in taverns in a children's quartet, later was a trick roller skater and dance teacher. Finally came vaudeville, and a succession of song-and-dance acts.

Gracie Allen was born in San Francisco, California, on July 26, 1906, the daughter of a vaudevillian. She did have three sisters and one brother, although any resemblance between them and the nitwit relatives in her routines is purely hilarious. She left school at fourteen to go into show business with her sisters, who had an act. They became members of a traveling Irish troupe, where Gracie developed an Irish brogue that she had the devil of a time losing. Leaving over an argument on billing, she enrolled in secretarial school. One night she accompanied a friend backstage after a show at the Union Hill Theater in New Jersey, and met George Burns who asked her to become his partner.

They were married three years later, in Cleveland, on January 7, 1926, but their marriage wasn't openly acknowledged on radio until the 1940s; up to that time, they thought they could get more comic mileage out of a courting premise.

Eddie Cantor brought Burns and Allen to radio in 1932; they were known to audiences from several films, and were so well received that they became regulars on the *Guy Lombardo Show*. In 1933 they got their own show, which ran uninterruptedly for 17 years. They also

George Burns and Gracie Allen

appeared in a number of films, especially during the thirties, such as *Big Broadcast of 1932* (and 1936 and 1937). In 1950 they made a smooth transition to television, where they enjoyed success until Gracie retired in 1958. She died in 1964.

Burns continued his career on TV in various shows, including *Wendy and Me,* which he produced. At the age of seventy-nine, he costarred with Walter Matthau in the film *The Sunshine Boys,* and won an Academy Award as the Best Supporting Actor of 1975. His many solo performances included a Carnegie Hall, New York, recital in 1976.

Burns' trademark was a cigar, held while he unleashed reminiscences and wisecracks, and ancient vaudeville songs delivered in his own style, making all the lyrics sound like one long word. His inability to carry a tune was impeccable, and was always a source of vilification—which of course, Burns pretended not to understand.

Let's go back to the good old days for a Burns and Allen routine.

GRACIE ALLEN: My brother Willie is going to join the army.

GEORGE BURNS: Well, if everyone else does their share, maybe we can win the war, anyway.

GRACIE: I've bought him some presents. A yo-yo, in case he goes to Egypt.

GEORGE: I don't understand.

GRACIE: Well, you know how lazy he is. He always wanted to play with a yo-yo, but doesn't like to move it up and down.

GEORGE: I still don't understand.

GRACIE: Well, they ride camels there, don't they? And they sway up and down all the time, so all he'll have to do is . . .

GEORGE: I get it, Gracie. Silly of me not to have figured it out for myself. What did you get him in case they send him to the Pacific islands?

GRACIE: A knife and a hatchet.

GEORGE: In case he has to hack his way through the jungle?

GRACIE: No. They grow bananas and coconuts there, don't they? Well, he likes banana splits with chopped nuts.

GEORGE: Say good night, Gracie.

GRACIE: Good night.

RED BUTTONS When he was sixteen, Aaron Chwatt answered an ad for "bell-boy and singer" at Dinty Moore's tavern on City Island in the Bronx, and was issued a uniform with forty-eight buttons. The customers immediately gave him the nickname he has kept ever since.

He was born on February 5, 1919, on New York's Lower East Side. He served his apprenticeship on the Borscht Circuit in the Catskills, and in Minsky's burlesque. By 1941 he worked his way up to a small role in a Hollywood film that was never released.

In 1942 he appeared in *Vickie,* a stage play starring Jose Ferrer, and a string of other minor roles followed. His comic talent was favorably noticed in an otherwise undistinguished musical *Hold It* in 1948, where he outshone the rest of the cast. It led to his appearance on television, where he portrayed Joe E. Lewis in a dramatization of that comedian's ill-fated career, and had several guest shots on variety shows like Milton Berle's.

For the 1953 fall season, CBS gave him his own half hour, probably as a low-key comedy alternative to NBC's exuberant Berle. He lasted only two seasons but made enough of an impression to assure himself a future in nightclubs, films, and theater. As he demonstrated in the film *Sayonara* (1957), he could handle a straight dramatic role, and from then on his career seesawed between drama and comedy. He also appeared in *The Longest Day* (1962) and *The Poseidon Adventure* (1973).

Here's some of Red's material:

Sophia Loren just had a baby. His first words were, "Gee, is that all for me?"

Most singers are Italian, and most comedians are Jewish. And yet there's not much difference between them—one year of high school.

You know the sorriest guy in history? He was the one who laughed when Lucretia Borgia said, "Name your poison."

Do you know what Venus de Milo said to Colonel Sanders? "Sure was finger-licking good!"

Do you know why Joe Torre is the manager of the Mets baseball team? Because he was too chicken to play catcher. He was afraid they would call him "Chicken Catcher Torre."

SID CAESAR One of his early bits was a complete wartime movie—the aerial battles between the always smiling American heroes and the grim-visaged evil Japs, the obligatory love interest, the wiping out of a machine-gun nest. He did all the sound effects, dialogue, and narration, and the whole sketch lasted just a few minutes, packed with laughs from start to finish. At first Caesar did this for the amusement of his buddies in the Coast Guard, but it was kept intact in the film *Tars and Spars,* which was a tribute to this branch of the Armed Forces.

This led to his breaking into TV in 1949. He might do, for a change of pace, a complete pantomime bit—such as his classic pianist who has everything go wrong, including hitting a sour note in a routine piece, nearly breaking his fingers striking the keyboard with its cover closed, and so on.

Out of a myriad of sketches with partner Imogene Coca, one that memory insists on dredging up is the time he is trying to dissuade her from jumping off a tall building. As she starts demonstrating what led her to it—continual knockdown fights with her husband—he gets progressively more and more disheveled, pummeled, and mauled. In the end, he is more than glad to help her execute her suicide plan.

Such was the world of Sid Caesar, the star of one of television's early highlights, *Your Show of Shows.* He and Coca—and also Howard Morris and Carl Reiner, who cut their baby TV teeth on the program—brought to the medium something that was practiced by many, but

Sid Caesar

rarely so well: the development of a simple basic gag to the limits of its comic potential. It was the same approach used in the movies by Laurel and Hardy.

Sid also appeared on Broadway in *Little Me* (1962) and was in a half-dozen or so films, including a leading role in *It's a Mad, Mad, Mad, Mad World* (1963).

Sid Caesar was born in Yonkers, New York, on September 8, 1922. His father owned a restaurant, and Sid claims he developed his gift for imitating the inflections of foreign languages without understanding them by eavesdropping on the conversations of foreign laborers who frequented the place. At first he wanted to be a musician, but when he joined the Coast Guard he found the men appreciated his humorous bits better, and he stuck to comedy ever since.

CHARLIE CALLAS One of the new breed, Greek-American Charlie Callas broke into show business against great odds. First of all, he looks like an imperfectly dried prune on a 90-pound frame; second, he was a shy kid and a stutterer in childhood. When he did overcome his shyness and tried for comedy, he took the odd route of doing impressions of things, rather than people: to my knowledge, he is the only comedian who does an impression of a bowl of cereal being heated.

Callas' first break came in New York in 1966 on the *Merv Griffin Show*. Jerry Lewis loved his impression of a nervous man shooting ducks, and took him to Hollywood. Subsequently, he appeared in *Big Mouth* with Lewis, got a featured role in the series *Switch* in the 1977 season, and was the voice (if strange sounds may be called "voice") of the dragon in Walt Disney's *Pete's Dragon* (1977). He appeared in person in *Silent Movie* (1976).

Ladies and gentlemen, Charlie Callas:

A Pole and an Italian jump from an airplane. The Pole pulls the cord—and the chute works perfectly. The Italian pulls the cord—and nothing happens. He keeps falling straight down. As he passes his friend, the Pole gets mad, unbuckles the harness, and shouts, "So you wanna race, eh?"

I come from a tough neighborhood. You could walk ten blocks in any direction and never leave the scene of a crime.

GODFREY CAMBRIDGE Godfrey Cambridge was one of the black social satirists who became a new thing on the comedy scene in the 1960s. He differed from the majority in that his racial humor was not bitter, and he was not above disparaging some of the characteristics of his race within the framework of social protest:

Now at last I can get the kind of job to which I can carry a briefcase—with fried chicken and watermelon in it, of course.

If I really want to scare the hell out of my white friends, I drive out to the suburb they live in and walk down their street slowly, carrying the real estate section of the *New York Times*.

Born February 26, 1933, in New York City, he attended Hofstra University and CCNY, but his first jobs were menial and clerical. He performed for the first time professionally in an off-Broadway revival of *Take a Giant Step* in 1956, after which he had a succession of minor roles until his friend Ossie Davis gave him his first role on Broadway in *Purlie Victorious* (1961). He also augmented his income by doing a nightclub routine, which led in 1964 to a brief appearance on the *Jack Paar Show*. After that, he basked in newly found national fame, recorded several albums for Epic, and acted in a number of films, including *The President's Analyst* (1967), *Bye Bye Braverman* (1968), and *Cotton Comes to Harlem* (1972). Godfrey Cambridge died in 1976, aged only 43.

JUDY CANOVA A cornball hillbilly style and vocal gymnastics distinguish a talented, versatile comedienne who was actually trained for opera. Born November 10, 1916, in Jacksonville, Florida, to a vaudeville family, she soon joined the act, together with sister Annie and brother Zeke. She sang on radio by the age of twelve, later went to the Cincinnati Conservatory to study opera.

During the Depression, the three children developed a hillbilly act that was good enough to be booked in a Greenwich Village nightclub. Judy's mugging and broad antics made her the star of the act, and she was offered a part in a

Judy Canova

Broadway musical, *Calling All Stars* (1934). From here on, she became one of the busiest entertainers in the business, making two dozen movies in Hollywood, among them *Scatterbrain* (1940), *Joan of the Ozarks* (1942), *Honeychile* (1951), and *Carolina Cannonball* (1955), two more Broadway shows, and hundreds of radio and television appearances in the next two decades. She had her own show on radio for ten years, and appeared on the first country music program ever to be televised, in 1939.

She continued appearing in rodeos and country music shows (such as *Grand Ole Opry*) in the 1950s and 1960s. Married twice, she has two daughters by her second husband.

EDDIE CANTOR Eddie Cantor was a dominant force in American show business for half a century. At one time or another he was number one or very close to it in vaudeville, the *Ziegfeld Follies,* musical comedy, radio, film, and television. He had an unsurpassed eye for new talent, and developed such protégés as George Burns and Gracie Allen, Bert Gordon (The Mad Russian), Parkyakarkus, Dinah Shore, Deanna Durbin, Eddie Fisher, Sammy Davis, Jr., Bobby Breen, and Rubinoff.

Cantor was born to an impoverished family on New York's Lower East Side on January 31, 1892. His real name was Edward Israel Iskowitz. A community welfare center sponsored a Surprise Lake Camp country vacation for the deprived youngster ("my first stretch of green that wasn't a pool table"), and the camp later became one of his many charitable causes.

Cantor started out in the lower depths of amateur contests and burlesque theaters, and came into his own as a blackface vaudeville comedian. He was a shrewd

Eddie Cantor (right) with Joe Franklin

showman with an intense, staccato, somewhat nervous style that kept the audience alert and involved. After headlining in the *Ziegfeld Follies,* he moved into musical comedy with a 1924–1926 smash, *Kid Boots.* He made the film version in 1926 with the "It Girl" herself, the flaming Clara Bow—of their love scenes, Cantor remarked, "She could kiss a tree and start a forest fire." Films yet to be made included *Whoopee* (1930), *The Kid from Spain* (1932), *Ali Baba Goes to Town* (1937), *Roman Scandals* (1933), *Strike Me Pink* (1936), and *Thank Your Lucky Stars* (1943).

Beginning in 1931 Cantor was a radio superstar, with an audience that peaked at 60 million. His humor and optimism helped Americans through the tortuous Depression era, and his skit about persuading a destitute human being to forget suicide and give life another try elicited several letters from listeners who were inspired by the skit to start anew. Cantor felt a responsibility to his brothers and sisters in the audience beyond singing and joking. But it wasn't all easy for Cantor in radio—at first his inability to stand still while performing meant the microphone missed a lot of his chatter, until someone gave him a portable mike. Cantor's fast-moving, bobbing style of entertaining was a hangover from his tomato-ducking days in vaudeville when he had to move fast or suffer the consequences.

In televisions's early days, when other established stars hesitated to venture into the new medium, Cantor appeared on the *Colgate Comedy Hour* in 1950. He was the first entertainer to be seen nationwide, via the coaxial cable, paving the way for Bob Hope, Jimmy Durante, and Jack Benny.

Cantor's declining years were marred by the deaths of his beloved wife, Ida, and one of his daughters, forever ending the famous joke about Ida and his five daughters. He was forced to retire by repeated heart attacks, and died in 1964.

Here's Eddie Cantor in 1929 A.C. (After Crash):

I am a very sick man. I was run over by General Motors, got burned by Westinghouse, and Otis Elevator left me off in the basement. As you can guess, I was in the market. In it nothing—I was *under* it. I went to J. P. Morgan and complained. He said, "My boy, just to show you that I have faith in the American economy, I'll give you these 1,000 shares of U.S. Steel." I thanked him and said, "Couldn't you make it something more substantial, like maybe ten bucks in cash?"

GEORGE CARLIN Along with Cheech and Chong and the Firesign Theater, George Carlin is one of the few comedians able to penetrate the hard core of rock freakdom in the early 1970s. He still enjoys a large—and, primarily, young—following for his concert appearances and record albums. In the tradition of his idol, Lenny Bruce, Carlin has undergone an obscenity bust.

He began in New York City coffeehouses and nightclubs as a typical, clean-cut, conservative comic, before deciding to let it all hang out. He promptly grew a pony tail, replaced his business suit and tie with a T-shirt, and found his comic identity in sex, weed, dirty words, and an underground comics type mentality. Why the change? On his 1973 TV special, *Monsanto Night Presents the* Real *George Carlin,* the long-haired, bearded, T-shirted Carlin pointed to a lifesize cardboard cutout photo of his former straight self and explained, "I used to be this guy and I liked him. I had fun and he did a lot for me. But he was just surface. I wasn't there. After a while I realized I wasn't in my own act. And then I discovered a much better character for me—myself."

The big change meant that in 1963 Carlin would do a Kennedy impersonation: "Lahst yea-h there was a $7 billion deficit—and that was just in my checking account." But in 1973 he would say, "Nixon is the perfect symbol for our country. He looks like he hasn't taken a shit in a month!"

Carlin is quick to point out that such change is natural, and to prove his point he describes how his whole generation did it: "And then pot came along and gang fights went away. In one semester in shop class guys went from making zip guns to hash pipes."

A Grammy Award–winning comedian, Carlin has released such albums as *Occu-*

pation: *Foole, Toledo Window Box,* and *Class Clown,* for which a high school teacher was fired after playing the album for his students.

ART CARNEY "The best second banana in the business" gained undying fame for his definitive portrayal of Ralph Kramden's upstairs neighbor on the durable show *The Honeymooners,* starring Jackie Gleason. His slouch, windmill gestures, slovenly mannerisms, and dimwitted remarks played a perfect counterpoint to Jackie Gleason's high-strung Kramden characterization, and despite Gleason's considerable skill at camera-hogging, it was a tossup as to who stole more scenes from whom.

Carney has had a versatile and distinguished career—far more than one top-rated television show. As a child, he liked to imitate film and radio personalities. He hoped to do that in show business, but his first job, at the age of nineteen, was as a straight singer with Horace Heidt's Orchestra (*Pot o' Gold,* 1937–40). Soon he began to look for humorous novelty material to try out on audiences. He also worked on many other radio shows.

Finally, his gift for mimicry came in handy. The producers of radio's *March of Time* documentaries needed people to imitate famous political figures of the

Art Carney

day. Carney tested out perfect as Franklin D. Roosevelt and worked on the program for two years, until he was drafted during World War II.

Reappearing on radio, (*Henry Morgan Show,* 1946–48), he became a second banana on Morey Amsterdam's show, which made the transition to television in 1949. This, in turn, led to his appearance on Jackie Gleason's variety hour, where "The Honeymooners" was at first an occasional sketch. It was so well received that it became a weekly half-hour situation comedy—and the rest is history.

Art Carney was born in Mount Vernon, New York, in 1918. As a teenager, he did amateur theatricals, then drifted into radio and nightclub work. In 1940 he married high school sweetheart Jean Myers; they have two sons and a daughter.

On radio, he appeared on eight shows as a regular, and on many others as guest comedian—including the shows of Fred Allen, Bert Lahr, and Milton Berle. In the late 1950s he did several Broadway shows, and in one year—1959—he appeared on *nine* television specials. The 1960s saw him once more on Broadway, where he created, in *The Odd Couple,* another unforgettable character (later taken over by Tony Randall for the TV series), with Walter Matthau in the role later given to Jack Klugman.

Art Carney has appeared in a number of films, such as *The Yellow Rolls Royce* (1965) and *A Guide for the Married Man* (1967), winning an Academy Award for his performance in *Harry and Tonto* (1974).

JACK CARSON His specialty was loud-mouthed boors and boneheads who think they are crafty when they are transparently dumb. This type of comedy depends on the actor being able to convince his audience that he is a genuine character, and in this, Carson excelled as few others.

John Elmer Carson was born in Carman, Manitoba, Canada, on October 27, 1910. He stumbled into a theatrical career on a friend's dare—at Carleton College in Minnesota. Teaming up with the friend, he went from small time to Broadway, then struck out on his own. Since vaudeville was dying, he made his way to Hollywood, and films.

Starting with RKO and later switching to Warner Brothers, Carson brightened nearly one hundred films, mostly light comedies, with his expert clowning. Nearly always he was the comic sidekick or supporting star, rarely the featured player. But, professional that he was, he played each role to the hilt. He perfected the double-take technique to a high polish, and used it to advantage in such programmers as *Bringing Up Baby* (1938), *The Bride Came C.O.D.* (1941), *The Male Animal* (1942), *Arsenic and Old Lace* (1944), and *Red Garters* (1954).

In 1951 he became an early supporter of television in Hollywood, and later he appeared in the theater, including the London Palladium. He was married four times.

When he tried to join the Service in 1945, a heart murmur was discovered that Carson never knew about. The condition deteriorated, and in the summer of 1962 he collapsed on stage during a rehearsal for a summer circuit theater appearance. He died on January 2, 1963, at the age of only fifty-two.

JOHNNY CARSON Reputedly the highest salaried star in TV history, Johnny Carson, of *Tonight Show* fame, is also one of the small screen's most intelligent and refreshing wits.

Johnny Carson

He was born on October 23, 1925, in Corning, Iowa, to an average middle-class family. His childhood hobby was magic, interspersed with ventriloquism and a foreshadowing of the wisecracks yet to come. As the mystifying "Great Carsoni," he earned as much as $5 a performance.

After a stint in the Navy, Carson earned a B.A. at the University of Nebraska, where he majored in drama and radio. His first significant foray into comedy, following a variety of television and radio jobs, was his 1951 TV program, *Carson's Cellar*. It was basically a satire of headline-making news, and it won a following among many famous comedians, some of whom, including Red Skelton and Groucho Marx, made free guest appearances on the show.

At the moment of *Carson's Cellar's* demise, Skelton hired Carson as a comedy writer for his popular television show. During an August 1954 rehearsal, Skelton suffered an injury, and on two hours' notice appointed Carson as his replacement. The response was such that CBS initiated the *Johnny Carson Show*, a 39-week ratings fiasco which demonstrated that Carson's talent was not for overpowering standup comedy, but for witty persiflage and skillfully humorous conversation.

Several successful quiz shows and dramatic roles later, Carson took over Jack Paar's seat on NBC's *Tonight Show*. Where sponsorship had been weak, the show was now booked solid. Anemic ratings soared. Johnny Carson had ascended to the throne of late-night television.

JACK CARTER Fast and funny with the one-liners, Jack Carter suffers from an affliction he shares with many top comics, notably Red Skelton and Milton Berle—the compulsive need to be "on" at all times, even if the audience is just one person. A perfectionist, he worries constantly how this or that gag will go over, how it could be improved, or whether it should be dropped. Such perfectionism has made him a top-of-the-mark headliner for many years in big nightclubs, Las Vegas, and other resorts, and on TV variety and talk shows and panel quiz programs.

The voracious need to be the main attraction may be an inheritance from the carnival atmosphere of Coney Island, where Jack Chakrin was born on June 24, 1923, to the owner of a candy store. In school he studied art and drama, playing the title role in a school production of *Cyrano de Bergerac*. In real life, he started his career on a far more prosaic level, as towel boy and shill for one of the boardwalk bathhouses at Coney Island.

His first crack at show biz was on *Major Bowes' Amateur Hour,* where he did imitations of Jimmy Durante and the Frankenstein monster. Later, he toured with one of the Major's units, and also did some summer stock work in comedy roles for Christopher Morley's group. For a while, he was announcer for Les Brown's dance band. During World War II, he was featured in the *Flying Varieties* soldier show throughout the Pacific.

In 1948 he started doing his comedy on television. He has remained there ever since, guesting on dozens of specials and variety shows, perhaps the biggest boost to his career being regular spots on the *Jack Paar Show* in the mid-1950s.

Carter's style is rapid delivery of one-liners punctuated by ego-deflating putdowns—of costars, hecklers, and most frequently himself, for Jack has a self-deprecating streak in his nature that never permits him to be satisfied with his success.

Jack Carter

"My mother drives me crazy. If I call her while I'm on the road, she hollers at me for spending the money on too many phone calls. If I don't call, she loves to go around the neighborhood and say, 'See what a rotten son I got—he never phones.' You can't win!"

And that about sums up his philosophy.

AJAX CASSIDY,

see FRED ALLEN

CAROL CHANNING Lorelei, the heroine of Anita Loos' book, *Gentlemen Prefer Blondes,* has been a quintessential American character ever since the novel first appeared in the 1920's. But it wasn't until 1948, when Carol Channing appeared in the Broadway version, that her characterization became definitive: Carol personified her, with the wide-eyed pretended innocence and husky voice of a little girl with a cold. The role has been hers for the asking ever since, and none of the other comediennes who have done it can escape being compared to her original comedy creation.

A measure of the admiration of her peers is that Carol Channing is the most imitated actress today—and many of the impressionists are men.

She was born in Seattle, Washington, on January 31, 1921, and attended Bennington College in Vermont. She always had a consuming ambition to be on the stage, and sang in a New York nightclub before she was twenty. In 1941 she almost made it on Broadway, obtaining the role of understudy in *Let's Face It,* but her big chance never came. So she tried Hollywood, where at first all she could get were modeling jobs for Los Angeles ad agencies.

Carol Channing

Eventually, she made it into the cast of a Hollywood revue, *Lend an Ear,* which went on the road and arrived on Broadway in 1948. This time she attracted favorable notices, and was offered the role of the "little girl from Little Rock."

Channing has remained at the top of her profession ever since—in films, casinos, and nightclubs, and on television, where she has appeared on everything from panel shows to her own specials. She bowled over Broadway again in *Hello, Dolly* in 1964, and ten years later in the revival of her greatest role, *Lorelei.*

CHARLIE CHAPLIN Charles Spencer Chaplin was born on April 16, 1889, in London. His parents were variety artists whose lives were beset by troubles. His father drank, and left the family when Charles was still a child; his mother lost her voice, and eventually her sanity. With elder brother Sidney, Charles grew up mostly in institutional environments, in poverty and squalor; their only escape was the world of make-believe. It led them at an early age to a thespian career; they had the good fortune to join the troupe of Fred Karno, who toured the English countryside with variety acts. He took a paternal interest in his charges.

In the years that followed, it became apparent that Charlie was Karno's best alumnus, with Stan Laurel a close second. Both left the troupe during a tour of the United States; Charlie left during the second such trip, in the latter part of 1913, after receiving an offer from Mack Sennett.

Charlie Chaplin (center) with Edna Purviance, Bud Jamison, Billy Armstrong, Margie Reiger

Arriving on the Keystone movie lot in Hollywood, early in 1914, Charlie revolutionized the world of film comedy for all time. Without fully knowing what he was doing, Charlie in his strange tramp costume—with the pathetic attempt at class with hat, cane, and frayed gloves, his unique shuffling gait, soon to become imitated all over the world, his wistful smile, and the facile transition from slapstick to pathos and back again—captured something on film that had never been there before. As analysts have pointed out ad nauseam, it was "everyman"—a sort of human common denominator.

Whatever it was, it made Charlie the most phenomenally meteoric star ascending in the Hollywood firmament. After a single year of apprenticeship at Keystone, during which he made 34 short films and one feature (the first full-length film comedy ever), he could practically write his own ticket—and he did.

In 1915 Essanay offered Chaplin ten times what he had been getting from Sennett, or $1,250 a week. In 1916 Mutual upgraded it to $10,000 a week; by 1918 he was making about $1 million a year and had his own producing company. (In 1918, $5 a day was the going rate for extras.)

He took the time to make full-length features: from 35 per year, he slowed down to one masterpiece every three or four years. There were *The Gold Rush* (1925), *City Lights* (1931), *Modern Times* (1936), and *The Great Dictator* (1940). He argued against sound; even with sound established for ten solid years, Chaplin in 1936 still made a feature that is, for all practical purposes, silent—although music and effects are on the sound track.

His enormous popularity in countries all over the world, where he became the single most universally recognizable person in the history of the motion pictures, overshadows the merits or demerits of Chaplin the man. The offscreen Chaplin was involved in painful controversies: moral, such as his admitted philanderings, predilection for young girls, illegitimate offspring, and so on; political, such as his early espousal of Communist causes; and artistic, such as his treatment of a controversial subject in *Monsieur Verdoux* (1947) and his sad decline in bombs like *The Countess from Hong Kong*. No matter. All of that came later, and could be blamed on many factors, such as the difficulty of adjusting to such sudden fame and fortune. And it is totally irrelevant to the fact that Charlie, the screen character, remains one of the noblest accomplishments of which the movies can boast.

George Bernard Shaw called Chaplin the only authentic genius the movies ever produced, and hardly anyone would care to dispute the claim.

He died on Christmas Day, 1977, in his home in Switzerland.

CHARLEY CHASE Second perhaps only to the legendary Max Linder, Charley Chase was a master of the comedy of social embarrassment. He was a dapper, likable young man, invariably courteous and helpful but somewhat naive; whether single or married, he always got into humiliating predicaments through no fault of his own. Of all the comedians whose output merits revival, he is perhaps the most neglected.

Born Charles Parrott in Baltimore in 1893, he became a vaudeville performer who did Irish monologue, sang, danced, and played several instruments. Approaching films in 1913 with his brother James, he was given work by Mack

Charley Chase

Sennett. His brother, using, for some reason, the name Paul Parrott, worked behind the camera. Charles performed as Charley Chase, and directed as Charles Parrott.

Later, at Roach Studios, Paul Parrott had a series of shorts, while Charles wrote and directed; but by 1924 Charley had his own series while Paul, now suddenly changing his name back to James (or Jimmie) Parrott, went permanently into directing. Not to be outdone, Charley became a director again, after

fifteen years for Roach, at Columbia; there he directed some Andy Clyde and The Three Stooges shorts, two Smith and Dale shorts, and several shorts in which he appeared.

He was married for years, but for never-disclosed reasons lived apart from his wife. He died on June 20, 1940, on the losing side of a bout with alcohol.

CHEECH and CHONG Cheech and Chong audiences don't read the *New*

Cheech (at wheel) and Chong

York Times and the *Wall Street Journal*, they read the *National Lampoon* and *Rolling Stone.* These are the comedians of the long-haired, stoned generation of rock aficionados (that is, of what is sometimes termed the counterculture). Booze, politics, television, and similarly conventional comic subject matter enter into their routines only peripherally, if at all. This is stoned comedy, and to appreciate it fully, one has either to be stoned (and I don't mean on liquor), or at least know the experience intimately.

Cheech (Richard Marin) was born in Watts in 1946, of Mexican descent. He sang with a group called Captain Shagnasty and His Lock Ness Pickles before splitting for Canada to dodge the Vietnam War draft. Chong (Tommy Chong) was born in Alberta, Canada, in 1940, of Chinese descent. He ran a topless club in Vancouver, where he met and teamed up with Cheech.

Together they developed their youth-oriented humor, and formed the only comedy act accepted by rock concert audiences. Cheech and Chong toured with top rock bands, where they first won a wide following. Then they began releasing recordings of their routines, which were invariably big sellers and strong chart performers.

Many of Cheech and Chong's jokes parody the drug culture:

CHEECH: My four-year-old told me I dress like a fag. I fixed her, though; I took away her lid [dose of dope]!

CHONG: So what did she do?

CHEECH: Now she chases cars like a dog. Gets stoned on the exhaust.

TOMMY CHONG,

see CHEECH and CHONG

SENATOR CLAGHORN Like Mrs. Nussbaum, Ajax Cassidy, and Titus Moody, Senator Claghorn was a character created by Fred Allen for the "Allen's Alley" section of his radio show. Since the "Alley" skit was always allotted five minutes, each of the four had only a minute and 15 seconds each week.

What the Senator—played by a fine dramatic actor, Kenny Delmar—did with this is amazing. His chauvinistic Southern bias, his blusteringly jovial manner, his repetitive peculiarity ("Senator, Ah say, Senator Claghorn heah"), his way of addressing everyone patronizingly as "son" ("That was a joke, son, Ah'm just too fast for you") became accepted as part of the national culture.

The Senate mailroom would get hundreds of letters addressed to Senator Claghorn, apparently in the belief that he was a real politician. A number of Southern towns vied for the privilege of renaming streets and plazas for him. The Warner Brothers cartoon department created a character, Foghorn the Rooster, copied faithfully from the original. Although intended as a caricature, the good Senator was not resented by most Southern-

ers; on the contrary, he was hailed as a true champion of the South:

When Ah go to New York Ah never come near the Yankee Stadium. And Ah won't see the Dodgers, either, unless Dixie Walker is playing, or they have a southpaw pitcher. In mah historical, Ah say historical ree-search Ah discovered that Horace Greeley was cross-eyed. When he said "Go West"—he was really facing South.

Fred Allen wrote the Senator's lines, but Delmar, a many-voiced radio veteran, delivered them with such gusto and mint julep–flavored accent that a robust new character sprang up over the airwaves.

SENATOR CLAGHORN: Ah've got to shake mah pegs, son. Ah'm the guest of honor at a concert of the Mobile Philharmonic, the finest, Ah say finest, musical aggregation of the South. The leader is Arturo Tuscaloosa. Instead of a baton, he conducts with a hoe handle. It's the only band in the world with a hounddog choir; when they play the Barcarolle you kin hear the barkin' twenty miles away.

FRED ALLEN: How is the woodwind section, Senator?

CLAGHORN: Ah never, Ah say never, seen so much wood and heard so much wind.

ALLEN: And the string section?

CLAGHORN: Son, they got rope, hemp, and twine. That's string aplenty.

ALLEN: And the brass?

CLAGHORN: They carry thirty spittoons. More brass than that is showin' off.

ALLEN: What do they play?

CLAGHORN: All the classics, son. Everythin' by Rimsky Culpepper. The Georgia Cracker Suite. The Flight of the Boll Weevil. The Poet and the Sharecropper. The Moonshine Sonata. Rhapsody in Grey. And no concert, Ah say, no concert is complete without the Claghorn Fifth.

ALLEN: You wrote it, Senator?

CLAGHORN: Ah drink it, son. You ain't got it upstairs, son, admit it, Ah'm too fast for ya.

CLARK and McCULLOUGH Their brand of nonsense was compared by critics with that of The Marx Brothers, and they were among the first Broadway headliners invited to do their act in sound movies in 1928. Bobby Clark and Paul McCullough specialized in rapid-fire dialogue that made no sense at all.

"I object, Your Honor," Bobby Clark would say, as a lawyer.

"On what grounds?" asks the judge.

"None!" Clark shoots back.

"Overruled."

"Content," says Clark triumphantly.

The next time the judge makes a statement, Clark jumps up to shout, "I don't object!"

Paul McCullough was born in Springfield, Ohio, in 1884, and Robert Edwin Clark in 1888. They met in school, and practiced their act at the YMCA. By 1900 they joined a minstrel troupe where they played instruments, did a song-and-dance act, a little tumbling, and, when necessary, shifted scenery. In 1905 they were hired by a circus, and began to mix a little comedy with their acrobatics.

Their vaudeville debut was in 1912 in New Brunswick, New Jersey, and for a while they also traveled the burlesque wheels. Somewhere along the way, Bobby Clark picked up a trademark that surpasses even Harold Lloyd's famous lensless glasses: he had glasses painted on his face.

They made a really big hit in England, where they played in *Peek-a-boo* and *Chuckles of 1922.* Among their audience was Irving Berlin, who hired them for the *Music Box Revue* in the fall of 1922. They won Broadway over, and returned for the 1924 edition of the show, as well as for the musical comedy *The Ramblers* (1926).

Then came sound movies, at first for Fox in 1928–29. They made 14, varying in length from one to five reels—an unusual length for a comedy act. More Broadway work followed, and 15 more shorts at RKO—this time all two-reelers—in the period between 1931 and 1935. In 1935 they toured the country; but the following year, March 25, 1926, McCullough, always the mixer and the sociable man, committed suicide.

Clark carried on alone in Broadway productions. He became interested in Restoration period comedy; he appeared in revivals from that era, and helped stage some of them. He lectured on the history of comedy at acting schools. During this period he acted in one film, *The Goldwyn Follies* (1938), but they made him abandon his painted-on glasses for a real pair, and made him abandon his comic flair for a Hollywood facsimile.

Bobby Clark died in February 1960.

IMOGENE COCA A fey five-foot-three pixie with a tinge of lunacy, Imogene Coca gained national fame as partner of Sid Caesar in the five-year run of *Your Show of Shows* (originally *Admiral Broadway Revue)* between 1949 and 1954. With astonishing versatility, she matched him expression for expression in their pantomime skits, carrying on inane conversations as his wife, girlfriend, neighbor, or total stranger; she satirized fads, fashions, foibles, and femmes fatales, and did solo routines that earned her recognition as the best comedienne in TV in 1951, according to the Radio and Television Editors of America.

Miss Coca was born in Philadelphia in 1909, and started taking piano, singing, and dancing lessons at an early age. At fifteen, she was a full-time trouper getting her first chorus job in a Broadway musical. It was only some ten years later, during rehearsals for *New Faces of 1934,* that she was seen by the producer while clowning around for the private amusement of the cast; she was given a comedy solo spot, and has worked at comedy ever since.

She amassed impressive credits in the theater, starting in 1925 with *When You Smile,* including *New Faces of 1934, New Faces of 1936,* and *New Faces of 1937,* and going on to *Happy Birthday* (1948), *The Girls in 509* (1958), ad infinitum. She also made a few forays into the movies, and in television A.C. (After Caesar) she had her own series for a while, in which she played a maid. But nothing could quite match the free-wheeling zaniness of *Your Show of Shows* and the chemistry between her and Caesar.

MYRON COHEN

MYRON COHEN Myron Cohen started telling stories when he was a salesman in New York's garment district. Encouraged by the laughs he was getting from customers and fellow employees, he kept at it more diligently than at pushing silk, until his boss told him, "Myron, you're a wonderful, funny guy and you should be paid for telling those stories of yours. But not by me!"

He became a professional comedian and in time developed into one of America's favorite raconteurs. He is at his best in the intimate atmosphere of a nightclub, telling a story with all the subtle dialect nuances of which he is an acknowledged master. There may be no belly-laugh punchlines: it is in creation of atmosphere that the raconteur excels.

Here is a relatively simple story that gains almost all of its impact from the way it's told:

It is a cold, cold evening, forty degrees below zero, a blizzard is blowing. The scene is a bakery. A small guy, all wrapped up from head to toe, comes in and says in a quivering voice [Jewish inflection], "Wun roll, please." The baker tries to make conversation: "You come a long way in this weather?" "Wun roll, please." The baker serves it to him, and tries again: "Is that all? Wouldn't you like a pie, or a piece of cake, or some cookies?" "Wun roll." The baker gives up, accepts the payment, and then has an afterthought: "Is that roll for someone else—your wife, maybe?" At last the little man speaks up: "Wot do you tink, on a night like this I would go out for wun roll for myself?"

JERRY COLONNA A bushy mustache, rolling eyes second only to Eddie Cantor's, a natural talent for zaniness, and silly catch phrases like "Who's Yehoodi?", yelled at the top of his lungs—and there you have the inspired nonsense of Jerry Colonna, long-time sidekick of Bob Hope.

Gerard Colonna was born in Boston in 1904. Even as a boy he had powerful lungs, and his first ambition was to play the trombone. He took lessons and became proficient enough to get into several college bands and be hired by Joe Herlihy's Orchestra.

On the side, in the mid-1930s, he began to perform comedy routines on radio. With an unerring sense for the absurd and an offbeat slant, he began to attract a small but devout following. This did not escape the notice of the producers of Bob Hope's show, and in 1938 he came on as Hope's sidekick.

A real trouper, he kept up with Hope through all his wartime and postwar tours to entertain servicemen, staying on for many Hope films—*The Road to Rio* (1947) was one. He also appeared on television shows with Hope.

Here is a typical exchange of Colonnialisms:

HOPE: Colonna, I hear you know all about horses.

Jerry Colonna

COLONNA: Of course. I've been riding side-saddle since I was two.

HOPE: That's a sissy way!

COLONNA: On an elephant?

HOPE: Colonna, you ruffle my dignity!

COLONNA: No, you ruffle mine—mine's got pleats in it.

HOPE: Look, Shrub Mug, how do you get along without brains?

COLONNA: I cheat. What's your excuse?

CHESTER CONKLIN The little man with the drooping mustache was always in trouble—kicked, pushed, and shoved by the Keystone Kops, abused by W. C. Fields, mangled in *Modern Times'* grinding machinery by Charlie Chaplin. He was beset, put upon, mortified.

One of the star graduates of Mack Sennett's inspired mayhem factory, Chester Conklin could elicit laughs by just appearing, with his hangdog mustache. Once in a while he burlesqued a villain, and a magnificent ball he had, too—but most of the time he got the pie in the face, serving as an ideal stooge for Sennett's more robust comedians. The absurd walrus mustache became a trademark almost as easily recognizable as Chaplin's hat and cane.

Ironically, the man who worked in pantomime prepared himself for show business by taking elocution lessons and winning first prize in his hometown Opera House amateur recital, where he did a takeoff on the speech and mannerisms of the famous pianist Arthur Rubinstein.

The hometown was Oskaloosa, Iowa, where he was born on January 11, 1886. It was a mining district, populated mostly by miners of Welsh ancestry, and the local Opera House was its only cultural outlet. Chester left home and supported himself with dozens of odd jobs in dozens of towns. He heard a circus was hiring people in Los Angeles. He went there and signed on as a clown.

He also heard that the film companies were hiring second- and third-rate actors (during the early years, most top performers wouldn't have been caught dead in "flickers"). He applied at Majestic Studios and got some work.

Later that year (1913), he switched to Mack Sennett's Keystone. Sennett knew how to bring out the best in his comedians, and the identity established for Conklin worked out to perfection. He was either "Droopington" the victim or "Walrus" the villain; he was teamed up with partners such as Mack Swain in his "Ambrose" characterization, and later Hank Mann.

In 1920 Conklin went to Fox, and later free-lanced at different studios. He made four silent features as second banana to W. C. Fields at Paramount; Chaplin used him in *Modern Times* and *The Great Dictator*. Only one director ever tried to use him in serious roles—Erich von Stroheim, who put him in *Greed* (1923), and *Woman of the World* (1925).

Conklin was married twice—first in 1914 (the marriage ended in 1933) and for the second time in 1965, when he was seventy-nine, to June Gunther. Conklin hated the idea of retiring: in 1954 a Los Angeles reporter found him working as Santa Claus for a department store. He found work in two films in the 1960s, *Li'l Abner* and *Big Hand for a Little Lady*.

JOE COOK He was sometimes billed as "one-man vaudeville," and was equally adept at telling jokes, acting in skits, singing, dancing, and mime. His comedy was good-natured, as was his infectious smile. Joe Cook was a thorough professional, and went through virtually all facets of show business except television before retiring in 1942.

Joe Cook

Four Hawaiians, which enjoyed a measure of success on the vaudeville circuits.

Joe Cook's Broadway debut was in *Hitchy-Koo* of 1919, and he stayed around for most of the twenties and thirties, appearing in *Earl Carroll's Vanities* several times (1923, 1924, 1926), in John Murray Anderson's *Fanfare* (1931), and in a number of other musical revues.

On film, he did some of the best comedies for Educational Pictures in the mid-1930s. He became a regular on many radio variety shows, and was the featured comic on a program called *Circus Night*.

He retired in 1942 and died on May 16, 1959.

Born Joseph Lopez in Evansville, Indiana, in 1890, he was orphaned at three and adopted by the Cook family. Like W. C. Fields and Fred Allen, he started as a comic juggler, at fourteen; he also trained himself in dancing and acrobatics, so as to be able to find jobs in vaudeville. For a while, he induced his half brother to join the act, which was billed as Joe Cook and Brother.

He sang novelty songs on occasions, and created an act with three others, The

PROFESSOR IRWIN COREY Master of the difficult art of double-talk, the good professor—he holds a Doctorate in Nothing from several asylums—can break up any audience with an authoritative lecture on any subject:

"We must first sublimate the imponderable eventualities, but only if we finalize the extemporaneous intricacies of the universal consciousness."

Corey is of indeterminate age, background, and education. As to his mind, it is necessary to realize that we cannot sustain, but can rise with impurity and render our unconditional acceptance—but we digress. He was born in Brooklyn and placed in an orphanage when he was one year old. He found he had the ability to entertain fellow inmates, and at the age of fifteen, when he left the orphanage, he had the same effect on fellow hobos with whom he traveled on freight trains.

Having made a little money in boxing (featherweight), he tried his professorial characterization in a few nightclubs, around 1943. His style was different, and eventually it landed him in the highly prestigious Blue Angel in New York, where he was held over for an incredible 55-week run.

Corey has done a lot of TV, and had a regular role in the series *Doc*. On Broadway he appeared in *New Faces, Flahooley, Happy as Larry, Mrs. McThing*, and *Thieves*. Film roles include *Thieves, Lips*, and *Car Wash*.

CHARLES CORRELL,

see AMOS 'n' ANDY

BILL COSBY He was born to a poor family in Philadelphia on July 12, 1938. His first job was building orange crates into a shoeshine box, buying polish and rags, and shining shoes. Today Bill Cosby lives in a lavish $1 million mansion crawling with butlers and filled with precious antiques. Yet his humble beginnings were essential for his later success, for it was in a substandard grammar school that Cosby met his buddies Fat Albert, Old Weird Harold, and the other prototypes for his brilliant comedy characters.

It was also in his early years that Cosby first felt the sting of prejudice, which was to shape the moral impetus of his comedy routines. Job-seeking during his freshman year at college, and tiring of the lame pretexts given by employers for not hiring him after he had invested time and money to travel to prospective job locations, Cosby recalls, "I just called up and asked over the phone, 'Do you hire Negroes?' 'No.'"

In the early 1960s Cosby was struggling to establish himself in second-rate nightspots in New York. As he polished his act the bookings became more frequent and prestigious, until he was spotted by network TV producers who in 1965 contracted Cosby to costar opposite Robert Culp

in the successful adventure series, *I Spy*. This made Cosby the first black performer to star in a dramatic TV series, and helped him to three Emmys.

The *Bill Cosby Show*, beginning in 1968, featured Cosby as Chet Kincaid, a modern-day teacher in a black community of real people, instead of the traditional stereotyped blacks that TV audiences had been fed on for decades. Cosby wanted the public to become sensitive to "the changes that have taken place regarding what we the black race are doing in today's society."

In 1972 Cosby began another network show, an hour of comedy and variety on CBS, which he saw as a vehicle for his new entertainment philosophy. "I don't follow anybody else," he explained. "My humor, whether you dig it or not, has got to be real, something that has happened or is now happening."

Cosby is attuned to children and education, especially in the ghetto, and these subjects surface frequently in his work. His beloved Fat Albert character was the genesis of the CBS cartoon show, *Fat Albert and the Cosby Kids*. *The Electric Company*, the National Educational Television Network series, is also a product of Cosby's genius.

In one episode of *Fat Albert*, the Cosby kids find a sackful of diamonds while playing in a garbage dump. Wide-eyed, they decide to buy all the toys and games in the world. Then one determines to buy his father a good pair of shoes to make his working day more comfortable. Another decides to present his mom with a washing machine to spare her hours of toil. Finally, they resolve to use the diamonds to make life a little better for everyone, everywhere. Says Cosby, "There's no harm in laughing while you learn. That is the key to the way I try to teach."

Today Cosby's nightclub performances

Bill Cosby

earn him from $50,000 to $100,000 per week; his comedy albums have won five Grammys and several gold records; and reruns of his television efforts continue to draw a dedicated audience. He is also big in motion pictures, starring in such films as *Uptown Saturday Night* (1974), *Let's Do It Again* (1975), and *A Piece of the Action* (1977).

This is a sample of Cosby's warm, wild, offbeat material:

As a kid, I grew up at a time when there were still radio dramas. I liked the horror shows, they made your hair stand on end and made your whole body tingle, especially if you were home alone. I remember one time I was listening to this horror show about the chicken heart—the heart of a chicken which got bigger and bigger until it broke out of its test tube—swallowed the scientist—ate up the

building—and the announcer was saying breathlessly: ". . . and the heart is going down the street, eating up all the people, and the cars. It's coming up the street, right up to your house, up the stairs, and it's behind your own door this very minute!"

When my father came home that night, he never did understand why I put the sofa against the door and set it on fire, and never even thanked me for saving our house from the big chicken heart.

Lou COSTELLO,

see ABBOTT and COSTELLO

WALLY COX Wally Cox was the famous "Mr. Peepers" of television. His characterizations were usually of the shy little man who despite these qualities holds his own against the world.

Wally Cox

His full name was Wallace Maynard Cox, and he was born in Detroit on December 6, 1924. As he recalled, his childhood experiences inspired his humor: "I was the smallest kid in the class. I had a high-pitched voice, good diction, good marks, and the teachers liked me. I was a perfect subject for getting beaten up. So I contrived a method whereby I could give the correct answers and make the guys laugh, without simultaneously offending the teacher. I had to dance between eggs."

After a stint in the army and studying botany at New York's City College, from which he dropped out, Cox formed his own business in which he made and sold cufflinks and related items. Despite his prosaic comic monologues at parties and informal gatherings he accumulated influential show business friends who interceded to launch his comedy career. One of his benefactors was childhood pal Marlon Brando. Cox made a stunning debut on the stage of the Village Vanguard in 1948.

His nightclub performances gained him the attention of high-level television producers, and helped him graduate to Broadway, radio, and the penning of successful books and plays. He began guesting on TV for Ed Sullivan, Arthur Godfrey, and Perry Como.

The network TV series *Mr. Peepers* had Cox cast in the title role, and its premiere show was aired on July 3, 1952; a nationwide poll named Cox that year's "Most Promising Male Star." When *Mr. Peepers* was canceled, the network was flooded with over 10,000 letters of protest from Cox's fans. A month later Wally Cox, Tony Randall, and Marion Lorne were restored to the airwaves.

Wally Cox appeared in a half dozen or so films, including *The Yellow Rolls-Royce* (1965) and *A Guide for the Married Man* (1967).

He died on February 15, 1973, at the age of forty-eight.

RICHY CRAIG, Jr. The son of a burlesque comedian turned theatrical producer and a musical comedy star, Richy ran away from a boarding school at seventeen to enter the family business. A year later he was a vaudeville headliner; at nineteen, he played the Palace.

At first he did a bit of everything—dancing, singing, playing the ukulele, and doing magic tricks—but then he took to heart an old vaudevillian's admonition that "the less you do on stage the more

Richy Craig Jr.

they seem to like you," and overnight became just a straight monologist. He played Texas Guinan's nightclub and other famous speakeasies during the 1920s, and appeared on radio. By the late twenties he started writing special material for several Broadway revues in which he was cast, including *Broadway Brevities, Animal Crackers* (1929) with the Marx Brothers, *Hey, Nonny, Nonny* (1933), and *Tattle Tales* (1933).

He was a regular on a radio program featuring singer Aileen Stanley when he died, on November 1, 1934.

DAGMAR,

see Jerry LESTER and DAGMAR

BILL DANA In 1959, a writer on the *Steve Allen Show* came up with the idea of a school for department store Santa Clauses. To make the sketch funnier, the instructor was supposed to be a Spanish-speaking immigrant who would write on the blackboard "Jo, jo, jo" when he wanted his students to pronounce it "Ho, ho, ho." When Allen was skeptical, the writer demonstrated how funny it would sound with the proper inflections. The rest is jistory: a brand-new ethnic character, Jose Jimenez, was born then and there.

The writer was Bill Dana, a "Jungarian Hew" whose real name was William Szathmary, a native of Quincy, Massa-

chusetts (born 1924). He graduated from Emerson College in Boston in 1950, started out as a small-time performer in local nightclubs in the 1952–53 season. He managed to get small parts on TV with Imogene Coca and Martha Raye, but a back injury interrupted his performing career. He turned to gag writing, contributed material to Don Adams and others, and finally landed a job on Steve Allen's staff in 1956.

Dana's Jose Jimenez characterization succeeded because he didn't put him down as stupid—merely confused, but earnestly trying to get along in his halting English, which is exactly what many immigrants were doing, and they could identify with it ("Did you bring your portfolio?" "No, I brought my lunch box.").

As Jimenez, he recorded five LP al-

Joan Davis (with Eddie Cantor)

bums, the first of which sold 90,000 copies in two months, a very respectable sale for a comedy album. Dana had Jimenez as an astronaut, or as a "financial typhoon" who wanted to merge Worthington Pump with International Nickel so he could manufacture pumpernickel. He got his own TV show in 1963, with Jimenez playing a hotel porter, but it was canceled after a mediocre season.

As the ethnic sensitivities of audiences became more pronounced during the 1960s, some grumblings began to be heard about the Jose Jimenez image. Finally, in 1970, Dana retired the character at a mock funeral in Los Angeles.

KARL DANE,

see CHESTER K. ARTHUR and KARL DANE

RODNEY DANGERFIELD He looks like a somewhat heavyset, completely middle-class, middle-aged restaurant owner. But he has one problem: "I don't get no respect!"

His pet rock died. He gets mail that starts, "You may already be a loser." At the racetrack, when they shoot off the starting gun, they kill his horse.

This kind of self-deprecating material is the stock-in-trade of a man who is exactly what he looks like, even down to the fact that he owns a restaurant—actually, a New York nightclub where he is always the featured attraction.

Dangerfield came into prominence in the late 1960s as a guest on a number of variety programs and talk shows, appearing often with Johnny Carson on the *Tonight Show*. He has made a small fortune by relentlessly putting himself down, and he continues to do so even though he is now a big success.

"I'm getting old. When I squeeze into a tight parking space, I'm sexually satisfied for the day."

JOAN DAVIS Joan Davis was a queen of slapstick, a comedienne whose zany exploits delighted her many fans for half a century, in diverse media that included vaudeville, film, radio, and television.

Born Madonna Josephine Davis to a St. Paul train dispatcher in 1908, Miss Davis began her performing career at age three with skillful song-and-dance routines. When she was six, her audience exploded into laughter during what was supposed to have been a serious recitation, and thenceforth Miss Davis was a comedienne. Before entering high school she was a smash hit touring the Pantages theater circuit.

In 1931 Joan Davis teamed up with actor Si Wills, and they were married soon after. Observing that vaudeville was in decline, Wills and Davis (as they were known professionally) moved to Hollywood to seek a career in the movies.

Her first film role was as a hillbilly in Mack Sennett's *Way Up Thar*. Over the next seven years her name became well known to film fans, thanks to her appearances in over two dozen films, including *Time Out for Romance, Thin Ice, Wake Up and Live,* and *Hold That Co-ed.*

After guesting on the Rudy Vallee radio program in 1941, Miss Davis took over the program two years later when Vallee left to serve in the Coast Guard. In 1944 she divorced Si Wills, and in 1945 the United Drug Company signed her to a four-year radio contract worth $4 million.

Later, Miss Davis worked for Joan Davis Productions, her own production company, on films and on her popular television series, *I Married Joan.*

Miss Davis' comedy relied heavily upon her visual, slapstick antics. In a typical sketch she would take violent pratfalls and make use of exaggerated facial contortions, cacophonous utterances, and generally burlesqued behavior.

On May 24, 1961, Miss Davis was stricken by a heart attack, dying at the age of fifty-three.

Here's a sample of her material:

Everything happens to me. I never win. With me, everything has been like a horse race. Why, in the race for life I was left at the post. In the race for love, I was scratched. And in the race for marriage, I can't even get out of the stable!

DEAD END KIDS,

see LEO GORCEY

SHERIFF DEADEYE,

see RED SKELTON

GABE DELL,

see LEO GORCEY

JOE DE RITA,

see THE THREE STOOGES

PHYLLIS DILLER The Phyllis Diller story might serve as inspiration for frustrated housewives everywhere. There she was, a thirty-seven-year-old frustrated housewife and mother of five, who began writing comedy routines between diaper changes. Suddenly, she was a star and a millionaire. She had *everything*—except men, she would probably remind us: "When I go to the beach wearing a bikini even the tide won't come in!"

Phyllis Driver (her maiden name) was born on July 17, 1917, in Lima, Ohio. At Ohio's Bluffton College she was editor of humor for the school paper. As the years passed, in her private life, Diller's natural sense of humor began emerging as an optimistic alternative to succumbing to life's manifold ills, such as the dreariness of a housewife's life. At the laundromat, she would bounce one-liners off fellow housewives. Typical thirty seconds with Phyllis Diller in a laundromat in 1954: "I bury a lot of my ironing out in the backyard. I finally found out how my neighbor—who I call Mrs. Clean—gets her laundry so much whiter looking than mine. She washes it."

In 1955 Diller took her comedy to San Francisco's Purple Onion nightclub, where her engagement was extended from two to 89 weeks. By the early 1960s she had made dozens of appearances on major television shows, including those of Jack Paar, Jack Benny, and Red Skelton.

Among her ventures have been attempts to get a successful TV series going, including a short-lived 1966 project, *The Pruitts of Southampton* (later renamed the *Phyllis Diller Show*); roles in numerous films, including a few with her idol, Bob Hope; best-selling comedy record albums, including *Great Moments of Comedy with Phyllis Diller;* and several books, including *Phyllis Diller Tells All About Fang* (Fang being an incisive nickname for her husband).

The distinctive brand of humor that rocketed her to fame consists of two thematically related parts, physical appearance and comic identity. Visually, she is a carefully coordinated mess, complete with weird costumes and outlandish hairstyles. ("I comb my hair with an electric toothbrush"). Her whole routine is geared to good-natured self-belittling, especially with regard to face and figure. Typically, she once said, "Everybody says that I'm a beautiful person *inside*. Just leave it to me to be born inside out!" Familiar characters in her routines through the years are Fang, Captain Bligh (a sister-in-law), and Moby Dick (a mother-in-law).

Of course, that Phyllis Diller is strictly a thing of the past. No more fright wigs, no more gawky garb. The new, sophisticated Phyllis Diller strives to be attractive; a face-lift, revamped wardrobe, and beautiful instead of bizarre makeup now aid her quest for a new image.

LEW DOCKSTADER Lew Dockstader was instrumental in converting the minstrel show from a crude caricature of Negro stereotypes into an instrument of social and political satire, giving it a fresh twist just before this form of entertainment disappeared from the American scene in the early part of the twentieth century.

Born George Alfred Clapp in 1856, he started out as a blackface minstrel in Hartford, Connecticut, as a teenager. He joined Bloodgood's Comic Alliance in 1873, later Emmett and Wilde's troupe; in 1876, organized his own troupe with Charles Dockstader. When the latter retired in 1883, Clapp kept the troupe's name intact, and later, for convenience, made it his own.

Phyllis Diller

He opened a theater on Broadway in 1886, but continued as a performer in vaudeville starting in 1890. Between 1898 and 1913, he had a partner, George Primrose; after that, he played solo on the Keith Circuit until 1923. He died on October 26, 1924.

His act combined blackface minstrel comedy with broad clowning: at one time he used a coat with a 30-foot tail, and shoes two feet long and a foot wide. Instead of making fun of the "darkies," as was then customary, however, he would do blackface takeoffs on leading figures of the day, such as Theodore Roosevelt.

TOM DREESEN Tom Dreesen is an average-looking fellow with dark hair who only recently started making the rounds of nightclubs and local TV shows in his native Midwest. In 1978 he got national TV exposure on an NBC comedy special, and he seems destined to find his place in the ranks of young comedy hopefuls. His comedy has that touch of madness and of the macabre that shows an active mind at work.

I come from Harvey, Illinois. We have 40,000 people, half of them black, half white. But we have no problems of racial nature. At least not now. We expect some in two years, however. That's when the 20,000 blacks will be released from jail.

My family is religious—we've never had a divorce. A few murders, yes—but no divorces.

My uncle and aunt had marital problems. At last my uncle agreed to go to a counselor. On the way, he got drunk and went into a transmission shop instead. They still have marital problems, but now he doesn't rattle.

MARIE DRESSLER A great woman of the legitimate theater in the late nineteenth century, Marie Dressler (1869–1934) teamed up with Mack Sennett and Charlie Chaplin to make a silent comedy classic in 1914, and went on to become a popular star of the early sound films.

"I was born homely," Ms. Dressler admitted, but her appearance helped her to become a favorite comedienne of turn-of-the-century theatergoers. She costarred with such immortals as Weber and Fields (in *Twiddle Twaddle* and *Higgledy-Piggledy*) and Eddie Foy (in *Little Robinson Crusoe*).

In 1914 Mack Sennett asked her to star in an adaptation of a play, *Tillie's Nightmare,* in which she had recently appeared. The film version, *Tillie's Punctured Romance,* became a classic thanks to both her broad caricature of an "innocent" country maiden being taken advantage of and the expert support of the best comedians on the Keystone lot, including Charlie Chaplin, Chester Conklin, Mabel Normand, Mack Swain, and the Keystone Kops.

In sound films, she was at first teamed up with Polly Moran in *The Callahans and the Murphys* (1927), in which the two played neighbors who enjoy an occasional snort together: "This stuff makes me see double and feel single." They did four films like that. She was also twice successfully teamed up with Wallace Beery; they were two lovable but irascible waterfront rats, in *Min and Bill* (1930), and *Tugboat Annie* (1933). In 1933 she also appeared in *Dinner at Eight,* with an all-star cast that included Wallace Beery, Jean Harlow, John Barrymore, and others.

THE DUNCAN SISTERS One of the most popular sister acts in vaudeville in the early 1920s, The Duncan Sisters are little heard of today because their most famous routine was the blackface Topsy

Marie Dressler (right) with Charlie Chaplin, Mabel Normand

and Eva act, which they made into a musical comedy and later a film. They were charming, talented comediennes, with a rare sense of timing and perfect rapport.

They poked gentle fun at fads and foibles of the day, and Vivian's rather dim-witted blackface Topsy was a perfect foil for Rosetta's straight-man Eva. The sisters are also remembered for several songs, including "Rememb'ring"— which they composed before either was twenty-four years old.

Rosetta Duncan was born on November 23, 1900, in Los Angeles, and Vivian on June 17, 1902. They played vaudeville

in Gus Edwards' *Kiddies Revue,* and made their New York debut in 1917, scoring an immediate success in that year's *Doing Our Bit.* They also conquered London in *Pins and Needles* in 1921, and stayed for more than a year.

Back in the United States, they wrote the book, lyrics, and music for an expanded version of their act, which came to Broadway in 1924 as *Topsy and Eva.* They also made it as a film in 1927, and continued appearing in productions of it in different towns and countries for many years. The Duncan Sisters appeared in the show *Clowns in Clover* in London in 1927 and in the road version of *New Faces* in 1934. They toured English music halls in 1937–38.

Rosetta was killed in a car accident on December 4, 1959.

JACK DURANT,

see MITCHELL and DURANT

JIMMY DURANTE Jimmy Durante is the comedian with the famous nose that was insured by Lloyd's of London for $1 million, included in *Who's Who,* and immortalized by being impressed in the concrete at Grauman's. But unlike Socrates, Cyrano de Bergerac, Oliver Cromwell, Tolstoy, and history's other proprietors of prominent probosces, Durante is not sensitve about his nose. Quite the contrary, he loves to have his olfactory organ the center of attention, and it has become the trademark of one of America's truly beloved comedians. As one columnist put it, "Durante has capitalized on such longcomings as his nose."

He was born in New York on February 10, 1893, and his full name is James Francis Durante. He accounts for his lack of schooling unabashedly: "I was tossed outuh duh winder in sec'n grade 'n didn't never come back." The expertly employed combination of heavily exaggerated New York accent, mispronunciations, and malapropisms became another Durante trademark. A third was his famous, and still not really explained, utterance at the end of each live performance, "Goodnight, folks, and goodnight, Mrs. Calabash, wherever you are."

Durante began his career as an ordinary nightclub pianist, but began to broaden his performing horizons when he teamed up with versatile nightclub entertainers Lou Clayton and Eddie Jackson. As Jimmy explains it, "Sometimes I would sing a song into one of dem dere megraphones—but I never had much of a verce." Well, "verce" or not, he became a favorite recording artist, with such songs as "So I Ups to Him," "I Can Do Without Broadway but Can Broadway Do Without ME?," and the classic "Inka Dinka Do" of his own composition:

Say it with flowers, say it with drink
But always be careful not to say it with . . .
ink. . . . -a-dinka-doo, . . .

Clayton, Jackson, and Durante became a hot act; much of their comedy was of the physical destruction variety. They might break a few chairs or pianos in the course of their act, entitled "Wood," in which anything made of wood was fair prey.

Durante, originally a ragtime pianist at Coney Island, had a separate career in music: he played with the New Orleans Jazz Band at the Alamo Cafe on 125th Street, with Bailey's Lucky Seven, and later with his own group, with whom he recorded for Gennett and Okeh.

Schnozzola's film debut came in 1930 in *Roadhouse Nights,* with Clayton and Jackson; thereafter, the movie producers had him carry the comedy alone, or teamed him up with other partners—several times with Buster Keaton, then on his way down. None of the films were major successes, but their shoddiness could not disguise the fact that Durante was a comedian of the first water.

He went on to a highly successful career in radio and later in television; in both he was for a time teamed up with the one partner who seemed least likely to hit it off with him—mild-mannered, crew-cut intellectual Garry Moore—and yet it was this unlikely combination that worked best.

Now here's Jimmy, talk-singing us off:

Jimmy Durante

Umbriago
Could be mayor of New York or of Chicago.
. . .

(*Interrupts song.*) The other day I saw my friend Umbriago milking a cow upside down. I asked him why and he said, "Why not? I want the cream to come up on top!"—Haha! I've got a million of 'em.

(*Resumes singing.*)
Umbriago

Raises Cain from Portland, Maine to Santiago
Ahhhh . . .

(*Interrupts again.*)
That note was given to me by Bing Crosby! And was he glad to get rid of it!

(*Chorus sings.*) Umbriago . . .

(*Interrupts chorus.*) How do you like that! Everybody wants t' get into th' act!

EAST SIDE KIDS,

see LEO GORCEY

EASY ACES,

see GOODMAN ACE

BOB ELLIOTT,

see BOB and RAY

LEON ERROL The impeccably dressed gentleman who got into trouble by flirting too much, drinking too much, and trying to preserve dignity at all costs in embarrassing situations was practically created by Leon Errol—although others, notably Max Linder and Charley Chase, also mined this rich lode of humor. Errol's rubbery legs, which seem to take him in several directions at once while he is inebriated, were in a class by themselves. Also, where most comedians doing henpecked husbands suspected of flirtation made it clear that they were innocent victims of coincidence, Errol generally let the comedy flow from an admitted weakness for extramarital spice.

A true funnyman whose inventiveness never flagged, Errol was a professional who reached the top in vaudeville, musical comedy, and social satire films. Born on July 3, 1881, in Sydney, Australia, he joined a theater group at a young age and learned every facet of stagecraft. A vaudeville headliner in all parts of the world, he reached the zenith in the glittering *Ziegfeld Follies* of the early 1910s. To demonstrate his versatility, he also directed the 1914 edition.

The movies used his many-faceted

talents in dozens of comedy features, starting in the silent years and on to the year of his death (1951). They included several with W. C. Fields, such as *Never Give a Sucker an Even Break* (1941). He was probably at his best in two-reel shorts, which gave him maximum artistic freedom and allowed him to show off his versatility, such as by playing contrasting dual roles, one of his favorite ploys. He made more than a hundred.

He was married, despite his flighty stage character, to just one woman for forty years: Stella Chatelaine, who died in 1946. Leon Errol died a few months after his seventieth birthday, on October 12, 1951.

FRANK FAY He is credited, among other things, with coining the term "master of ceremonies" where previously "interlocutor" was used. He created on Broadway the original part of Elwood P. Dowd, the genial inebriate who is accompanied by an invisible six-foot-tall rabbit named Harvey. In 1917 he tried something quite startling for the times: he delivered a humorous monologue on stage without clown makeup, using no dialect or fractured English, and not once falling down or getting kicked in the rear; on the contrary, he was meticulously dressed in top hat and tails and spoke intimately, and sophisticatedly, to the audience.

All subsequent emcees are indebted to Frank Fay, because he went far beyond merely introducing the acts: he would walk onto the stage during each number, involve the performers in impromptu patter, fill the time between numbers with witty remarks, and become a dominant force throughout the show. He married a chorus girl from a Texas Guinan club, named Ruby Stevens, who admitted that she was "a nobody until Frank came along, and probably would have remained a nobody if he had not taught me most of what I know about show business." Changing her name to Barbara Stanwyck, she proved that this was quite a lot.

His reputation for agility with the ad lib was deserved; he is said to have rarely used the same line twice in his routines. When Milton Berle, who had a similar reputation for being able to come up with off-the-cuff punchlines, challenged him to a duel of ad libs, Fay declined, saying it was against his principles to fight an unarmed man.

He was born in San Francisco on

November 17, 1897, the son of stock company actors. His parents made him a child performer from the age of four, and at eight he made his Broadway debut in *The Redemption of David Corson* (1906). After a brief try at regular school education, he went with a Shakespearean stock company, and by the age of fifteen was in vaudeville. In 1918 he made it into Broadway musical comedy, where he wrote and produced his own show, *Frank Fay's Fables,* for the 1922 season. Then back to vaudeville, where his notable success as an emcee enabled him to break all records at the famous Palace; he played there for 26 weeks in a single year.

As the 1920s came to a close, he moved to Hollywood, appearing in a number of films over the next decade and a half. His biggest personal and financial success, however, was on Broadway; *Harvey* (1944) was a smash hit that stayed on for 1,775 performances.

Fay died in 1961, having lived in semi-retirement for the last few years.

JOEY FAYE The Boswell of burlesque, Joey Faye has collected 18,000 sketches and routines, and is the only person alive who can listen to Henny Youngman and credit each line to its originator—which in some cases, he claims, is Shakespeare or even Aristophanes. He proved his love for his training ground by writing, directing, and acting in *Anatomy of Burlesque* in 1967, and again in *That Wonderful World of Burlesque* in 1975.

Joey Faye was born Joseph Anthony Palladino in New York on July 12, 1910. His stage debut was on a vaudeville bill in New Haven in 1931. His next job was with Minsky's burlesque, and he stayed there for seven seasons, spending his summers as a "toomler" in the Borscht Belt. At Camp Copake, writer Alan

Joey Faye

Boritz saw some of his routines, and asked if he could use them in the show he was writing, *Room Service* (1938). In return, he got Joey a role in it.

Leaving Minsky for Broadway may have been a step up in prestige, but it took a hefty bite out of Joey's paycheck; he was a top burlesque headliner, making $300 a week, whereas his Broadway bit paid only $100. "If I had stayed where I was, I might have been a highly paid nightclub comedian. But I stayed on Broadway, and was rewarded by always being the second banana."

Faye toured for the USO in World War II, and afterward made a few movies, always interspersed with small Broadway roles. He also did a lot of television: 32 guest shots for Ed Sullivan; emcee on *Kraft Music Hall;* his own variety hour on CBS, *The 54th Street Revue;* and appearances with the *Milton Berle Show.* He also supported Phil Silvers in both stage and screen versions of *Top Banana.*

One of his favorite stage skits had the distinction of making it into a prizewinning play. In his burlesque routines, he would say to a straight man that he was going to have a drink, and the following exchange would take place:

Straight Man: What are you going to have?
Joey: Whisky.
Straight Man: You should not drink it, you should drink milk.
Joey: Why?
Straight Man: Whisky will ruin you. Look at me—I'm fifty-one and people take me for thirty, because I have never taken a drink of whisky in my life.
Joey: Well, I had an uncle who drank whisky every day of his life and lived to be eighty-three. When he died, we buried him, and then three weeks later we opened the grave again, and he *still* looked better than you do.

About a year after Joey did this routine in the Catskills, Moss Hart paid him the compliment of incorporating it into *The Man Who Came to Dinner.* The irascible Sheridan Whiteside opens a box of candy, and his nurse tells him he shouldn't eat it. There follows an almost word-for-word rendition of Joey's bit. And how do we know the story's true? "I toured in the show for two years, didn't I?" says Joey.

FERNANDEL In 1931 the French filmed an extraordinary, biting satire of small-town morality, *Le Rosier de Mme. Husson,* released here originally as *He,* and later reissued as *The Virgin Man.* Madame Husson is a small-town society matron who holds an annual nomination of the most virtuous girl in town; one year, having run out of virgins, her clique has to settle for the village idiot, who has obviously been untouched by sin. Enter Fernandel—in his second film appearance—and a major new comic talent was on the way.

Fernandel's face as he depicts the imbecile's earnest, slow-witted efforts to comprehend what is going on is a study in theatrical craftsmanship. The eyes like those of a frightened horse, with a physiognomy to match; the ripple of wrinkles and the tilt of the face as he anxiously scrambles in his gray matter for some hint of the proceedings; the bashful smile slowly, oh ever so slowly, hueing the roseate countenance as he is offered flowers and handshakes. It is a formidable face, and Fernandel utilizes it like a musical instrument of unbelievable range.

He never quite scaled the same heights since, but he has delighted millions of movie viewers on both sides of the Atlantic by his portrayal of Don Camillo in *The*

Little World of Don Camillo (1952) and *The Return of Don Camillo* (1953).

His full name was Fernand Contandin, and he was born in Marseille on May 8, 1903, where he got an early exposure to show business from his father, a cabaret singer. He tried to earn a living as a bank clerk for a while, but the lure of the theater was too strong, and in 1922 he joined the Eldorado Theater in Nice, and that was the end of any attempt to find an ordinary job.

When he courted Henriette Manse, who became his wife and bore him four children, the future mother-in-law did not approve and referred to him rather contemptuously as "Fernand d'elle" (which translates roughly, "that Fernand of hers"); he shortened it to Fernandel and adopted it as his stage name. He made about one hundred films, at least half of which were shown in the United States. There were also French plays, operettas, British music hall appearances, and tours of the United States and Canada. Many moviegoers will recall *The Well-digger's Daughter* (1940) and *The Sheep Has Five Legs* (1954). In the extravaganza *Around the World in 80 Days* (1956), he appeared only briefly but with dazzling effect.

Fernandel died in 1971 in Paris.

STEPIN FETCHIT What insane political persecution did to some performers in the McCarthy era of the 1950s, equally insane overreaction against racial stereotypes did to others in the socially conscious 1970s. Audiences are steeped in graphic sex, violence, and streetwise realism, but on the subject of ethnic humor, they are treated like a bunch of unsophisticated rubes who might actually believe that some individual's comic portrayal of a character is a realistic appraisal of a whole race or class.

Nowhere is this fatuous oversensitivity better demonstrated than in the case of Stepin Fetchit, a talented and versatile comedian with excellent credits and stage knowhow. Suddenly, it has become fashionable for people—especially blacks—to despise him, and a recent alleged "encyclopedia" of black performers contained not a single word about him.

Yet when one of the major studios, Fox, reluctantly gave director Paul Sloane permission to make an all-black musical short in 1929, it was Stepin Fetchit's hilarious performance as Gummy, the ultimate lazybones, that persuaded the company brass to make it a full-length feature. It became the first feature film with an all-black cast made by a big studio: *Hearts in Dixie* paved the way for future efforts like *Hallelujah, Cabin in the Sky,* and *Stormy Weather,* and in its way pioneered the slow and painful process of racial integration.

At a time when blacks were reduced to crumbs, Fetchit's deliberately overemphasized portrayal of the shiftless, lethargic, superstitious good-for-nothing breached the racial barrier and got him to Hollywood. He was probably the first black performer recognized and loved by a majority of white movie audiences. While the immortal Bert Williams had long before that acquired fame in white vaudeville, theatrical audiences were numerically quite insignificant compared to audiences for the mass film medium. This breakthrough alone should assure Stepin Fetchit's immortality; that he should be vilified for selling out, when he was shrewd enough to realize that if audiences laugh at you they cannot hate you, easing the acceptance process of the black, is ironic.

He was born Lincoln Theodore Perry in Key West, Florida, in 1896 (although he later preferred to claim it was 1902).

After a thorough training on the TOBA vaudeville circuit, he became a headliner in Harlem nightspots and revues, and appeared in films made by Harlem's black film maker, Oscar Micheaux. Then Hollywood beckoned, and he slouched his way through approximately forty films between 1929 and 1954. During World War II, he played clubs and army bases in the GI show *Flamingo Follies.* He was rarely heard from during the 1960s, when his image was at its lowest, and his passing in 1977 was hardly noticed by the media.

GRACIE FIELDS This British music hall favorite gained fame by entertaining GIs during World War II and appearing on radio and on the nightclub circuit in the United States, singing humorous ditties.

Born Grace Stansfield in Rochdale, Lancashire, England, on January 9, 1898, she started as a cinema vocalist in 1906, toured with various juvenile troupes, and soloed for the first time in music halls at the age of fifteen. In 1914 she was in a pantomime, *Dick Whittington,* touring English towns; she made her London debut a year later in a revue titled *Yes I Think So.* Many more tours followed, one of which, in 1930, brought her to the Palace on Broadway.

During the thirties and forties, she appeared in a number of films, made in England and in the United States, including *Looking on the Bright Side* (1932), *The Show Goes On* (1937), and *Molly and Me* (1944).

She came to the United States a second time for a prolonged wartime stay in 1940, worked for the USO, and toured armed forces camps with their shows. She received a number of honors for her tireless efforts, including the title of Commander of the British Empire. A great humanitarian, she worked for many causes and founded an orphanage.

TOTIE FIELDS Her favorite meal was "breakfast, lunch, dinner, and in-between," and she was affectionately referred to as the only show business fat woman since Sophie Tucker with sex appeal. A favorite in the Las Vegas nightclub scene and on the talk show circuit, the hefty comedienne's success was due partly to the way people identified with her, through lines like, "I've been on a diet for two weeks and all I lost was two weeks."

Totie Fields

Her real name was Sophie Feldman, "Totie" being the way she mispronounced "Sophie" as a toddler in Hartford, Connecticut, where she was born in 1931. She began singing in high school, and later in small clubs. With her husband, she moved to the land of show business opportunity, New York, but found instead three years of bad luck. Finally, there was a booking at the Copa in 1963, and then the *Ed Sullivan Show.*

By then the cute one-liners between songs had mushroomed into full-blown comedy routines, and her music was forced to take a back seat. In 1970 Earl Wilson called her "the hottest comedienne in the country," and in 1975 *Playgirl* magazine described her as "the number one stand-up comedienne on the saloon circuit." The magazine pointed out that she drew a bigger paycheck than either Phyllis Diller or Joanie Rivers.

In 1976 Totie Fields had her leg amputated, but endured the ordeal with characteristic good humor. From her hospital bed she began formulating her new act, and insisting that her daughter's wedding plans not be interrupted on her account.

She died on August 2, 1978, after a protracted illness.

W. C. FIELDS W. C. Fields was born William Claude Dukenfield on January 29, 1880, in Philadelphia. At the age of eleven, he ran away from home after an altercation with his father. He lived off the streets, sometimes selling papers; even then, his bizarre sense of humor began to assert itself and, instead of shouting out the headlines like other newsboys, he would confront passersby with obscure items from the inside pages.

His Philadelphia experiences did not endear the city to him, and later he panned his hometown mercilessly. "Last weekend I went to Philadelphia but it was closed," he remarked on one of his radio appearances in the early forties. In the film *My Little Chickadee,* he is caught cheating at cards and is about to be hanged in a Western town. As a last request, he says, "I would like to see Paris before I die," but, noting a hostile reaction on the faces of the posse, he adds hastily, "but Philadelphia will do." In the mid-1920s, the magazine *Vanity Fair* asked a number of prominent personalities to select the epitaph for their tombstone. Fields: "On the whole, I'd rather be in Philadelphia."

He became a showman by teaching himself how to juggle at fourteen, and getting a job at an amusement park. For two decades he crisscrossed the world as a comic juggler, becoming so good that he was the first American to be headlined at the *Folies-Bergère* above the names of all other attractions. (The second one was Josephine Baker.)

By adding lines to his juggling routines, he upgraded his act until it was ready for Broadway, where he arrived with assorted sketches of his own design, including a golf lesson in which the ball is never hit, a pool game with trick balls, and a line of muttered asides as mordant as they were hilarious. He practically monopolized the comedy chores in the *Ziegfeld Follies* for nine years.

He was ready now for a third career, as the star of a legitimate play. The vehicle was *Poppy* (1923), and in it he created the irascible, fraudulent, misanthropic character that he used, with minor variations, for the rest of his life. Many of his incomparable sarcastic digs at sheriffs, mothers-in-law, insurance salesmen, relatives, cops, judges, and officials reflected his own jaundiced views, influenced by bitter memories of the times he had been cheated during the early vaudeville days

W.C. Fields

and ill treated by his own family. "The world is fraught with marauders," he once mused to Mae West, and that sums up his philosophy.

The success of *Poppy,* which stayed on Broadway for two seasons, established him with the movie magnates, and Paramount featured him in a series of silents filmed at the Astoria studios in New York, so that he could make them while at the same time staying in the play. He didn't really hit his stride in films until sound added the bonus of his dire imprecations and vitriolic maledictions.

When the sound revolution came, Fields moved to Hollywood so that he could devote himself full time to films, which he would write under assorted pen names (few comedians were as positive about what was right for their screen character as Fields, or fought with such determination to be allowed to stick to it; it is fortunate that Fields usually prevailed, as what he wrote invariably came out best; the few films in which compromises were made, such as *My Little Chickadee,* where Mae West insisted on having a virtually separate role, are poorest as comedies). His shorts included *The Dentist* and *The Fatal Glass of Beer* (both made in 1932), and many moviegoers will remember full-length features like *The Man on the Flying Trapeze* (1935), *You Can't Cheat an Honest Man* (1939), and *The Bank Dick* (1940), a classic shown again and again on television reruns.

Fields married in the early 1900s and had a son, but the union was unhappy and he lived apart from his wife for most of his life. For the last fourteen years of his Hollywood stay, he had the company of a Mexican starlet, Carlotta Monti.

By the late 1930s, his fondness for an occasional snort was approaching the dimensions of chronic alcoholism, but he still had one world to conquer: radio.

This he did as a frequent guest on the Edgar Bergen show, where he engaged in a running feud with Charlie McCarthy:

CHARLIE MCCARTHY: Is that your nose, Mr. Fields, or are you eating a tomato?

W. C. FIELDS: Quiet, you woodpecker's snack, or I'll take you for a ride on a buzzsaw and slice you into Venetian blinds.

CHARLIE MCCARTHY: Oh, Mr. Fields, you make me shutter!

Fields made a recording of one of his funniest bits, a "Temperance Lecture," a few months before his death, on Christmas Day of 1946.

Actor Thomas Mitchell, one of the last to see him, was shocked to find Fields, the incorrigible atheist and reprobate, propped up in bed perusing the Bible. Imperturbably, Fields explained, his breath laced with *spiritus frumenti:* "Just looking for loopholes!" A worthy exit line for a magnificent American character.

Some famous Fieldsiana:

If at first you don't succeed, try again. Then quit. There's no use being a fool about it.

There comes a time in the affairs of man when you have to catch the bull by the tail and face the situation.

I like children—girl children, about eighteen or twenty.

There's no question as to which is man's best friend—whisky or dogs. After all, when two or more boon companions meet, do they sit around petting dogs?

LARRY FINE,

see THE THREE STOOGES

MICHAEL FLANDERS and DONALD SWANN The piano playing (by Flanders) did not have quite the classic virtuosity of Victor Borge, and the singing (chiefly by Swann, but frequently by both) did not have quite the sardonic bite of Tom Lehrer. But, using these talents, the gentle British songwriters struck gold in a satirical revue titled *At the Drop of a Hat,* which became one of the all-time sleepers of show business on both sides of the Atlantic.

Opening for the first time on New Year's Eve of 1956 in a small London theater club, the show was an instant hit. It was transferred to a large West End theater for a two-year run, to be followed by a season on Broadway and still another year on a world tour. The inevitable sequel, *At the Drop of Another Hat,* enjoyed a similar success between 1963 and 1967.

Swann looked like a bespectacled, overaged cherub, while Flanders cut an imposing patriarchal figure with his beard and portly, seated corpulence (he was confined to a wheelchair by polio). In style, they ranged from mild political messages, such as that of the nonconforming cannibal,

I won't eat people, I won't eat people,
Eating people is bad!

to highly refined references to amorous peccadillos, such as the wine connoisseur's guide to seduction,

Have some Madeira, m'dear,
It's ever so much better than beer!

to utter nonsense, play on words, and what have you, as in the misunderstood zoo denizen's lament:

I'm a g-nu, I'm a g-nu,
The g-nicest work of g-nature in the zoo.

Donald Swann was born September 30, 1923, in Llanelly, Wales, started performing in dramatic productions at Oxford University after service in World War II, and became a free-lance composer.

As a lyricist, he found Michael Flanders, who was born in London on March 1, 1922, and was a radio writer and broadcaster after recovering partially from a crippling attack of polio, which had put him in an iron lung in 1943.

Together, they started performing their own songs at parties, and found them so warmly received that they decided to do them for paying audiences.

Swann married Janet Oxborrow in 1955, Flanders married Claudia Cockburn Davis in 1959.

PHIL FOSTER Phil Feldman is a roving ambassador from Brooklyn; even his stage name comes from Foster Avenue in the Flatbush section where he was born in 1913. He specializes in human interest stories with local color, infused with sentiment, rather than in gags and punchlines. "As boys in Brooklyn, we used to hang around the candy store so long we formed a father-and-son club," is a good example.

During the years Brooklyn was caught up in baseball fever, Foster told a story which captured the individuality of the borough: "This guy comes to Ebbets Field three days before the opening day. For three days and nights he stands by the ticket window, rain and shine. Finally, they open the window and he asks for a specific seat. Since he is first in line, he gets it. A reporter gets interested, follows him into the stands, finds out it is the only seat in the place behind an obstruction, so you can't even see the field from there. Naturally, he asks why. 'Gotta root for

Phil Foster

the Dodgers, ain't I? But I hate baseball, so I don't look!' "

Foster notes the changes in Brooklyn: "In my old neighborhood, many new minorities have moved in. But my mother still keeps going every week to the local movie house. 'But Mama, why do you see these shows, you don't understand Spanish!' I said. 'So, did I understand when they were in English?' "

Phil came into show business via that time-honored route—the amateur contest. "Had a sketch with another guy, and we tried it out at the RKO Tilyou down by Coney Island. Would you believe it, we won—it was the first time in living memory the accordion player lost on amateur night!" But he finished school (Erasmus High) and did a stint in the Army before making his professional

debut at Maxim's ("the one in the Bronx, naturally—what did you think?"). He scored at Grossinger's and other Borscht Belt resorts, and was in off-Broadway shows.

He had guest spots on radio with Kate Smith and Tallulah Bankhead, and handled the comic chores on NBC Radio's long-running *Monitor*. On TV, he was on Tallulah's *Big Show* for 26 weeks, went on *Caesar Presents* in 1955, and made appearances with Kate Smith, Steve Allen, Garry Moore, Jack Paar, Ed Sullivan, and Perry Como. During the 1978 season, he played Laverne's father in the top-ranking sitcom, *Laverne and Shirley*.

A favorite true story concerns a famous actress he and his wife knew when she was an unknown. She got a TV series, and stopped seeing the Fosters. Then the show was canceled, she became unemployed, and she renewed her friendship with them as if nothing had happened. A couple of years later, she played a supporting role in a film and won an Academy Award for it. Phil Foster sent her the following wire:

CONGRATULATIONS—AND
GOODBYE AGAIN.

REDD FOXX For years, he was known only to black audiences who saw him at the Apollo Theater in Harlem or other stops of the black comedy circuit, or who bought one of his dozens of strong-selling LPs, all with strictly blue material definitely not for the family trade.

After decades of being buried in black and blue obscurity, Foxx suddenly blossomed out on a television series, *Sanford and Son,* as a decidedly lovable (although cantankerous and devious) character. And, in this entirely unexpected field, he became an "overnight" smash hit.

Sanford is his real name—John Elroy Sanford. He was born in St. Louis on December 9, 1922, and ran away from home in his teens to join a washboard band. It won second prize once on *Major Bowes' Amateur Hour* on radio.

When Foxx switched to comedy, which he practiced in Harlem niteries, he was among the first to abandon the rural black humor approach and do urban ghetto material of which he had first-hand knowledge. He was even jailed once, when bookings were scarce and he committed a robbery. But slowly he became established in the black community as a top-notch entertainer in the risqué vein; starting in 1955, he recorded a prodigious number of his routines on more than fifty albums.

Next came the equalizing sixties, and blacks could appear on TV as equals. Taking full advantage of this, Foxx brought in a winner with his portrayal of a scheming junkman in *Sanford and Son*, which had its debut in 1972.

He had roles in a few films, including *Cotton Comes to Harlem* (1973) and *Norman . . . Is That You?* (1976).

During the 1977 TV season, Foxx switched to a revue format, and resumed his career in the resort hotels in Las Vegas and so on, where he can use his risqué style to advantage.

Some of Foxx's lines to a nightclub audience:

Aren't you happy knowing that while you're here laughing at my dirty jokes, your children are safe at home . . . listening to my records?

I don't usually go for white women but I ain't stupid, neither. I'd grab Elizabeth Taylor before Moms Mabley any day.

Even my worst critics have to admit I'm as American as apple pie: my name is Redd, my hair is white, and my stories are blue!

A gentleman shouldn't argue with a lady—he should dicker!

EDDIE FOY In the rough-and-tumble vaudeville before the turn of the century, the average clown relied heavily on prat-falls, contortions, kicks in the face and to the opposite end, and similar stock-in-trade. By contrast, Eddie Foy was described by a contemporary critic as "the least obtrusive comedian of the stage," with his droll antics, absurd pantomime, and farcical singing and dancing. "His is the art that conceals art," concluded the critic.

He was born Edward Fitzgerald in New York on March 9, 1854, and moved with his family to Chicago in 1865. Thus he experienced the great Chicago fire in 1871; much later, in 1903, he was appearing in a theater that caught fire, and became the hero of the hour by retaining control and talking at least some of the audience out of panicking.

Foy tasted the thrill of show business at twelve as a clog dancer, and worked his way up slowly through provincial vaudeville and burlesque, long before the latter degenerated into a sex tease. By 1884, he started appearing regularly in stage vehicles; around 1887, he developed the stage makeup for which he became famous, with a face "that reminds one of a cat suffering from colic." Starting in 1889, he toured with David Henderson's musical extravaganzas, and between 1901 and 1913, he was the toast of Broadway in a series of musical comedies. They included *The Strollers* (1901), *Mr. Bluebeard* (1903), *Mr. Hamlet of Broadway* (1908), and *Over the River* (1911).

He was married four times (Rose Howland, 1879; Lola Sefton, 1886; Madeline Moranda, 1895; and Marie Combs, 1923). It was his third wife who gave him the reason for returning to vaudeville in 1913: she presented him with seven children, so that he could form his own act, "Eddie Foy and the Seven Little Foys." He opened with it in Bayside. As the curtain opened, he simply stood there with the children around him and said, "If I ever move to Bayside, it will be a big city." This got such a laugh he used it afterward in every town, adding other remarks to soften up the audience:

My wife and I live in New Rochelle, and every time someone finds a lost kid there, they always first call "The Foyer" and ask if it's one of ours. Strangers passing our place by bus often ask the driver if that is the town's orphan asylum. One big problem is that every morning I wake up with a start, sure that it is someone's birthday and I had forgotten it.

Eddie Foy passed away on February 16, 1928, soon after being booked by the Keith–Albee–Orpheum circuit for his longest tour ever in the vehicle *The Fallen Star*.

WILLIAM FRAWLEY,

see LUCILLE BALL

STAN FREBERG Having flunked history in high school (Alhambra, California, 1944), Stan Freberg became a satirist. He even got back at history:

LOOKOUT: Land Ho!
COLUMBUS: Quick, hand me the glass. —No, no, the other one. (*Sound of pouring*) Well, here's to the New World!

He had a series on CBS Radio in the mid-1950s doing takeoffs on historical figures as well as current political personalities and on show business.

His satiric recordings of the rock-and-roll hits of the day zoomed to the tops of the charts:

PIANIST: Look, man, I think there's a mistake in my part. It has the same chord over and over again, like plink-plink-plink, plink-plink-plink.

ROCK-AND-ROLL ARTIST: That's right. That's what I want!

PIANIST: Man, I don't dig that jive. I'm from a different school, George Shearing and like that. I ain't playing that plink-plink stuff.

ROCK-AND-ROLL ARTIST: You play that plink-plink jazz or we're getting a new piano man.

PIANIST: (*after a pregnant pause*): Plink-plink-plink.

A big seller was his satire on *Dragnet,* called *St. George and the Dragonet* ("How are you going to catch that dragon, St. George?" "I thought you'd never ask. Dragon net!"). He also scored in a takeoff on silly soap operas in the song "John and Marsha," which consisted entirely of the two names, spoken in more and more passionate tones and with rising repetitiveness. An early r-&-r favorite, "Sh-boom," came in for a merciless ribbing ("When do I come in?" "In this song, it don't matter. Wise up, eh!").

This led to more singles, LPs, and a TV show. Eventually, Freberg settled in the world of Madison Avenue, producing humorous commercials. (When asked to supply a title for his own LP, he said: "Let's make it commercially safe and call it 'Guy Lombardo Plays Francis Scott Key's Little Women'!")

FREDDIE the FREELOADER,

see RED SKELTON

JOE FRISCO Joe Frisco was America's famous stuttering comedian. His other trademarks were his large cigar and derby hat. Over four decades Frisco was a favorite on the vaudeville and nightclub circuits.

Born in 1890 in Milan, Illinois, his real name was Louis Wilson Josephs. At the age of fifteen, in Chicago, Frisco developed soft-shoe routines that brought him loose change tossed by audiences. Soon he and a partner were calling themselves "Coffee and Doughnuts," and this was probably the extent of Frisco's diet during those lean years.

Subsequent acts included "Frisco and His Jazz Band," and a comedy-dance act called "Frisco with McDermott and Cox." With this last act he made his debut as a verbal comic, and his sharp wit and stuttering delivery (each stutter was precisely timed to enhance the punchline) catapulted him to better jobs, higher fees, and (starting in the twenties) stardom.

Frisco's peak engagements were as a headliner under such legendary banners as the *Ziegfeld Follies*, the Orpheum circuit, and *Earl Carroll's Vanities*.

An inveterate racetrack gambler, Fris-

Joe Frisco

co received $40,000 from Warner Brothers for two months of film making in the twenties, and promptly lost every penny.

Only the world's highest paid comic—which many say Frisco was during the early days of the Hoover administration—could afford such extravagance. When a booking agent offered him $1,000 a week, Frisco demanded $3,000. He was accused of asking for more money than President Hoover made. "S-s-sure," Frisco stammered, "b-b-but he didn't m-m-make g-g-good yet!"

His stutter may have slowed his speech, but his mind was quicker than mercury. One day the sidewalk in front of the Palace was being torn up, and an unemployed comedian who hung out in that area asked Joe if he knew what was going on. "I d-don't know, I g-guess Albee's k-k-kid must have l-l-lost a b-ball," said Frisco, referring to the Palace owner's well known autocratic ways. Frisco was a favorite among fellow performers, whom he could break up any time. Many said his "in" jokes were funnier than most of his stage material.

Up until his death, of cancer in 1958, Frisco was still telling jokes. A month before his death he was honored at a large Hollywood Masquers Club testimonial dinner and awarded a plaque inscribed, "To Joe Frisco, America's Greatest Wit."

DAVID FRYE Born David Shapiro in Brooklyn in 1934, David Frye started imitating people in his teens and has been at it ever since. He played nightclubs in the Village and around the New York area in the early 1960s, and in 1962 got a spot on the *Johnny Carson Show* imitating John F. Kennedy, though he considers a 1966 appearance on the *Merv Griffin Show* the turning point in his career. He was invited back many times.

He is not only good at mimicking his victims, but also at giving them lines with quite a vicious bite. While doing an impression of presidential aspirant George Wallace, he would drawl:

Ah'm heah to say Ah'm sick and tard of the lootin' and riotin'. Last week they burned down mah library down in Alabama—both books! And one of them Ah ain't even colored yet!

But he reserved his sharpest venom for his impression of Richard Nixon—and his record *I Am the President* sold nearly as well during the Nixon administration as Vaughn Meader's *The First Family* did during the Kennedy era.

They call me "Tricky Dicky," but I don't know why. I've got two perfectly good legs, two arms, two faces . . .

I want my administration to be remembered as the one which took crime off the streets and put it in the White House where I can keep an eye on it.

I love America. You always hurt the one you love.

Although it may be inferred from these lines that he did not care for the President, Frye was sorry to see him go in 1974. As he explained in a TV interview, he couldn't see any of the upcoming political personalities providing such great material for caricature.

His premonition proved correct. In another uncanny parallel to Vaughn Meader, Frye's vogue also faded somewhat when his favorite target disappeared from the national scene, and he (Frye, that is) has been seen less frequently in recent months.

G

GALLAGHER and SHEAN Perhaps nobody demonstrates the difference between old-time vaudeville and today's show business better than the still remembered duo of Ed Gallagher and Al Shean. Their fame rests on one single number, which was more recitative than melodic, featuring topical matter and the immortal tagline, "Positively, Mr. Gallagher?" "Absolutely, Mr. Shean!"

Granting that the song's format permitted endless permutations of the topical content, that was all there was to it; the two men were not even permanent partners, working together only from 1910 to 1912, and again from 1922 to 1926. But no one remembers Shean and Warren, Shean and Carson, Gallagher and Barrett; and hardly anyone knows that in the only film featuring a Gallagher and Shean routine, *Atlantic City* (1944), Shean was actually doing it with Jack Kenny.

In vaudeville, it was possible to build a whole act on a single routine like that, and have it last a number of years, because it was presented to different audiences every day; today, with television's instant exposure to millions, such a one-time routine could not create so disproportionate a renown.

Of the two, Al Shean was the more creative artist. Born in 1868 in Dornum, Germany, he arrived in this country as a young man and drifted into vaudeville. When his nephews, The Marx Brothers, showed signs of talent, he helped them get bookings and wrote some of their early routines (a favorite legend is that he forgot to put in lines for Harpo, whereupon the imaginative lad created a pantomime character that remained in the act for good).

Somewhere in his tours of the circuits, Shean picked up Gallagher around 1910, and they played as a team for the next two years, capitalizing on the ethnic contrast between an Irishman and a Jew. Their act got them a Broadway job, in *The Rose Maid* in 1912; afterward, they went their separate ways.

In 1922 Shean wrote a song for the upcoming edition of the *Ziegfeld Follies;* he thought it would go over best if done by a team, so he reunited with Gallagher, and they made history. They were offered top bookings, such as the pinnacle of vaudeville, the Palace Theater on Broadway; Victor recorded the routine; and they had three years of solid gold success with it, including the pleasure of seeing dozens try to imitate it. Their last appearance with it was in the touring edition of the 1925 *Greenwich Village Follies,* where they worked the French soubrette Fifi d'Orsay into the act. They tried it again in a 1926 show (again with D'Orsay), named *In Dutch,* but this had a very short run, and the partners abandoned the routine and split up permanently. Neither ever recaptured their early success.

Shean died in 1949.

Their routine went something like this:

SHEAN: Oh, Mr. Gallagher, Mr. Gallagher!
If you're a friend of mine please lend me a couple of bucks.
I'm so broke I'm badly bent,
I haven't got a cent,
I'm as clean as if I'd just been washed with Lux!
GALLAGHER: Oh, Mr. Shean, Mr. Shean!
You don't mean to say you haven't got a bean?
On my word as I'm alive

I intended touching you for five!
SHEAN: Positively, Mr. Gallagher?
GALLAGHER: Absolutely, Mr. Shean!

ED GARDNER "Hello. Duffy's Tavern—where the elite meet and eat. Archie the manager speaking; Duffy ain't here—oh, hello, Duffy. Guess who just walked in—Adolphe Menjou. Wot a terrific guy! Very suave. Huh? . . . Your wife says you're suave? Duffy, I hate to tell you, but she means 'a big fat suave' in your case."

How come Duffy always "ain't here" when it's his tavern? And who is Duffy, anyway? These questions were asked by millions of faithful listeners to one of radio's most colorful shows, the long-running *Duffy's Tavern*, created by Ed Gardner, who played Archie.

Ed Gardner's humor was Runyonesque: his "elite" included Broadway-wise types like "Brains" Finnegan, played by Charlie Cantor, Eddie the handyman (Eddie Green), and the simple-minded Miss Duffy, who tended the cash register and dished out straight lines for Gardner. A favorite elbow bender at the make-believe tavern was Two-Top Griskin, the two-headed baseball player—"the only pitcher who could watch second base and home plate at the same time." The types were lovable, and their mayhem upon the language was unforgettable: puns and malapropisms were scattered on the sawdust floor with abandon; Archie's accent, a mixture of tough-guy slang and Brooklyn cabdriver Newyorkese, his own creation, was a definite artistic improvement on the genuine article.

Why was the tavern run by an absentee owner? Gardner offered the explanation that Duffy was a buddy with whom he had intended to start a real tavern after World War II, but that he got killed in

142

action and so, in memoriam . . . A terrific publicity story, but given out around '48 or '49, by which time many listeners had forgotten that the show had started *before* the war, in 1941, so that it is at best suspect.

Edward Francis Gardner, born in Astoria on June 29, 1905, did have a real connection with taverns: he played piano in a bar at the age of sixteen. He didn't have show business ambitions, but when he was about nineteen, he was smitten by a comely young lady who was a member of a small theater group; just to be near her, he joined the company and toured with it, and in 1929 married the girl. Her name? Shirley Booth.

Still not seeing himself as an actor, Gardner stayed in touch with show business by becoming a producer; the play, created from Dorothy Parker's book *After Such Pleasures,* enjoyed a three-week run at the Barbizon Plaza Hotel. Then he directed a theater group for the Federal Theater Project of the WPA. Then he joined an advertising agency, buying radio time for sponsors.

Gardner knew just the kind of program he wanted to buy time on—but no one had a show about a diamond-in-the-rough New York type. In 1939, therefore, Ed created it himself, called it *This Is New York* and offered it to CBS, which then previewed likely series on the air for sponsors to hear under broadcast conditions. But no one bought it.

Ed knew what he wanted, but none of the radio actors auditioned for Archie's part had the right combination of Brooklyn brass and Broadway polish. He kept demonstrating what he had in mind for the various hopefuls, until someone asked him why not do the part himself. Ed did, revised the format to include the absent tavern owner, and suddenly had a huge success.

Shirley Booth played Miss Duffy for the first two seasons. Then she divorced Ed, and the role was done by Florence Halop and Florence Robinson. Gardner married Simone Hegeman in 1943.

BILLY GILBERT His trademark was The Sneeze—a magnificent production, with copious preparatory heaves, thunderous execution, and after-the-fact embarrassment. No one could sneeze as funny. Gilbert sneezed endlessly in more than three hundred films and thousands of personal appearances. Needless to say, he was the voice of Sneezy in Walt Disney's *Snow White and the Seven Dwarfs*—who else?

But although he was most famous for the sneeze bit, he was no Johnny One Note; his comic versatility was considerable, and he proved it in such roles as W. C. Fields' comically pompous minister and would-be successor in the mythical country of Klopstokia in *Million Dollar Legs,* and as Air Marshal Herring in the Land of the Double Cross run by Charlie Chaplin's dictator Hynkle in *The Great Dictator* (1940), as well as in *Block-Heads* (1938), as Oliver Hardy's next-door neighbor, and in *His Girl Friday,* as a confused innocent being manipulated by politicians.

Born in Louisville, Kentucky, in 1894, Gilbert was on stage practically all his life, since his father was lead tenor of an opera company and his mother was in the chorus. He joined a traveling show with them at the age of twelve, and at eighteen was on his own with a troupe for which he could do more comedy. However, he was not a success in small-time vaudeville and burlesque until one matinee in Wilkes-Barre, Pennsylvania, when he tried to arouse the inattentive audience by sneezing through his act. It got a big laugh, and he worked at it ever since.

Billy Gilbert (right) with Victor McLaglen and Leo Carillo in a scene from Rio *(1939)*

Movies provided Gilbert with a comfortable living since 1929, and he made only occasional forays into radio and TV, with one single time on Broadway (in the role of Panisse in *Fanny,* 1956).

He married Ella McKensie in 1937. He died in 1971.

JACKIE GLEASON Besides being among television's most successful, most boisterous buffoons, Jackie Gleason has excelled in straight dramatic motion picture roles, for which he once occupied the *Time* magazine cover.

He was born on February 26, 1916, on the seamy side of Brooklyn. His father abandoned the family when Jackie was eight, so his mother went to work as a subway token clerk to support them.

Gleason made his show business debut at sixteen, as emcee for a vaudeville theater. He recalls that customers threw plates at him during these humble beginnings. Subsequently, he worked as a daredevil driver, disc jockey, and carnival barker.

His first regular nightclub engagements were at the Miami Club in Newark, New Jersey. Gleason started at $8 per week, and in three years worked his way up to $75. At the Miami Club he was spotted by Jack Warner, the motion picture producer.

Jackie Gleason (with Audrey Meadows)

After several unspectacular film roles in Hollywood, Gleason returned to New York, where he joined the ranks of the legendary show, *Hellzapoppin'*. He became widely known through his performance in *Follow the Girls,* in 1945, and was signed up for network television.

On TV Gleason rose steadily through the ranks until his role as Ralph Kramden on *The Honeymooners* netted him a two-year $7 million contract. Ralph was a bus driver who was generally preoccupied with one get-rich-quick scheme or another, until rescued (or skeptically observed) by his acidulous but affectionate wife Alice, played by Audrey Meadows. Not to be forgotten is Art Carney, who as sewer worker Ed Norton played the perfect foil for Gleason.

His most popular characterizations besides Ralph Kramden include the haut-monde playboy, Reginald Van Gleason, the Third; The Poor Soul, a perennial nebbish for whom everything goes awry; and Joe the Bartender, an amusing but less robust echo of *Archie* from radio's legendary *Duffy's Tavern.*

Filmwise, Gleason earned critical acclaim for his performances in *The Hustler* (1961) and *Requiem for a Heavyweight* (1962).

GEORGE GOBEL "Well, I'll be a dirty bird," said George Gobel in his characteristically wry intonation, and a new catch phrase took root in America. Beyond that, Gobel contributed thousands of memorable comedy sketches to television viewers during the 1950s and 1960s, on his own comedy-variety program.

The crew-cut comic was born in Chicago, Illinois, on May 20, 1920. A barndance bit on a small Chicago radio station was one of his earliest entertainment endeavors, and soon Gobel was singing frequently on radio and in nightclubs. After serving in the air force he did nine more years of nightclub work, earning as much as $3,500 a night, before NBC grabbed him for an appearance on *Who Said That?* When the networks discovered that ratings jumped whenever Gobel made guest appearances, he became a much-sought-after guest star, appearing principally, but not exclusively, on the *Garry Moore Show.*

In 1954 he won his own TV series, and his sympathetic "Lonesome George" character, in mild confrontations with his wife (played by Jeff Donnell, and subsequently by Phyllis Avery), kept viewers tuning in for nearly a decade. "Lonesome George" was singularly unaggressive, a fact underscored by his TV wife being taller than he was.

Gobel's mobile face, and his ability to act out a punchline, rather than just grinning, leering, or playing the buffoon, differentiated him from most of his contemporaries. His was easygoing comedy, with no brass knuckles, no message or controversy, just pure entertainment. So easygoing was Gobel, in fact, that he probably told fewer jokes per minute than any other comedian of his day—yet rarely failed to sustain interest. It was "Lonesome George," not a constant barrage of jokes or a gimmicky format, that attracted a generation of fans.

A couple of free samples:

I've never been drunk . . . but often I've been overserved!

My uncle was the town drunk . . . and we lived in Chicago!

NORMAN GOFF,

see LUM and ABNER

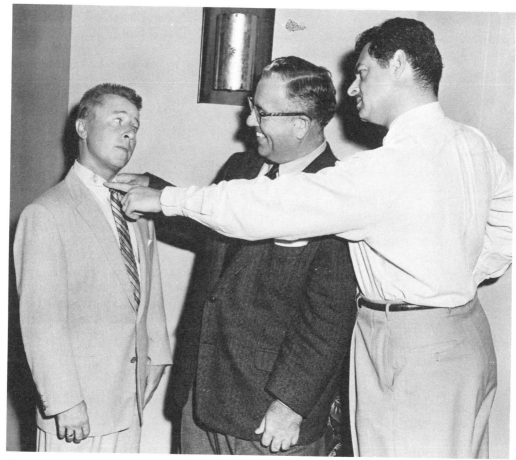

George Gobel (left) with Hal Kanter and John Trotter

MOLLY GOLDBERG,

see GERTRUDE BERG

RUBE GOLDBERG It's rare when the full name of a comic genius becomes part of the language. A "rube goldberg" is a contraption designed to accomplish something simple with a maximum expenditure of time, energy, and weird goings-on; thus, removing the cotton from the top of a bottle of aspirin may involve levers, trap doors, locomotives, marching armies, moon rockets—plus a trained flea, or perhaps a match or pin; all, of course, illustrated by the crackpot inventor.

The world's unchallenged top inefficiency expert started out as a cartoonist. Reuben Goldberg was born in San Francisco on July 4, 1883, and became a cartoon contributor for the *San Francisco Chronicle* and *Bulletin*. In 1907 he came to New York to join the staff of Hearst's *Evening Mail*, where he stayed until 1921. Later his drawings were sold by a syndicate, and his last job was as editorial cartoonist for the *New York Sun* in 1938;

for these, he won the Pulitzer Prize in 1948.

Around 1912 Goldberg wrote a hit comedy number "I'm the Guy," and started a side career appearing in clubs and vaudeville as a comedian. He also recorded one record, and wrote and appeared in one film, *Soup to Nuts* (1930). But his forte was his cartoon inventions; no one ever approached solutions to simple problems with such fiendish determination to move heaven and earth.

LEO GORCEY The wisecracking, tough-talking chief of The Dead End Kids (later also known as Bowery Boys and East Side Kids), whose worst crime was moidering the King's English ("I'm dilapidated to meet you"), was to the manner born: he really came from one of New York's tough neighbor hoods, and many mannerisms that he used as an actor were picked up from the neighbor hoods.

Born in 1917 to a Russian-Jewish actor (the diminutive Bernard Gorcey, who usually appears as the candy store

Leo Gorcey (with hat in hand about to strike Huntz Hall)

owner in The Bowery Boys' films), Leo had no formal training in acting, but learned a lot from his father, who played Papa Cohen in the long-running *Abie's Irish Rose* on Broadway. Gorcey, Senior, made young Leo try out for the role of Spit in Sidney Kingsley's *Dead End* (1935); there he met the other members of the gang, Huntz Hall, Gabe Dell, and Bobby Jordan. All repeated their role in the 1937 film version, and the success of that picture led to a brief stint at Warners, where they were billed as The Dead End Kids in serious melodramas: *Crime School* (1938), *Angels with Dirty Faces* (1938), and *Hell's Kitchen* (1939).

In 1940 they switched to Monogram Pictures, where they could play the same roles for laughs; to distinguish their new approach from their old identity, they now called themselves The Bowery Boys. Leo was the driving force behind the group, which lasted as a unit for fifteen years, although only Leo and Huntz Hall stayed with it all the way.

The formula was simple: Huntz Hall, with his goofy ungainliness, would do something foolish, and then the rest of the boys took the rest of the picture extricating themselves from the mess he got them into. Leo would be talking tough out of the side of his mouth, mangling syntax with fluid dexterity as he was pummeling Huntz Hall with his hat or any other handy object.

When Bernard Gorcey died in 1955, Leo called it quits, appearing only in a bit part in *It's a Mad, Mad, Mad, Mad World* (1963), and finally in *The Phynx* in the year of his death, 1969. He had been married four times, always unsuccessfully.

BERT GORDON In 1935, Eddie Cantor had on his evening radio show a guest comedian who was introduced only as The Mad Russian. He came out and said "How Do You Do" with an accent you could stir borscht with; audiences lapped it up, and the preposterous character remained with Cantor for the remainder of his radio career—14 years.

Bert Gordon, who had not thought much of The Mad Russian character, and had other bits ready, wisely chose not to argue with success, and became one of the most durable sidekicks in radio.

Born Barney Gorodetsky in 1900 on the Lower East Side of New York, the

Bert Gordon (The Mad Russian)

Frank Gorshin

son of a real Russian immigrant, he appeared at fourteen in Gus Edwards' "Newsboy Sextette" act, where his colleagues were Walter Winchell, Georgie Price, and Bert Wheeler. The act broke up, and Barney went with a similar one, "Nine Crazy Kids," which included Jack Pearl and Bert Lahr.

Since Barney looked funny and had unusually big ears, he developed an act in which his homeliness was contrasted with a tall, beautiful girl's charm (she had to be dumb to compensate). This went over in vaudeville, and later he had a funny Western act, "Desperate Sam."

He made it to Broadway in the 1920s, and toured Europe for two years with *George White's Scandals*. His first radio break came on the *Jack Benny Show,* but it was the appearance on Cantor's program that changed his life permanently.

FRANK GORSHIN Master impressionist Frank Gorshin (also a comedian, pantomimist, actor, and singer) admits that "I secretly crave to be like many of the people I impersonate." A few of his many subjects are Richard Burton, Alfred Hitchcock, Richard Widmark, Jackie Gleason, and George C. Scott. His impressions are remarkably accurate; he sounds like and even looks the parts. Among his varied television and film credits was the role of the notorious Riddler on the *Batman* series.

Born in Pittsburgh in 1935, Gorshin first found inspiration while working as an usher in a movie house when he saw Kirk Douglas in *Champion.* He recalls, "I entered the theater happy and left intense. I was gritting my teeth." He began doing impressions of Douglas for his friends that very day, and from that moment was hooked.

After serving in the army's Special Services Division in 1955, Gorshin began pounding the pavements in search of acting jobs. He found occasional work in such shows as *Naked City* and *The Untouchables,* but had to work in a post-office to pay his rent. Then Steve Allen caught his nightclub impersonations routine, invited Gorshin on his show, and this proved to be the versatile comedian's breakthrough to steady work at the top. His film credits include *The Great Impostor* (1961) and *Sail a Crooked Ship* (1962), and he joined Rich Little, George Kirby, and other impressionists in a wild TV series called *The Kopykats* (1975).

FREEMANGOSDEN,

see AMOS 'n' ANDY

RAY GOULDING,

see BOB and RAY

SHECKY GREEN Shecky Green (real name: Greenfield) is one of the Las Vegas comedy superstars, of the six-figure weekly paycheck elite. He earns every penny of it as one of the hardest working comedians around, jumping, mugging, singing, creating waves of sight gags.

The spoof is his modus operandi, and no person or phenomenon in the limelight can hope to escape the bite of his satire. His repertoire has included Richard Burton's Henry the Ninth, Dean Martin (spilling a drink on his shirt), Clark Gable, *Fiddler on the Roof,* sex symbols, *Madame Butterfly,* Sammy Davis, Jr., Frank Sinatra, and Sophie Tucker.

Even his wife is fair game: "I've finally discovered a way to make my wife drive more carefully. I warn her that if she has

Shecky Greene

an accident in Las Vegas, all the newspapers will print her age."

Here's some of his material:

I went to a nudist wedding. People were hard to tell apart but everyone could see who was the best man.

We vacationed in the South Pacific but it was no good. I swam out to the sand bar but it was closed.

CHARLOTTE GREENWOOD At the age of eleven, she was five feet ten and thin as a beanpole, but her mother, who managed a theatrical hotel in the Times Square area, put her into a sister act anyway (with Eunice Burnham). Once

they followed a dog act, and one of the dogs was not housebroken. Charlotte did not see the mess, and did an entirely unplanned split. The house laughed appreciatively, and that was the end of the sweet, sisterly song-and-dance.

Within two months, Charlotte got ten times her previous salary by exploiting her lanky frame and long legs, doing an arm-waving, high-kicking routine with new partner Sidney Grant, an experienced vaudevillian who was only five feet two. "I'm the only woman in the world who can kick a giraffe in the face," she used to claim.

In 1914 she was in the play *Pretty Mrs. Smith,* in which there was a character named Letitia Proudfoot, lanky and long-legged. Charlotte was so successful in the role that a playwright turned a straight but unsuccessful play, *Your Neighbor's Wife,* into a musical *So Long, Letty,* as a vehicle for her. After that, she made the Letty character her own and appeared in a number of sequels, such as *Linger Longer, Letty* and *Let 'er Go, Letty.* With one of these, *Leaning on Letty,* she toured the world for five years.

She also enjoyed a long career in Hollywood, where she made 40 features and a number of short comedies. In 1944 she had a *Miss Charlotte* series on NBC Radio.

She was married twice. Her first husband was songwriter Martin Broome, who composed the songs for the *Ritz Revue,* in which she played in 1924. She died on January 18, 1978, at the age of eighty-seven.

Charlotte Greenwood's comedy derived from that old reliable stereotype, a homely girl trying to snare a husband. Here's a typical exchange between her as a waitress and a customer:

CUSTOMER: Stop winking at me.
CHARLOTTE: Can't a girl get a hair in her eye?

Charlotte Greenwood (with Bert Roach)

CUSTOMER: You must be man-crazy.

CHARLOTTE: Well, a girl can't go through life with a tray of food on her arm. Say, haven't I seen you around?

CUSTOMER: No, I usually eat in good restaurants.

CHARLOTTE: I'm glad you came in here. I'm looking for a man.

CUSTOMER: I doubt you'll find one here.

CHARLOTTE: I guess you're right, now that I see you better. Look, you're a guy and I'm a girl. Doesn't that suggest something to you?

CUSTOMER: Yeah, I want my check so I can get out of here.

DICK GREGORY A brilliant comic mind and an unrelenting determination to help black (and other) people help themselves are two factors that make Dick Gregory one of the few comedians of real social importance. While most entertainers who have made it quarantine themselves within plush mansions, Gregory has suffered physical exhaustion, extreme starvation, police brutality, and imprisonment while fighting for those in need.

Born in St. Louis on October 12, 1932, he spoke of his childhood decades later: "This is the only country in the world where a man can grow up in a ghetto, go to the worst schools, be forced to ride in the back of the bus, then get paid $5,000 a week to tell about it." In high school he didn't get enough good food to eat, and nevertheless became a champion distance runner. These years were good preparation for Gregory's projects of later years—going without food for extended periods (once tipping the scales at under one hundred pounds) and running across the United States from coast to coast, to dramatize such worthy causes as the plight of the hungry and poor.

Gregory had washed a thousand cars and shined a thousand pair of shoes before finding the inspiration to become a comedian in the late 1950s. In 1961 he won wide recognition, and introduced to America the "healthy racial joke" which doesn't belittle one race or another, but cuts through the layers of hypocrisy and prejudice to make caustic social commentary. "When I land on the moon," he quips, "a six-legged, *green*-skinned man is sure to come up and tell me he don't want me marrying his sister." Gregory analyzes why Madison Avenue advertising has no pull in Harlem: "We're the only ones who know what it means to *be* Brand X."

After achieving fame, Gregory phased out his lucrative nightclub appearances to take on less profitable college engagements (when not out on the street working for his people). His rationale is that younger people will be more receptive to his message, and to change.

Working in an era when racial relationships were still touchy, Gregory did much to scale the problem down to size by ridiculing it:

Now, if there is any resentment in the house about my appearing tonight, please burn your cross now and go so that we can get on with it.

Wouldn't it be hell if all this was burnt cork and you people were being tolerant for nothing?

I know the South very well. I spent twenty years there one night.

I waited all these years to be admitted to the Woolworth lunch counter, and now I find I don't like anything on their menu!

The waitress said to me, "Sorry, we don't serve colored people here." I said to her, "That's all right, I don't want to eat any, bring me a chicken."

Dick Gregory

H

BUDDY HACKETT At five feet six, weighing over two hundred pounds, Buddy Hackett has been affectionately called "a baked potato out for a short troll." He is one of the wittiest of the ad libbers, and he expertly combines his wit with hilarious facial and body clowning, for which his rubber face and round physique are ideally suited. "I'm not really a human being, I'm a cartoon. And when I say something serious it still comes out funny," he once said.

His real name is Leonard Hacker, and he was born in Brooklyn on August 31, 1924. After high school, where he directed his class play, was a member of the football squad, and graduated by the skin of his teeth, Hackett and his father, an upholsterer, toured the Borscht Belt servicing upholstery. He returned to the Catskills as a bellhop who doubled as a professional party enlivener. After seeing

the Broadway show *Oklahoma* in 1945, Hackett realized he wanted to be an actor.

With a new name, a retinue of songs and jokes, and a prayer, he got $40-a-week work at a Brooklyn café called the Pink Elephant. He worked steadily thereafter, but his spectacular rise started when his manager realized that "nobody can write for Buddy Hackett except Buddy Hackett." Hackett came up with his now famous Chinese waiter impersonation (accidentally, while trading jests with Red Buttons). He immortalized the routine on wax, and it became one of the all-time best-selling comedy recordings.

In 1954 Hackett began branching out into other media. First came the play, *Lunatics and Lovers,* after seeing which the famed *New York Times* drama critic, the late Brooks Atkinson, described Hackett as "a large, soft, messy comic

Buddy Hackett

with a glib tongue and a pair of inquiring eyes," who plays his role with "exuberance."

Next was the first of several film roles, in *God's Little Acre* (1958), for which Hackett was lauded for managing to inject deep meaning into an absurd character. Then came two relatively short-lived TV ventures, his own 1956–57 series called *Stanley,* and a regular role on the *Jackie Gleason Show* a year later.

In the 1960s Hackett discovered and concentrated on his forte—conversation. His spontaneous wit became the delight of nightclub patrons and talk show viewers.

Also in the sixties, Buddy's antics enlivened a number of films, such as *The Music Man* (1962) and, paired with Mickey Rooney, *It's a Mad, Mad, Mad, Mad World* (1963). He appeared with Harvey Korman in a TV-movie, *Bud and Lou* (1978), an adaptation of the life of Abbott and Costello.

A few of his gags:

In Las Vegas, everything is gambling and luxury. They have slot machines even in the toilet. You put in the quarter, pull the lever, and if you win you get extra-soft tissue.

No, I didn't use a dirty word there, madam. That's a medical term, abbreviation for "anterior superior spine," or A.S.S.

JACK HALEY Bright and likable as a puppy, Jack Haley was a consistently underrated comic talent. After eight good years on Broadway (from *Round the Town,* 1924, to *Follow Thru,* 1929–32), he was invited to Hollywood, where they kept him on ice for five years as second banana in second-rate films before giving him his first good role (in *Wake Up and Live,* 1937, with Alice Faye). He is most fondly remembered by several generations of TV watchers for his role of the Tin Woodman in *Wizard of Oz* (1939). He was a capable standup comedian and interpreter of comedy roles. His diffidence in boosting his talents, his mild-mannered personality, made it difficult for him to claw his way to the top in the rough world of show business.

Haley was born on August 10, 1902, in Boston. At the age of six he got up at a church meeting and sang a song. His first frontal attacks on the stage failed, and he spent some time plugging songs for a Philadelphia music publisher. Finally, he put together a song-and-chatter routine and entered vaudeville in Hoboken, New Jersey. After a year on the Keith circuit, he was booked in the revue *Round the Town* on the Century Roof in New York, then in the second edition of *Gay Paree* (1925), and finally in the Chicago production of *Good News,* where he played the lead. Then came *Follow Thru* (1929); he also did the film version, and this led him to try Hollywood for a while. He was in many films of the mid-thirties, including *Mr. Broadway* (1933), *Sitting Pretty* (1933), *Here Comes the Groom* (1934), *Poor Little Rich Girl* (1935), *She Had To Eat* (1937), *Alexander's Ragtime Band* (1938), and *Hold That Coed!* (1938).

In radio, he appeared on the *Maxwell House Show Boat* and the *Wonder Show,* starting in 1937, and was a guest star on variety programs. He returned to Broadway in *Higher and Higher* (1940), and took on more film roles up to 1949. He married Florence McFadden in 1923; their son, Jack Haley, Jr., became a producer and in 1969 coaxed his father out of retirement for a final film appearance in *Norwood.*

Haley was considered a master at timing a gag, a difficult art that he may have picked up from his two best friends,

Jack Haley (with Ginger Rogers)

George Burns and Jack Benny; when the three were newly married and struggling, they lived close to each other at Central Park South in New York, and in the thirties, when they all moved to Hollywood, they bought houses close together. Legend has it that for several years, George Burns, convinced that Haley's talent outstripped his roles, kept introducing Haley to a producer who would murmur some vague promise and forget it. Finally, Haley made it big in *Follow Thru,* and the same producer saw Burns with Haley at a restaurant. Indignantly, he came up to Burns and said, "Why didn't you tell me you knew such a talented guy? I could have put him on contract years ago!"

Perhaps Haley's misfortune was that he was blessed with average looks; no one could tell at a glance that he was a comedian.

HUNTZ HALL

See LEO GORCEY

THE HAPPINESS BOYS On October 18, 1921, one of the first radio stations in the country, WJZ in Newark, New Jersey, had been on the air a little over two weeks. That evening, two small-time vaudeville singers who had made a few records came to the studio and for an hour and a half sang, talked, and joked in front of a microphone. They were the first comic duo to perform in radio—

ahead of such teams as Coon and Sanders, Lum and Abner, Amos 'n' Andy, or Bob and Ray.

Their easygoing style lent itself best to radio: they poked gentle fun at current events, politics, and even early radio itself, and wrote topical songs like "Henry's Made a Lady out of Lizzie" (about Henry Ford's Model A), "When Lindy Comes Home" (about Lindbergh's overseas flight), and "I Can't Sleep in Movies Any More" (about sound film).

Billy Jones was born on March 15, 1889, in New York City. Of Welsh ancestry, he sang whenever he could, even while working at odd jobs; finally, someone sent him to Lew Fields (of Weber and Fields), who gave Billy a job singing in a Broadway musical comedy in 1909. Then came a period eking out a living as a singer on hundreds of records for various companies; the recording industry was still new and paid very little.

In 1920 he met Ernest Hare, of Norfolk, Virginia (born March 16, 1881), in a recording studio, and the two struck up a friendship; they would often record together as a duo, and that's how WJZ heard of them.

Hare had a brief fling at a business career before the call of show business became strong and he started hanging around Broadway casting offices. After some chorus jobs, he was given credit on the program of *The Passing Show of 1912,* but he didn't make a big enough hit to become a star—just to get steady jobs as a nameless chorus member in future productions. Like Jones, he started haunting recording studios.

When their WJZ stint produced hundreds of listeners' letters, Jones and Hare realized they had found their niche. In 1923 they picked up a sponsor, the Happiness Candy Company, and henceforth called themselves The Happiness Boys—another first, they were the first performers of any type identified by the name of their sponsor. Their five-week contract with the candy maker stretched to five and a half years, and after that they stayed on radio for other sponsors.

In 1933 they were scheduled for a two-week appearance at New York's Roxy Theater, and stayed for 19 weeks. In 1936 they made a cross-country tour that resulted in an offer to lead a community singing program on the CBS radio network, where their cohost was a rising comedian named Milton Berle.

In 1939, after a brief illness during which his sixteen-year-old daughter filled in for him, Hare died. Jones did not wish to continue the program without his partner, but eventually agreed to join another program already on the air, *The Three Sachs* (for the Sachs Furniture Company). Jones was carrying a script of the show in his pocket when, barely a year after his friend's death, he was stricken with a fatal heart attack while walking along Broadway.

This is the way it was:

BILLY JONES: Good evening fiends—er, friends. This is station O.U.C.H. of the Neurotic Tres-passing, er National Broadcasting Company, operating on a wavelength of 600 motorcycles.

ERNEST HARE: We are your friendly announcers, Pete and Re-pete. Our next future, er feature, will be the song "People Who Live in Glass Houses Shouldn't." It will be sung by Howl and Bellow, the silver-plated tenor and the gold-filled baritone, courtesy of station B.U.N.K.

BILLY JONES: Ladies and gentlemen, owing to an emergency, S.O.U.S.E., there will be a slight pause in our program.

OLIVER HARDY,

see LAUREL and HARDY

ERNEST HARE,

see The HAPPINESS BOYS

PHIL HARRIS,

see JACK BENNY

GOLDIE HAWN Goldie Hawn won fame as TV audiences' favorite among the regular madcap maniacs on Rowan and Martin's *Laugh-In.* From 1967 to 1969 her blonde hair, plastic face, shapely figure, and wacky words, were among *Laugh-In's* prime commodities. In motion pictures she has proven that her talent as an actress and comedienne extends beyond the surface layer of zaniness.

On November 21, 1945, Goldie Jeanne Hawn was born in Washington, D.C. Ballet and tap-dancing lessons began during her third year, and eventually led to go-go dancing in New York and Las Vegas nightclubs.

From a dance bit in the chorus of a 1967 Andy Griffith TV special, she was cast in a supporting role in a CBS-TV series, *Good Morning, World,* whose birth and death (in 1967) were nearly simultaneous.

That same year came *Laugh-In,* where Ms. Hawn's paradoxical combination of sophisticated sexuality and complete innocence made for one intriguing dumb blonde.

She left *Laugh-In* for Hollywood, and her film debut was in *Cactus Flower* (1969). Her second screen effort (and the first in which she starred) was *There's a Girl in My Soup* (1970). Her subsequent films include *Butterflies Are Free* (1972), *The Sugarland Express* (1974), *The Girl from Petrovka* (1974), two Warren Beatty vehicles, *Dollars* (1971) and *Shampoo*

(1975), and *The Dutchess and the Dirtwater Fox* (1976).

TED HEALY,

see The THREE STOOGES

HARRY HERSHFIELD A well known raconteur and humorist, Hershfield reached the height of his popularity at the time of World War I with his character, Abe Kabibble, in the comic strip *Desperate Desmond* that he was doing for the Hearst papers. Afterward, he hung around for many years, as a sort of comedians' comedian, emcee, and TV panelist.

Born in 1886 in Cedar Rapids, Iowa, he became a cartoonist on the *Chicago Daily News* by the age of thirteen, and stayed on for ten years. In 1908 he came to New York for the Hearst papers, and having heard Fannie Brice use the Yiddish expression *"nischt gefiddle"* (I should worry), he used part of it to create "Kabibble," then added a first name. (Later, singer Merwyn Bogue used the whole expression for his stage name, Ish Kabibble.)

Hershfield appeared on an early talking short made by radio pioneer Lee De Forest between 1922 and 1927; the film also featured President Coolidge and Adolph Zukor. He also participated in the first experimental television program demonstrated to the press, in 1926, when a show featuring George Jessel, Sid Garuman, and Harry was beamed from Jersey City to a receiver in Times Square.

In 1939 Hershfield created another cartoon series, *According to Hoyle,* which ran in the *Herald Tribune* for two years. In the fifties he appeared on the TV comedians' program, *Can You Top This?,* as a regular panelist.

Goldie Hawn

163

Harry married Jane Isdell in 1917—his only marriage. He died in New York City on December 15, 1974.

But his humor lives on after his death. Like so:

Two neighbors are discussing an incident in their block.

"It was terrible. Joe found his wife with Charlie. He knocked him unconscious, pulled all his teeth out with a pair of pliers, and gave him third-degree burns with a blowtorch."

"It could have been worse."

"How could it have been worse?"

"The night before, *I* was with Joe's wife!"

The General was giving instructions to his troops before a big battle:

"All right, men, don't worry, I'm with you all the way. Remember, wait until you see the whites of their eyes, then start firing. Of course, being colorblind, I had better stay out of it. Then, if the enemy gets within a hundred yards, you retreat. Well, since I am a little lame, I'd better start now."

Love is the only thing where the imitation is much more expensive than the real thing.

Strike your child regularly every day. You may not know why, but the kid does!

PORTLAND HOFFA,

see FRED ALLEN

JUDY HOLIDAY *Born Yesterday* was a stage play about a dumb-blonde golddigger who snares a rich slob on the strength of her brainless act, and later regrets it when a better man comes along. The show was meant as a vehicle for Jean Arthur, but she became ill during the Boston run, and had to be replaced for the Broadway opening by a comparative unknown, Judy Holliday.

A show biz legend resulted. With an impeccable sense of timing, a few inflec-tions, a forlorn, plaintive, whining voice, and a bewildered look, Judy created an unforgettable role, and was basically responsible for the show's four-year run in New York, and the resounding success of the film. It established her as a comedienne of the first water, and earned her an Academy Award for best female performance of 1950.

She was born Judith Tuvim (Hebrew for "holiday") on July 21, 1922. Her first contact with the theater was as switchboard operator at the Mercury Theater; then she joined a Betty Comden–Adolph Green group, The Revuers, and performed with them in clubs and small theaters. Her talent began to break through when she obtained a small role in the Broadway show *Kiss Them for Me;* she stole the show, gained critical acclaim, and won the Derwent Award. Then came *Born Yesterday.*

Judy was very funny in a supporting role in the Tracy–Hepburn film *Adam's Rib* (1949) and sparkled as the star of *The Solid Gold Cadillac* (1956). Among her other films were *Phfft* (1954) and *Bells Are Ringing* (1960).

In 1948 she married David Oppenheim; they had one child, were divorced in 1958. Judy died in 1965.

STERLING HOLLOWAY The professional bumpkin was born in Cedartown, Georgia, in 1905, and studied drama in New York. He wanted to be a serious actor but his hayseed face predestined him for the type of role that he played for five years as Waldo on the *Life of Riley* show on television.

He earned his first actors' salary in walkons in Theater Guild productions. In 1925 he and several others wrote a few burlesques of the Broadway plays currently playing in New York, for what they

Judy Holliday

hoped would be several Sunday afternoons of just plain fun for which they could be paid. The result, called *Garrick Gaieties,* became so popular that the group took over the theater full time for four years. Sterling played only in the 1925 and 1926 versions, then went to Hollywood.

Out west, Holloway tried some silent two-reelers, and was in *Casey at the Bat* with Wallace Beery. Some more vaudeville and a few plays later, Holloway returned permanently to Hollywood as talkies took over, making more than one hundred films. He also did voices for some Walt Disney cartoon characters, and put out a very popular series of children's records.

In the 1950s, he appeared from time to time in the Pasadena Playhouse, the Los Angeles Civic Light Opera productions, and summer stock in Sacramento.

LOU HOLTZ An all-round vaudeville topliner with an inexhaustible supply of jokes, anecdotes, and dialect comedy, Lou Holtz is best remembered for singing old jokes set to music (with an incongruous "O Sole Mio" at the tag end), and for his "maharaja" stories—in which the alleged maharaja would mumble some nonsense, and Lou would "interpret." He played the Palace many times, and was a favorite emcee there.

Holtz was born in San Francisco on April 11, 1898, had his first job at The Crest (a beachside inn), and had the good fortune to be seen there by Elsie Janis, then a vaudeville star of the first magnitude. She induced him to make the trip to New York and put in a good word for him with some agents. He worked Miller's Hotel on Forty-third Street and the College Inn in Harlem, and finally hit the vaudeville circuits starting in Newark. In the 1919 edition of *George White's Scandals,* when the leading comedian became ill, Holtz substituted for him, and stayed on for three seasons. Eventually, he formed his own revues and toured the country with them. He was instrumental in developing the natural comic talent of Polish-born Lyda Roberti and letting her loose on the Broadway musical stage.

Holtz remained near the top of his profession as long as vaudeville had any life left in it, and thereafter made the hotel and resort rounds. He rarely ventured into other media, making only a few appearances on film.

Here's some of his typical material:

My talk tonight asks the question, "Do married men make the best husbands?" Now, I don't want to say anything against marriage; I don't use that kind of language! I have been married myself for four years, and we're so happy it doesn't seem like more than ten or twelve. The other night we sat in the parlor and I held her hands for two hours. If I had let go, she'd have killed me! I was introduced to her by a scoundrel who knew I would never pay him back the $3 I owed him, and he thought this would be a way to get his revenge. I married her because she told me her father was a retired bank president; then I found out he was "retired" by a judge for twenty years.

HOOSIER HOT SHOTS Playing music in a funny way, without sacrificing musicianship, is a sporadically practiced, difficult art. There was Spike Jones in the swing-era field, Firehouse Five Plus Two in dixieland, and Johnny Puleo. In the field of country and western music, the Hoosier Hot Shots were by far the funniest such aggregation—and, surprisingly, one with an impeccable taste for the jazz idiom in hillbilly disguise.

The originator of the combo was Rudy

Trietsch, known as Ken, who plays banjo and guitar and composes most of the group's original numbers. His brother Paul, known as Hezzie, is the clown of the outfit, with percussion instruments that include the washboard, auto horns, slide whistle, and other noisemakers. The band's frequent exhortation, "Are you ready, Hezzie?", became a trademark of the Hot Shots.

The other members of the original quartet were Otto Ward, known as Gabe, on the clarinet (and, occasionally, saxophone), and Frank Kettering, who usually plucked the bass but could also play the piano, banjo, or flute.

They first appeared on a radio station in Fort Wayne, Indiana (where a fellow Hoosier, Herb Shriner, got his start), and quickly ascended to the hillbilly heaven, the *National Barn Dance* radio show, in 1935. They remained unfailingly popular through the years, never varying their cornball act, which was received with equal warmth by audiences in all corners of the globe. In the mid-1970s they were still at it, even putting out LPs on their own label.

BOB HOPE Ask any GI from the last three wars, and you'll find that Bob Hope is revered as a sort of patron saint. He told his jokes—always topical and carefully custom made for the audience and the locale—for the amusement of the Armed Forces in the remotest corners of the world, during World War II, Korea, and Vietnam, often just a few miles back of the front lines.

His specialty is the machine-gun monologue: a series of quick quips on any number of current subjects and personalities, fired at the audience as fast as they can absorb them.

In the Sahara, during World War II, he told the GIs at a desert encampment: "I wanted to mail a letter home but it's so hot here I had no spit to use on the stamp—so I pinned it to the letter."

On a ship in the mid-Pacific: "I just left Hawaii, the world's hardest place to leave. Everywhere else, they wave with their hands. But I'm here because my grandfather was a naval hero. He shouted when the battle was approaching: 'I have not yet begun to fight!' And, you know, he never did!"

In a Greenland arctic weather station: "They don't bother with roll call here. No sense counting noses, nobody's got one. You can also do away with marriage ceremonies here. You just wet your lips, kiss your girl—and till death do you part."

Following the troops was routine for Bob, who always hotfooted it to where the action was. He started in vaudeville, when that was big; stepped into radio as soon as that showed signs of life, and became one of its major stars; left that for television with undiminished success. He also appeared in Broadway musicals and more than fifty films, and authored half a dozen books.

Hope was born in Eltham, Kent, England, on May 29, 1903, as Leslie Townes Hope, but his family moved to Cleveland when he was only four. He broke into show business in a local Chaplin impersonation contest, and later formed a song-and-dance act with various partners. He made it to Broadway by 1932 in the show *Ballyhoo,* and the following year he did *Roberta.*

In 1934 he went into radio and started making films. The radio program became memorable for his barbed monologues, which were now familiar to the whole country for the first time, and for the colorful sidekicks developed over the years, such as the master of non sequi-

Bob Hope (with Shirley Ross)

turs, Jerry Colonna, and the lame-brained spinster Vera Vague. It was radio's top-rated show of 1944.

In 1950 Hope started on television. He has remained on it ever since, with hour-long specials, broadcasts from overseas tours, and guest appearances. He has entertained several presidents, amassed a huge fortune, and scaled the heights of success and fame.

A fabulous career for any comedian, without really going down the list of his many film successes—and Hope was one of the great movie comics. The "Road" pictures, with Bing Crosby and Dorothy Lamour, were big hits, with Bob and Bing getting into trouble in Singapore, Morocco, and all kinds of remote places. Hope's other film credits include *My Favorite Blonde* (1942), *They Got Me Covered* (1943), *My Favorite Brunette* (1947), *Fancy Pants* (1950), *The Lemon Drop Kid* (1951), and *The Facts of Life* (1960). His films remain extremely popular, appearing over and over on TV reruns.

DE WOLF HOPPER A big man with a booming bass voice, he was best known for reciting Ernest L. Thayer's famous "Casey at the Bat," which he delivered for the first time at Wallack's Theater in New York in May of 1888, and repeated by his own count at least 10,000 times more during the next forty years.

Born March 30, 1858, in New York City, William d'Wolf began his career in theatrical stock companies, where he specialized in Gilbert and Sullivan patter songs. He reached Broadway in *Desiree* in 1884 and stayed on for many more productions. He created his most famous role in *Wang* (1891). After 1900, no musical comedy on Broadway seemed to be complete without him, including the Dillingham shows at the Hippodrome and many Gilbert and Sullivan revivals.

He was married to Edna Wallace Hopper and later to Hedda Hopper, the columnist. He died on September 23, 1935.

EDWARD EVERETT HORTON He was the master of understated concern amidst absurd situations in scores of comedies; he seemed to have been always worried, and often downright shocked, but he was far too gentlemanly to show undue alarm. Because he was always an island of nervous calm in a sea of frenzy, he could get more comic mileage out of a simple raised eyebrow than most comedians could out of major grimaces.

Horton was born on March 18, 1886, in Brooklyn, and attended college at Baltimore City and at Oberlin before switching to Columbia. There he appeared in the *Varsity Show* of 1909, and was bitten by the theater bug. His first outside job was in the chorus of a Broadway musical comedy, *The Newlyweds and Their Baby,* in which he met another chorus boy just starting out, Wallace Beery.

Edward's first lead part was as the Japanese prince in *The Typhoon* in 1913. He toured the country, spending two years in Portland, Maine, three years in Pittsburgh, and six in Los Angeles. In the 1920s, he took over the Majestic Theater there and did his own directing.

He made several silent films, starting at Vitagraph with *Too Much Business,* including the original *Ruggles of Red Gap* (1923). He did a Western for Harold Lloyd when he was still making two-reelers. At the end of 1927, Horton appeared in one of the first all-out talkies, *The Terror,* rushed into production at Warners as the sound revolution hit all

Edward Everett Horton

studios. It costarred Louise Fazenda and May McAvoy.

Horton's best films were made during Hollywood's madcap comedy years: he worked five times for Ernst Lubitsch in pictures like *Trouble in Paradise* (1932) and *Merry Widow* (1934); was in *Design for Living* (1933) with Gary Cooper; and in *Reaching for the Moon* (1930) was Douglas Fairbanks' butler, one of his favorite roles. He also appeared, apprehensive and jittery, in several Astaire–Rogers films.

In the late 1930s, he made films in England, the last of which was *The Gang's All Here* (1939).

EUGENE HOWARD,

see WILLIE HOWARD

JERRY (Curly) HOWARD,

see The THREE STOOGES

MOE HOWARD,

see The THREE STOOGES

SAMUEL (Shemp) HOWARD,

see The THREE STOOGES

WILLIE HOWARD One of the giants of vaudeville, Willie Howard was equally adept at parody, farce, and musical comedy; his favorites were devastating take-offs on popular singers and show biz personalities of his day. He was often teamed with older brother Eugene; but Eugene later tired of being the straight man and became Willie's manager. A third brother, Sam, was overshadowed by Willie and never went far in show business.

Willie was born in Neustadt, Germany, on April 13, 1886, and came to this country with his family at an early age (the family name was Levkowitz). His theatrical debut took place at the age of fifteen at Proctor's 125th Street Theater in *The Little Duchess* (1901). He toured vaudeville with his brother Eugene for ten years before winding up on Broadway in the newly opened Winter Garden. The brothers Howard were among the most regularly employed comics on the Great White Way. Among their credits were

George White's Scandals of 1926, and ditto for 1928, 1929, 1936, and 1939, plus the *Ziegfeld Follies of 1933.*

Respected by fellow comedians, Willie Howard was among those recorded on experimental sound film by Vitaphone in 1926, and featured on early television in the 1930s. He died on January 12, 1949.

Here's one of Willie's routines:

A Communist speaker in Union Square: ". . . and when we take over, this will be a paradise on earth, and everybody will be able to eat strawberries for breakfast!"

Voice from the crowd: "But I don't like strawberries."

The speaker: "And that's another marvelous thing about the Communist system. Under our regime, you will eat strawberries *and like it!*"

BUDD HULICK,

see COLONEL STOOPNAGLE

GEORGE JESSEL Star of vaudeville, Broadway, movies, radio, television, and books, George Jessel is a show business perennial. The years have not detracted from his vigorous career; in 1975 he published an autobiography, *The World I Lived In.* A *Variety* reviewer wrote that it "might as easily have been called 'The Beds I Slept In.'" His romantic interests as detailed in the book included Norma Talmadge, Lupe Velez, Helen Morgan, and Pola Negri.

An acerbic critic of today's entertainment, Jessel is a nostalgic fan of the grand old days of live entertainment when over 15,000 vaudeville theaters graced the United States. "Vaudeville is the only place where the artist is in full control," he said recently. "In television, you have to say what the sponsor wants you to. In theater, you have to do what the audience wants. In vaudeville you do what

you want to do. You can change things. You can ad lib."

Jessel was born in New York City on April 3, 1898. His father, who lost his shirt in show business, told the seven-year-old boy, "You will never be an actor as long as I live." The next year his father died, and at age nine Jessel was singing professionally. Three years later he appeared with a neighbor kid, Eddie Cantor, in Gus Edwards' revue *School Days.*

An accomplished dramatic actor, Jessel scored with *The Jazz Singer,* on stage in 1925. Among his many other milestones are having produced films for Twentieth Century–Fox, being named Toastmaster General of the United States by President Truman, and inventing that unique show business celebration, the "roast."

Films weren't really his thing, but

George Jessel (with a film bit player)

Jessel appeared in over a dozen, mostly in the twenties, with corny titles like *Ginsberg the Great* (1928) and *George Washington Cohen* (1929). He also produced something like twenty films in the forties.

Jessel had scores of famous jokes and routines, including "Watch the Owl." He tells of an old-time Chicago vaudeville duo who rejoice to learn that they've been booked for 38 weeks in Dubuque. One fellow vaudevillian warns them to watch for the owl in the balcony: "There's a great attachment between this owl and the owner of the theater. No matter how great your act is, no matter how much the audience screams and laughs and applauds, if the owl hunches his shoulders, you get canceled immediately." Another seasoned vaudevillian warns one of them to watch out for the stage manager whose good looks are a sure bet to lure away his wife. Undaunted, the team brings their act to Dubuque and, sure enough, just as he's about to deliver the big punchline, the husband sees the stage manager in the wings "doing it" to his wife. He whispers, horrified to his partner, "Look what that guy's doing to my wife!" The reply: "Never mind him—watch the owl!"

CHIC JOHNSON,

see OLSEN and JOHNSON

BILL JONES,

see The HAPPINESS BOYS

SPIKE JONES Outside of Charlie Chaplin's *The Great Dictator,* probably the funniest parody to come out of World War II was the 1942 song "Der Fuehrer's Face." An inspired bit of nonsense featuring a resounding Bronx cheer, written

Spike Jones (left)

by a comparatively unknown bandleader with only five records to his credit, it took off in sales and radio requests like wildfire—because the wartime audience was starved for humor.

This plus subsequent hits like "Cocktails for Two" and "Chlo-e" assured many years of popularity to perhaps the zaniest band ever assembled, which used a workshopful of sound effects and controlled vocal insanity in devilishly clever takeoffs on big songs of the day. To do parody well took fine musicianship, and only a talented person with a sense of humor could play third pistol for Spike Jones and His City Slickers.

The leader and first pistol of "the band that played just for fun" was born Lindsay Armstrong Jones in Long Beach, California, on December 14, 1911. He led his first combo on radio while still in high school, and by the early thirties played drums in the bands of Ray West, Everett Hoagland, and Earl Burtnett.

Finally, he landed a job with the NBC Radio studio band, which accompanied the top comedy shows. Perhaps the humor of Fred Allen, Bob Burns, Fibber McGee and Molly, and Al Jolson was infectious, because Spike started rehearsing the band in off hours, doing funny renditions of popular standards.

An NBC executive heard the band murdering "Red Wing" one day in 1941, and asked them to cut a record of it on the Bluebird label. It sold enough to keep the band together until their big hit gave them national notice—if that's the right word. NBC then gave them their own show, which usually featured banjoist Freddy Morgan, singers Doodles Weaver, Red Ingle, and Dorothy Shay, and various band members who managed to free themselves from their straitjackets.

The City Slickers appeared in several low-budget comedies in the next few years, and recorded on V-Discs for the Armed Forces. In the fifties, there was plenty of television exposure, and in the early sixties, Spike held court in Las Vegas and so forth.

Spike Jones married Patricia Ann Middleton in the thirties, and they had one child. In the forties he married the band's vocalist, Helen Grayco, and they had three children. He died on May 1, 1964.

BOBBY JORDAN,

see LEO GORCEY

JIM JORDAN,

see FIBBER MCGEE and MOLLY

ABE KABIBBLE,

see HARRY HERSHFIELD

ISH KABIBBLE In 1937 an inane little ditty called "Three Little Fishes" took off like a rocket: five million copies later, it justified vocalist Merwyn Bogue's conviction that you need a gimmick to make it to the top.

A capable trumpet player and fair vocalist, Bogue (born January 19, 1908, in Erie, Pennsylvania) did not feel his talent was good enough for more than playing and singing for fun at West Virginia University where he was studying law and economics. He graduated in 1930 when professional jobs were scarce, and accepted an offer from Kay Kyser's band.

To overcome his inferiority complex, he evolved a comedy character: hair cut in bangs a little like Moe Howard's (of The Three Stooges fame), name taken from Yiddish vaudeville via Harry Hershfield (q.v.), and novelty songs. He became a leading exponent of the nonsense song, bestowing on the public such mind-boggling gems as "Hold Tight, Boorri-yaki-taki" and the evergreen "Mairzy Doats."

Ish Kabibble appeared with Kay Kyser on radio and in films such as *That's Right, You're Wrong* (1939). Later, during the 1940s, he worked single and led a band of his own in Los Angeles. In the 1950s, he formed a combo called The Shy Guys. In the 1960s, he retired from show business to go into real estate and public relations.

CLEM KADIDDLEHOPPER,

see RED SKELTON

MILT KAMEN Combining his love for movies with a flair for comedy, Milt Kamen did funny movie reviews—perhaps he was the only nationally known practitioner of this offbeat genre:

As a boy I was in love with Fay Wray, but I couldn't see what she saw in King Kong. He had no imagination: on their first date, he takes her to the Empire State Building like a regular tourist. I knew nothing would come of it.

Kamen was born in Hurleyville, New York, in 1922. He studied music and played French horn in a theater pit orchestra. But when he saw Ray Bolger perform in the theater, he tried his hand at comedy.

He first appeared at The Purple Onion in San Francisco, and got booked for Sid Caesar's *Show of Shows*. This led to a featured spot in New York's Blue Angel, and then the *Tonight Show* and *Merv Griffin*. He also appeared off-Broadway, and in such plays as *A Thurber Carnival, The Typist, The Tiger,* and *The Passion of Joseph D.*

He died in Beverly Hills, California, on February 25, 1977.

HELEN KANE She was the quintessential flapper cutie of the 1920s: pert and saucy, complete with turned-up nose, rolled-down hose, and flirty dark eyes. The cartoon strip *Betty Boop* was modeled after her, and so was its animated

Helen Kane

counterpart in the movies. She became a national institution virtually overnight, and stage-struck mothers would have their little girls imitate her as the best way to get an audition—until Shirley Temple came along.

And all this happened by accident. Helen Kane (born Helen Schroeder in 1904) was an obscure songstress; in 1924 she made her show business debut in a Marx Brothers revue (*I'll Say She Is*), but no one seemed to notice her in the general bedlam. Then, in 1927, she got a part in another Broadway production, *A Night in Spain,* but it closed after 22 performances.

Then came the 1928 show, *Good Boy,* where she was teamed up with Dan Healy (whom she later married). While rendering the song "I Wanna Be Loved by You," she was at a loss what to do at the end of the lyrics, and so she ad libbed a timid little "Boop-boop-a-doop." For reasons better left to sociologists, it became a sensation. Her appearance at the Paramount Theater in New York with the Paul Ash Orchestra created a riot; she made eight feature films and several shorts within the next two years.

The lasting impression she left during her meteoric career can be gleaned from the fact that twenty years later, when Debbie Reynolds filmed *Three Little Words* at MGM, which called for her to sing "I Wanna Be Loved by You," it was Helen Kane who dubbed the lyrics for her.

Helen died in 1966.

GABE KAPLAN Gabe Kaplan attained the apex of commercial comedy as cocreator and star of ABC-TV's smash show, *Welcome Back, Kotter.* The show is based on his nightclub material, which was drawn from his personal childhood experiences with the oppressive nature of our school system.

Welcome Back, Kotter is the story of a formerly loud street punk type who returns home to Brooklyn to teach a remedial class, helping out rowdy gangs like the ones he had belonged to, whose insults (toned down for television) include, "Your mother's so low she can play handball against the curb," and "Up your nose with a garden hose!" Yet Kaplan's theme is serious. "What I try to show is I don't believe in the school system because the kids can't achieve anything when they're thrown together in such a class. I can recall a sense of hopelessness."

In one episode a robot-like female career counselor refuses to counsel one of Kotter's students for a career as a veterinarian, because the computer's results show him fit for "the highly rewarding field of manual labor." Numbers are the highest authority, and she ignores the fact that the student has cared for a wide variety of animals. Despite her urgent protestation that "I never go in classes where there are real people," Kotter marches her to the classroom where the student has just supervised the birth of baby hamsters. Dumfounded, she reconsiders her verdict and grants the student another counseling session. "Only this time," the student begs, "could you please talk in English? I don't understand computer."

Born in 1946, Kaplan dropped out of school to become a professional baseball player, but never made it past the minor leagues. "I just didn't have it," he said. He turned to bellhopping in Lakewood, New Jersey, while trying out comedy material in coffeehouses. His fresh approach to standup comedy made him an "in" comic among sophisticated younger audiences. Kaplan provided one of the

Gabe Kaplan (center) – John Travolta is at his left

best among a thousand and one comedians' impressions of Ed Sullivan. In Kaplan's version, Sullivan is soused on his very last broadcast and tipsily insults his guest stars, even the dignified Kate Smith.

Like many comedians, Kaplan at first fell into the trap of using vulgar language for shock value, rather than developing and communicating ideas. He refined his style to become one of the most original standup comedians on the scene.

DANNY KAYE Danny Kaye is a singularly talented comic stylist who estab-

lished himself as a top-rate comedian without ever telling a joke. His performances consist of novelty songs, mimicry, and dancing. One of the rare entertainers with a strong sense of social responsibility, he has devoted a large portion of his time for more than two decades to working with the United Nations International Children's Emergency Fund (UNICEF).

He was born David Daniel Kominski in Brooklyn on January 18, 1913. His show business debut came when he played a watermelon seed in an elementary school play. At thirteen he ran away from home, and by fifteen he was a combination bus boy and comedian on the Borscht Circuit.

Danny Kaye

In 1940 Kaye achieved a milestone and the breakthrough to fame, when he came onstage in Moss Hart's *Lady in the Dark*. He managed to uncork the names of 54 Russian composers in a mere 38 seconds, speaking in his characteristic rapid-fire gobbledygook.

Although Hollywood had an enduring love affair with him, Kaye's reputed dislike for motion picture work impelled him to accept no more than one film per year. The films he did deign to appear in include *Up in Arms* (1944), *The Kid From Brooklyn* (1946), *The Secret Life of Walter Mitty* (1947), *The Inspector General* (1949), *Hans Christian Andersen* (1952), and *The Five Pennies* (1959).

At least one film was a labor of love for Danny Kaye, his documentary for UNICEF called *Assignment Children*. To make the film he traveled around the world with a cameraman, showing the plight of underprivileged children everywhere.

BUSTER KEATON The year is 1922. The film is *Cops*. A bomb is thrown into Buster Keaton's moving vehicle. With perfect serenity and his trademark deadpan face, Keaton grasps the bomb and applies its sizzling fuse to his unlit cigarette. Then he discards his impromptu cigarette lighter, and it lands smack in the middle of a parade of policemen. Such is the prototype Keaton situation: the quasi-rationally motivated act, its fortuitous and suspense-producing ramifications (in this film, the constant ire of the cops), presided over by a deadpan face that is equally intent whether peering into a loaded cannon or facing a marriage ceremony. But, though his face was still, Keaton had one of the most mobile and dexterous bodies of any film comedian.

Buster Keaton

During one stunt he literally broke his neck, without becoming aware of the injury until a physician detected it, long after it had healed!

Joseph Frank Keaton was born on October 4, 1896, in Piqua, Kansas. He was a professional acrobat at age three, working with his parents as The Three Keatons. His entrance to films was in 1917 playing the stooge for Fatty Arbuckle, by then a veteran who taught Keaton the techniques for adopting stage know-how to the screen.

Two of Keaton's favorite comic catalysts were chase scenes and girls; his films testify to his passion for both. But the wild daredevil stunt was his real forte, and he refused to employ a double. For *Steamboat Bill, Jr.* (1928), he planned to have a two-ton building facade crash down around him. A small window opening would barely save him from being pulverized into dust. The stunt was so dangerous that the film's director and half the crew left, when they couldn't convince Keaton to invent a safer thrill. But when it came to his art, Buster's placid visage told no lie; he had no fear, and the crashing building stunt stands among the most spectacular of the silent era. Today, of course, it would have been shot with a miniature building and trick photography.

Keaton and his colleagues in the 1920s represented a new wave in film comedy, a wave of maturity that strove to be funny through comic ingenuity instead of relying on the slapstick tradition. "A comedian today," said Keaton, "no longer finds his dressing room filled with slapstick property bricks, stuffed clubs and exploding cigars. Comic situations have taken the place of these veteran laugh getters." During his life, Keaton made about sixty films, including *The Navigators* (1924),

Sherlock, Jr. (1924), *The General* (1926), and *The Cameraman* (1928).

When his vogue had passed, he continued to act whenever he could secure decent work, right up to his death on February 1, 1966.

AL KELLY Al Kelly probably coined more nonsense phrases than anyone since Etaoin Shrdlu made his linotype debut. He was a broodlebiss who could fraspilate the language in such a crastering manner that he left his audiences in a state of strismic gallooble, as he would have put it. His words were almost real, but not quite—and his greatest joy was to befuddle specialized audiences, such as conventioneers who were supposedly expert in some field, into believing that he was actually a fellow specialist. Once some medical friends of his arranged his surprise appearance at a medical convention, where he stated with the utmost conviction that he "was able to rehabilitate diabetics with daily injections of triprobe into the right differnarium, which translucentizes the stoline, producing a black greel which enables you to stame the klobium." To his delight, he had some of the assembled doctors later approach him for details of his new treatment.

His real name was Al Kalish, and he went into show business in 1914 on his native Lower East Side of New York City, as one of the Nine Crazy Kids. Later, he served years of apprenticeship in the Borscht Belt with a regular standup routine. One day, driving to one of the Catskill resorts, he developed his specialty: he stopped to ask a state trooper the way, but mispronounced the name of both hotel and location. Before he had a chance to correct himself, the policeman

Al Kelly

started looking for the nonexistent place on a map, and Al realized it would be funny if a whole audience could be so fooled.

The double-talk act was a sensation, and brought him an offer from Willie Howard; together they toured the country between 1936 and 1948. Kelly also appeared in several revues, including *Crazy With the Heat, Priorities of 1942, Hilarities,* and *Star and Garter,* and in one film, *Singing in the Dark* (1956). On television, he made virtually all the early variety shows, including Jackie Gleason, Milton Berle, Ed Sullivan, Steve Allen, and Jack Paar.

Al claimed that the real start of his fascination with topsy-turvy language came when he was a kid of about seven or eight and wanted to join one of the many children's clubs in the area: the one he chose was called Sufolla, which is the reverse spelling of "All of us."

He died on September 7, 1966, at the age of sixty-seven.

EMMETT KELLY The art of the circus clown is too specialized to warrant the inclusion of a representative sampling of clowns in a volume on general comedy, but America's greatest living clown, Emmett Kelly, may be a justifiable exception. He developed a character, Weary Willie, who was the direct inspiration for one of television's well remembered comedy creations, Red Skelton's Freddie the Freeloader.

Weary Willie so captivated the audiences of America's largest circus that the Ringling Brothers granted him a unique privilege in that he was allowed to remain in the arena throughout the entire performance, at liberty to do any of his pantomime bits or enter into the act and interfere with the performers in his own special way. Spectators throughout the world never failed to respond to his untiring efforts to sweep up a circle of light thrown by a spotlight. As he kept sweeping, the circle got smaller, and he would chase it under a rug or into a dustbin; satisfied, he would start leaving, only to find another circle of the original size right in his path.

Kelly was unusually versatile, and is the only clown to make it to Broadway (*Keep Off the Grass,* with Jimmy Durante, in 1940), to films (*The Fat Man,* 1950, *The Greatest Show on Earth,* 1952, and *Wind Across the Everglades,* 1958), into print (autobiography *Clown,* 1954), and even into baseball (for a few seasons, he was the Dodgers' official pre-game clown).

He was born on December 9, 1898, in Sedan, Kansas. In school, he exhibited a talent for drawing, and in 1917 he went to Kansas City with the intention of becoming a professional cartoonist. Finding only a limited outlet for his talent in newspapers, he started supplementing his income by giving "chalk talks" at fairs and circuses—children's shows in which he would tell a tale while sketching a picture on a blackboard.

This led to his joining a traveling circus on a permanent basis. Since all circus personnel then had to do more than just one act, he also doubled on the trapeze. In 1923, he married a fellow trapeze artist, Eva Moore, and they had a son. The marriage broke up in 1935, and later he was married for a short time to another fellow performer, Mildred Ritchie.

Kelly switched permanently to clowning in 1931, with the Hagenbeck-Wallace Circus, with whom he traveled to Europe several times. In 1942, he came to the Ringling Brothers Barnum and Bailey Circus. His conception of the clown was not a jolly fellow full of laughs, but essentially a rather sad reject who is always trying to find a bit of dignity and respect. It was Weary Willie's pathos that made him the best clown in the business.

He died in Sarasota, Florida, in 1979.

PATSY KELLY

PATSY KELLY She was at her best as the heroine's best friend, always ready to help with the wisecrack, straighten out the irresolute girl, or come through with sound, if a bit loud-mouthed, advice. She had the best chance to demonstrate it in a series of two-reel shorts with the beauteous Thelma Todd; perhaps she did it too well because she became typed as the greatest second female lead around and never reached stardom in her own right.

Born in 1910 in New York City, she attended dancing school—but even there she was overshadowed by a classmate, Ruby Keeler. Patsy got a job with comedian Frank Fay, who made her his vaudeville partner; later, she had small roles in several Broadway productions.

In 1931 she made a Vitaphone short, Hal Roach hired her for the Thelma Todd two-reelers, and later she played second fiddle to Lyda Roberti, ZaSu Pitts, Jean Harlow, and many others.

After two decades of solid movie making, with more than fifty films to her credit, she took time out in 1955 to tour with Tallulah Bankhead in *Dear Charlie*, and to do a few TV shows and specials. Back in Hollywood, she had small parts in *The Crowded Sky* (1960), *Please Don't Eat the Daisies* (1960), in which she was the maid, *The Ghost in the Invisible Bikini* (1966), *C'mon Let's Live a Little* (1967), *Rosemary's Baby* (1968), and *Freaky Friday* (1977).

WALTER C. KELLY

VIRGINIAN JUDGE: You're charged with stealing half a dozen eggs. What do you have to say about it?

DEFENDANT: Well, Your Honor, I was coming home last night and took a short cut through the fields, and there they were—must have been laid by some of them wild hens.

JUDGE: Oh, yes, those wild hens are very dangerous. So I'm going to protect you against them for the next thirty days. But you are also charged with assault by your neighbor. How do you plead on that charge?

DEFENDANT: Your Honor, he made some disparaging remarks about my Irish ancestry, so naturally I got a little vexed.

JUDGE: A little vexed, eh? Looks like you vexed him right under a freight car. That'll cost you five dollars.

DEFENDANT: But, Your Honor, that's an awful price for beating an Englishman.

JUDGE: I know it is, but that comes under the heading of "luxuries" to us Irish.

Such was the justice dispensed by the Virginian Judge, Walter C. Kelly. Born in Minerville, New York, on October 29, 1873, he ran a café in Virginia as a young man, and thus his observations about various human types were firsthand. In time, he became a master dialectician doing Negro, Scandinavian, Italian, and other ethnic tales, but he is best remembered for his Virginian Judge character—in which he would do the voices of all the plaintiffs and defendants, male and female, and then deliver the verdict in his own voice. He toured the vaudeville circuit for forty years, and appeared in several films, including *Laughing Irish Eyes* (1936).

Kelly died in Philadelphia on January 6, 1939.

ALAN KING

ALAN KING Topical nightclub monologist and star of over thirty television specials, Alan King is at his caustic best when talking about marriage, suburbia, and the economy. In the early days of

Alan King

moon flights he lamented the billions squandered on space travel since "for a couple more dollars I could have taken a cab crosstown."

He was born Irwin Alan Kniberg in Brooklyn on December 26, 1927. He entered show business in his middle teens as a professional musician at the Gradus Hotel in the Catskills, later switched to comedy, and first became widely recognized as a top-flight comedian during the 1950s.

King's talents extend far beyond his brilliant monologue: his acting debut saw him re-create the role of Nathan Detroit in a 1965 production of *Guys and Dolls.* His film roles include a rabbi in *Bye Bye Braverman* (1968), and a mobster in *The Anderson Tapes* (1975). Among his many TV credits are frequent appearances as guest star and host of the *Tonight Show,* and his fondly remembered work on *Kraft Music Hall* and *Comedy Is King.* Alan has written two books, *Anybody Who Owns His Own Home Deserves It,* and *Help! I'm a Prisoner in a Chinese Bakery!*

This is the kind of material that King has used so effectively on television:

My wife has two weaknesses: she's on a cleanliness kick, and she can't resist bargains. She's always cleaning up after me; how would you like to get up at five o'clock in the morning to go to the bathroom, and when you come back the bed is made? And when it comes to sales, she's the all-time champion. Our local supermarket now advertises sales by posters that say, "Dear Mrs. King: . . ."

The KINGFISH,

see AMOS 'n' ANDY

MEL KLEE Klee was a vaudeville headliner for twenty years, from 1915 to 1935.

He was born in 1893, and started in show business as a song plugger for Al Herman. Later he inherited Herman's act when the latter went to the west coast. He started as a single, at first making use of blackface. For years he was the top comedy star with Fanchon and Marco Ideas, and he also appeared with other girl acts.

His real name was Mel Lefkowicz. He died on April 8, 1935, at the tender age of forty-two.

ROBERT KLEIN Robert Klein is one of America's new wave of comedians who has shown his talents in nightclubs, films, and recording. He has received only sporadic television work, including *Comedy Tonight,* his own CBS series for the summer of 1970, which went virtually, and underservedly, unnoticed.

Born in the Bronx in 1942, Klein attended De Witt Clinton High School, received his B.A. in history and political science from Alfred University, and enrolled at the Yale Drama School to study comedy. Disillusioned, he later said, "Yale is no place for a comedian to learn his trade. The only way is to go out and do it." He dropped out.

In a 1963 off-Broadway Circle in the Square production of *Six Characters in Search of an Author,* Klein made his professional stage debut. His acting commanded all of $5 a week, and Klein had to work on the side as a substitute teacher, which later inspired some fine comedy routines.

During the run of the show, Klein's ambition to be a standup comic intensified, and he began writing routines and feeding them into a tape recorder before testing them at such clubs as the Improvisation and The Bitter End. "Every night for the next three years," he recalled, "there I was at The Improvisation with my tape recorder, honing my craft." During an appearance he was spotted by Rodney Dangerfield, who brought him up to a more lucrative echelon of show business. Impressive nightclub engagements and roles in Broadway shows followed.

Because his Broadway performances received good reviews, Klein began appearing frequently on TV shows hosted by Johnny Carson, Dick Cavett, David Frost, Merv Griffin, Ed Sullivan, Joey Bishop, Flip Wilson, and others. Then came roles in four movies, *The Owl and the Pussycat*, *Pursuit of Happiness* (1971), *Rivals* (1972), and *The Landlord*, followed by his short-lived *Comedy Tonight* TV series. His first of several comedy albums, *Child of the Fifties*, received a Grammy nomination.

His demeanor has often verged on the "countercultural," but Klein's comedy is as American as apple pie. Who else still jokes about the sweet scent of Navy bean soup wafting through the corridors? "I'm not a preacher, teacher, or prophet," explains Robert Klein, who is now making nearly one hundred live performances a year—with this kind of material:

The art of the panhandler in New York is something fantastic. There's this guy hangs around Broadway who comes right up to you and shouts, "PLEAAAAASE, PLEAAASE, help me!" But he blew it the other day. I saw him being picked up after his regular hours in a '78 Eldorado. A couple of weeks later, I flew to L.A. for a TV taping, and there on the street I see a guy going "PLEAAAAASE, PLEAAAASE!" It was a franchise.

Do you know my definition of patience? That's a guy sitting by the Hudson River at 125th Street, actually hoping he will catch a fish.

EFFIE KLINKER,

see EDGAR BERGEN and CHARLIE MCCARTHY

DON KNOTTS His own comedy preferences are tongue twisters, malapropisms, spoonerisms, and bloopers. Waiting to go on with a humorous monologue on the *Tonight Show* for Steve Allen in the 1950s, he did an imitation of a man stricken with paralyzing stage fright; it was so hilarious that Allen asked him to make it a running gag on the show, and Don Knotts suddenly found himself quivering and shaking all over the tube.

In 1958 he played in the film *No Time for Sergeants* with Andy Griffith; Griffith liked his style, and in 1960 made him his comic sidekick on the *Andy Griffith Show* on television. In 1970 Don Knotts tried his own show, but it failed.

He was born in 1924 in Morgantown, West Virginia.

Even the titles of his films show that he has been typecast as a timid jellyfish for all time. There were, for example, *The Ghost and Mr. Chicken* (1966), *The Shakiest Gun in the West* (1968), and *The Apple Dumpling Gang* (1975).

Now, here's Knotts tied up in knots:

Good evening, er afternoon, jades and lemons, er ladies and gentlemen, this is your announcer, Loose Usedtothink, bringing you a by-play, er play-by-play prescription, er description of today's fame, er flame, er game between New York Pen and Used State, er NYU and Penn State. It's a grand day in the greatstand, er great day in the grandstand, with the gunshine beaming on the fectators' paces, er sunshine beaming on . . . what a fright! What a sight! I plee the sayers, er see the players warming up. The ball is now scoring sky in the high, er soaring high in the sky, and it comes down on the five-clothes line, er five-yard line. And here comes No. 37, and he's on the louse, er on the loose, but they catch him with a fish and tackle, er flying tickle; what a cackle, er tackle! He's been up there in the State pen for two years now, I mean Penn State for two years now. And now the players are in a puddle, er huddle, but oh-oh, someone's been hurt, he's flying on the bat of his fleck, er lying on the flat of his back, and here comes the doctor running across the bag with a stadium in his hand. And now a beer comes from, I mean a cheer comes from the grandstand: the doctor just shaved the player's wife, er saved the player's life.

ERNIE KOVACS Ernie was the first genuine creative genius to be developed wholly in the field of television. His visual comedy gift was nothing short of brilliant. He would construct a complete room tilted at a 20-degree angle, then have the camera shoot it at the same tilt so that the image on the screen would appear perfectly level, but liquids and round objects would roll crazily down the table, and it took a while to figure out the whole insanity.

He did one 15-minute segment in which he browsed through a library without saying a word. He picked up a thick book: on opening the front part, a miniature cannon shot a puff of smoke at him; he opened the book further back, and a live dove flew out. He closed the book and put it back on the shelf so that the title would show: *War and Peace*. Another book started out with a light cough,

Ernie Kovacs

which got progressively worse as he turned the pages (*Camille,* of course).

The Nairobi Trio were three orangoutans in full dress and bowler hats playing a mournful tune, with the percussionist always pummeling the gentleman in front of him instead of the drum in deadpan earnestness.

Kovacs was a genius far beyond his time, and regrettably stayed around for too short a while. He was the only TV personality within memory who strove to present visual comedy, as opposed to the "talking heads" type of shows done by virtually everyone else.

Born on January 23, 1919, in Trenton, New Jersey, he started out as a disc jockey on a local radio station, and worked his way up to sports announcing by the time television began to pick up steam in the late 1940s. He wanted to try the new medium but all he could get was the host spot on a cooking show; eventually, a local Philadelphia station gave him a quarter-hour slot in the early evening for comedy. His bizarre sense of humor immediately asserted itself—he had his guests, for example, freeze in midsentence while commercials were on, then resume as if time had stood still.

The successful show went network, and by 1956 Kovacs was hosting his own one-hour prime-time show on CBS. He was soon making movies, such as *Operation Mad Ball* (1957), with Jack Lemmon and Mickey Rooney, and the fey *Bell, Book and Candle* (1958), in which he played an author of books on magic.

In 1955 he married Edie Adams, who started out as one of his stooges in the early programs. Tragically, he died in a car accident on January 13, 1962.

BERT LAHR Bert Lahr is generally remembered as the Cowardly Lion in *The Wizard of Oz,* and as the old man in the potato chip commercials who "can't eat just one." Yet his career spanned half a century and was as diversified and succeesful as it was long.

Born Irving Lahrheim in New York City on August 13, 1895, Lahr joined the Nine Crazy Kids, a child vaudeville ensemble, in his teens. He worked his way up through vaudeville and burlesque to the legitimate theater, where he won the distinction of being named best Shakespearean performer of the year by the American Shakespeare Theater and Academy.

His favorite role was in Samuel Beckett's classic *Waiting for Godot.* Lahr said, "The play was controversial. Those that hated it, spit at it. But it had its cult and

created a different type of audience for me." On Broadway, he was also in *Foxy* (1964), which won a Tony Award.

Lahr played several fine comic screen roles, although only his Cowardly Lion is commonly remembered. Despite his distinguished career, he was never stopped on the street by admirers until he began making those famous potato chip commercials late in life.

The great drama critic Brooks Atkinson described Lahr as a "clown who fills a theater with wonderful nonsense without crouching behind the microphone or assaulting his audience with murderous drumfires of wisecracks. He radiates a kind of genial though lunatic good nature."

Despite being one of the comedians who attempted to broaden his artistic scope (he did Shakespeare, Beckett, and

Bert Lahr with Claudette Colbert in the film Zaza *(1938)*

Aristophanes), Lahr claimed that he was first and foremost a businessman, a commercial entertainer. "Will you cut out this artistic stuff?" Lahr scolded frequently, continuing, "I'm a pure mercenary. . . . Put me into a jockstrap for an hour or so, and if I entertain people, if it's a big hit, that's the extent of what I care about." Commercial he was; he once developed a get-rich-quick plan to manufacture popsicles molded to resemble famous starlets' breasts. Said Lahr, "We'll get Lana Turner and Betty Grable to endorse our venture."

Bert Lahr died on December 4, 1967, at the age of seventy-two.

STEVE LANDESBERG On the *Barney Miller* show, where he plays a detective, Steve might offhandedly make a remark like, "I have this neighbor who likes to go for long walks. Yesterday he was gone nearly the whole day."

Whereupon Barney (or one of the other detectives) would ask, "Well, what's wrong with that? He came back, didn't he?"

Casually, Steve comes back with, "Yep. Tide brought him in."

This slight touch of the macabre, which makes it risky to pursue any conversation with him, is what he likes. He has possibly the driest and at the same time the flakiest sense of humor of all the comedians working in television today, and even coperformers are never quite sure what to expect from him next.

Landesberg grew up in the Bronx where he was born some thirty or so years ago, and after a period of odd jobs following his graduation from high school, entered show business via an open audition for the *Tonight Show,* with a Wild West routine featuring all the accents he learned in his father's grocery near Yankee Stadium. He didn't make

Steve Landesberg

In 1971 Johnny Carson was so intrigued with Steve's style of comedy ("slightly wacko," he called it) that he gave him four guest spots. His most popular bit, the crazed German psychiatrist, was featured on the *Bobby Darin Amusement Company,* and modified slightly to fit the character of a German violinist who was a regular on a short-lived TV series, *Paul Sands in Friends and Lovers.*

This is where the producer of the *Barney Miller* show saw him, offering him a niche that, according to Steve, allows him practically to play himself.

LUPINO LANE An extremely gifted English comedian from a distinguished old acting family, Lupino Lane is little known because much of his early film work in England was not preserved. But he was appreciated in the trade, and a number of comedians, Chaplin among them, expressed admiration of his talent.

He had something in common—particularly in appearance, white facial makeup, and studied awkwardness—with both Larry Semon and Harry Langdon; but his characterizations went deeper than Semon's, which may explain why his popularity went up as Semon's declined in the second half of the 1920s, and he had more poise and decisiveness than the baby-faced Langdon. He was a skillful acrobat, like Keaton, though not as inventive.

His American debut took place in 1922 with Fox, and between 1925 and 1929 he was with Educational Pictures, producing near brilliant parodies. It is one of the mysteries of the erratic movie business why so few Lupino Lane comedies are available to the public.

His real name was Henry Lane, and he was born in London in 1892. He wa

the show, but got hooked on comedy, and talked some Greenwich Village nightspots into giving him a chance to try out before the public. In 1969 he began working out at The Improvisation, alongside Jimmy Walker and Dave Brenner. Together, they and three other would-be comics formed a company called The New York Stickball Team, and toured with it for nearly two years.

Brenner confided to a reporter that Landesberg had the most original comic mind in the sextet. But also the laziest: "Many a time, he would have us in stitches for twenty minutes with some outlandish routine which he improvised while we were having lunch or something. We'd all tell him he simply had to do it on stage, and he'd amiably agree, yes, sure. Then you'd never hear it again.

worked into the music hall act of his cousin, Stanley Lupino, at age four, and became a knockabout acrobatic comic. His brother Wallace appeared in some of his two dozen plus films; eventually, both were overshadowed in fame by Henry's daughter Ida Lupino, who became a distinguished actress and director.

Henry Lane turned to directing when he returned to England in 1931, and he died in 1959.

HARRY LANGDON Harry Langdon was once hailed as a possible successor to Chaplin. Had he not begun to believe that this made him the best judge of what he should play in films, he might have scaled the lofty heights of his profession. Sadly, he took the publicity too seriously, and arrogantly controlled the reins of production long before he was ready—if he would ever have been ready. He was not really quite sure what special talent he had; a shrewd director was needed to bring out the unique Langdon touch and make the most of it.

By sheer chance, Langdon did find such a director almost as soon as he got into the movies—a youngster working for Mack Sennett's studio, by the name of Frank Capra. Together, they made several shorts, and then a feature, *The Strong Man.* It stunned the public; what they saw was an epicene creature, partly man but mostly a sort of baby in man's clothing, who could create wistfulness and pathos out of less material than any comedian alive.

Perhaps nowhere was this uncanny ability to depict one hundred percent pure innocence on camera better demonstrated than in his third feature, *Long Pants.* He is a country bumpkin who blunders into a streetwise showgirl, and she takes him to town. He has a scene in her dressing room where he sits with his back fully to the camera so that no portion of his face is seen, and he is looking at the girl who is changing for her number. The idea is that he never expected her to take off her clothes in front of him, but she obviously has no scruples about it. What is stunning is that Langdon manages to convey to us, merely by the slightest stiffening of his back, and then a somewhat dejected slump of his shoulders, what is happening to him: he has been incredibly shocked, and finally has lost his illusions about this beautiful but not innocent girl. To say this much without facing the camera is an artistic achievement of the first water, and Langdon does it almost effortlessly.

It is too bad that he was not satisfied with Capra, but wanted to be in charge of his own destiny. He fired everyone, and hired some relatives to work with him. Having eaten up the critical raves about "pathos" and "feeling" in his two big films, he asked the writers to smear a lot of that stuff around; this they did, and his next film, *Three's a Crowd,* wallowed in maudlin sentiment but did not have the slightest spark of creative humor. A few more like this, and Langdon was finished. He hung on, desperately, finding work in progressively less and less inspired turkeys in poverty-row studios; the public couldn't care less, and no critic would waste a breath on him.

Harry was a veteran vaudeville trouper when he came to film. He was born on June 15, 1884, in Council Bluffs, Iowa, and ran away from home when he was twelve or thirteen years old to join a medicine show passing through town. In 1903 he toured vaudeville with an act called "Johnny's New Car," which was so successful that he kept doing it for twenty years. In 1923 he was hired by Principal Pictures to make a series of comedies, but

Harry Langdon

the contract was sold to Mack Sennett. Thus, he was seen for the first time in a 1924 Sennett short called *Picking Peaches.*

Two dozen shorts and two years later, Capra and Langdon made *The Strong Man* and *Tramp, Tramp, Tramp,* and in 1927, *Long Pants,* and the world of comedy was at their feet.

Langdon appeared in 57 films in 17 years after his failures. He was working on Republic's *Swinging on a Rainbow,* in 1944, when he was stricken with a head pain and had to be taken from the set. On December 22 he died of a cerebral hemorrhage, virtually unmourned by the public.

He was married three times. The first two marriages ended bitterly, with disputes over alimony. His third wife Mabel (married in 1934) presented him with his only child, Harry, Jr.

CHESTER LAUCK,

see LUM and ABNER

HARRY LAUDER The master of the comic Scotch song became a one-man goodwill ambassador for his native land in more than half a century of circling the globe. There is hardly a music hall, theater, or auditorium in the English-speaking world where he hasn't appeared, from the Palladium in London and the Palace on Broadway to small-town pubs in Australia and South Africa. He has made hundreds of records; toured the United States 25 times in one 23-year period (1909–1932); organized a front-line entertainment unit in World War I; appeared in films (*Auld Lang Syne,* 1929; *Song of the Road,* 1940); and was knighted in 1919.

Lauder was born in Portobello, Scotland, on August 4, 1870, and worked in a flax mill and in a coal mine for ten years before his fellow workers' demand for his singing convinced him he could make it in show business. At first he had to stick to Scotland, because his thick Scotch burr was not understandable to the English; finally, he learned to use "stage Scotch," which seems to be acceptable everywhere. He made his London debut at the age of thirty, and became the highest paid British artist of his day.

Lauder died in Strathaven, Scotland, in February 1950.

LAUREL and HARDY Comedy teams have been around as long as comedy itself, but Stan Laurel and Oliver Hardy brought a new dimension to the partnership, which propelled them to the very top.

The chief ingredient distinguishing their comedy from others was dignity. They recognized that laughs in comic situations are generally related to someone's loss of dignity (we won't laugh when a toddling baby falls down, since the baby has no dignity to begin with, but we laugh when a pompous ass falls down). In order to lose dignity, you must first show that you have it; Laurel and Hardy always did this, addressing each other with utmost courtesy even in the most trying situations, and always introducing each other as *Mister* Laurel and *Mister* Hardy to any outsider.

It is strange that the soundness of their formula was not recognized by others. For example, Abbott and Costello had to work much harder to milk laughs from their audiences, because Costello acted like an idiot, and so Abbott's slapping him around was not particularly amusing. However, when Hardy finally got exasperated enough with Laurel to resort to violence, the audience realized the provocation had to be extreme.

Laurel (right) and Hardy

Laurel and Hardy's specialty was taking a simple controversy and developing it carefully, almost lovingly, into a big hassle. An instructive example is the short film *Big Business* in which, as Christmas tree salesmen, they get one tiny twig caught in a prospective customer's door. They ring his door again to get the twig released; he cuts it off instead with a scissors. They retaliate by cutting his tie; and, within the 20-minute running time of the film, they progress to cathartic mayhem, demolishing his house brick by brick, while he is taking apart their

delivery truck and reducing the trees to kindling.

They also used several trademark bits of business, such as Hardy's embarrassed tie twiddle, Laurel's crying jags, and Hardy's way of looking straight into the camera as if to say, in utter exasperation,

Why was I saddled with this imbecile?

In reality, Stan Laurel, an earnest student of comedy, originated most of their routines, while Hardy had few ambitions beyond enjoying an occasional round of golf.

However, the courteous deference he showed in addressing Laurel or in speaking to ladies was quite natural with him. His full name, which he used in many of the films, was Oliver Norvell Hardy, and he was born into the family of a small-town Southern lawyer in the hamlet of Harlem, Georgia, on January 18, 1892. He got into the habit of watching people in the lobby of a hotel his mother operated after his father's death, and learned to imitate their manners and speech patterns.

As a boy, Hardy had a singing talent, and his mother let him travel with Coburn's Minstrels when he was about eight. Later, he studied music at the Atlanta Conservatory.

He entered show business in an unusual way—as a business. In 1910 his family moved to Milledgeville, Georgia, and finding no movie theaters there, Hardy opened one. When he saw the quality of films being made then, he was sure he could supply better product himself, and in 1913 went to work for Lubin, a Philadelphia-based film company with a unit working in Florida. In 1917 he was in New York working for King Bee, a company making imitation Chaplins. Hardy played villains at this time, and later did the same for Larry Semon in California. In 1926 he joined the Hal Roach studio, where Stan Laurel had been working off and on since 1918.

Stan was Arthur Stanley Jefferson, born in Ulverston, Fngland, on June 16, 1890, the son of a theatrical entrepreneur who introduced him to stage life from infancy. He came to the United States as a member of the Fred Karno troupe, which also included Charlie Chaplin, whom Stan understudied. Stranded in Chicago when the company broke up, Stan worked in vaudeville and teamed up with an Australian dancer, Mae Dahlberg, who became his common-law wife and suggested that he change his name to Laurel. He tried several forays into film, and in 1926 Roach offered him a long-term contract. Tired of the vaudeville circuits, he accepted.

As contract players, Laurel and Hardy appeared in several films in various roles before anyone began to notice a special chemistry developing between them. By 1928 they were an inseparable duo. They worked together in 77 shorts and 28 feature films, the last made in 1951. Among them were *Pardon Us* (1931), *Pack Up Your Troubles* (1932), *Sons of the Desert* (1933), *Babes in Toyland* (1934), *Way Out West* (1937), and one of their best, *Block-Heads* (1938).

Television revived interest in their work, and in their retirement they found themselves as beloved as ever. Hardy died on August 7, 1957, and Laurel passed away on February 23, 1965.

A key element of Laurel and Hardy's comedy was the premise that Stan could come up with a coherent thought but that it would disintegrate under close scrutiny. A typical exchange (from *Towed in a Hole*) went like this:

OLLIE: For the first time in our life, we're a success. A nice little fish business, and making money!

STAN: You know, I've been thinking.

OLLIE: What about?

STAN: I know how we could make a lot more money.

OLLIE: How?

STAN: Well, if we caught our own fish, we wouldn't have to pay for it. Then, whoever we sold it to, it would be clear profit.

OLLIE (*thoughtfully*): Tell me that again.

STAN: Well—if you caught a fish—and whoever you sold it to they wouldn't have to pay for it—and the profit goes to—the fish—and—

OLLIE (*jubilantly*): I know exactly what you mean!

JOE LAURIE, JR. Before the term "superstar" had been coined, Joe Laurie, Jr., was a superstar of vaudeville. Like George Burns and Alan King he always had a cigar, and smoked it while delivering the most imaginative monologue in vaudeville. Laurie's dry humor contained no one-liners and wisecracks; neither did he need a trick voice or funny delivery. His inventive stories stood up on their own, and made him one of vaudeville's favorite personalities.

When Laurie did employ stooges in his act, it was perhaps the only time in vaudeville history that they were used as decorative props who didn't contribute to the act. They were usually two actors, an older man and woman, introduced as Laurie's father and mother. Most stooges were all-purpose clowns who danced, sang, took pratfalls, and goofed in every way imaginable, but his alleged mother and father simply stood there on stage while Laurie went into a routine about his parents.

Vaudeville died, and Laurie managed the transition to radio without appreciable difficulty. He was an occasional guest on *Information Please*, and a regular, along with Harry Hershfield, Peter Donald, and Ed Ford, on *Can You Top This?* In the latter program the four panelists would attempt to top comical stories submitted by the audience. This gave Laurie ample opportunity to exploit his encyclopedic command of comedy material.

In retirement, the well-to-do Laurie would spend every afternoon with his show biz cronies at New York's Lambs Club, reminiscing about the glory days, optimistically, even piously, awaiting the second coming of vaudeville, about which he wrote the definitive history in 1953. It never did come back, though, and Laurie passed away on April 19, 1954.

PINKY LEE Milton Berle's successful invasion of television from the world of burlesque, with that medium's broad bag of broad antics, paved the way for other burlesque veterans to make the transition. Pinky Lee was a lisping zany who became very popular on TV in the early fifties, ending up with a successful kiddie show.

Pinky Lee

Pincus Leff was born in St. Paul, Minnesota, in 1916. As a child he danced, sang, and played the xylophone. At thirteen he joined Gus Edwards' *School Days* revue, and during the 1930s traveled Harold Minsky's eastern and western burlesque wheels with Milton Schuster.

In 1942 Pinky Lee appeared at Earl Carroll's Hollywood theater-restaurant; then followed a few films, such as *Earl Carroll's Vanities* (1945), and finally television. As late as 1967, he toured in the show *This Was Burlesque*. He married Bebe Dancis in 1932.

TOM LEHRER A most unusual, original humorist of the intellectual variety emerged out of Harvard University in 1953, clutching a master's degree in mathematics. Long popular around the campus for his offbeat, slightly cynical, droll comments on the college scene, he was prone to compose songs on such subjects as "Nicolai Ivanovich Lobachevsky," a real Russian mathematician (1793–1856)—clearly a challenge to any songwriter—and other academic matters.

Here, in a more earthy vein, is his advice to Boy Scouts:

Be prepared—
Don't make book if you can't cover bets;
Don't write naughty words on walls that you can't spell;
Keep those reefers hidden when the Scout Master's around
For he'll only insist that they be shared—
Be prepared.

Be prepared—
Don't solicit for your sister, that's not nice—
Unless you get a good percentage of her price;
If you're looking for adventure of a new and different kind

And come across a Girl Scout who's similarly inclined—
Don't be nervous, don't be flustered, don't be scared:
Be prepared!

Recording these and other songs at his own expense, he saw sales soar surprisingly ("more than forty copies in the United States alone," as he put it), and for several years was in great demand on campuses, avant-garde nightclubs, and auditoriums. He toured England with his act in 1959, Australia and New Zealand in 1960 ("I also gave lessons on ukulele da gamba on the side," he is apt to remark).

JACK E. LEONARD Jack E. Leonard was a nightclub and television favorite famous for his one-liner insults. A typical insult was leveled at his intimate pal Ed Sullivan: "There's absolutely nothing wrong with you that reincarnation won't cure." But Leonard's insults were always good-natured, and Sullivan bore him no malice. He commented, "Jack is always on. He's identical with his stage image. He's just a wonderfully amusing guy."

Leonard was born in Chicago on April 24, 1911, named Leonard Lebitsky. After working as a lifeguard he began participating in Charleston contests. The little fat man's comical dancing won him an invitation to vaudeville, where he quickly rose in the ranks. During World War II, Leonard made his contribution by working tirelessly for USO camp shows.

In the next stage of his career, Leonard accompanied prominent big bands on their nationwide nightclub tours. With the advent of television he became a much-sought-after guest star on major programs, and his popularity and earnings ballooned—the latter to about $250,000 for five months' work per year.

Jack E. Leonard

"Money doesn't mean much to me," Leonard quipped, "because I bought Polaroid at 11. And you can be sure that it's tough carrying 11 Polaroids around."

Leonard also did some motion picture work. He played a character named Porky in *Three Sailors and a Girl,* had a cameo part in Jerry Lewis' *The Disorderly Orderly,* and narrated Universal's *The World of Abbott and Costello.*

Fat Jack (340 pounds and known as "The Lump") dieted determinedly and became Flat Jack (205 pounds). "No pills, no injections," he claimed proudly, "just pure willpower." "I've had thirty years of good meals," Leonard responded to a heckler who shouted that he looked like he needed one, "and now I wanna live to enjoy them."

Jack E. Leonard died on May 10, 1975, after a heart failure and diabetic troubles.

But his insults live on after his death:

What is this—an audience or a painted backdrop? Thank you for the applau—I can't put an *s* at the end of that word because that would imply there was more than one person clapping. You at the piano, must you play in the cracks? What a crowd—if Moses had seen you, he would have thought up another commandment! You there, sir—I always wanted to know how long a man can live without brains—would you mind telling us your age?

JERRY LESTER and DAGMAR On *Broadway Open House* they were one of the funniest comic combos of early television. Dagmar, the amply endowed dumb-blonde giantess whose stock in trade was sex, and Jerry Lester, the energetic funnyman-interviewer-juggler, were perhaps the first team able to keep millions of Americans glued to their televisions until midnight.

Lester was born in Chicago in 1911, and Dagmar (Virginia Ruth Egnor) was born in West Virginia in 1926. In nightclubs, radio, and film, Lester never quite made it, and was selected for *Broadway Open House* only when the first choice died of polio. Dagmar had had a small part as a stooge in Olsen and Johnson's *Laffing Room Only* before *Open House,* and had a show of her own after the partnership with Lester, *Dagmar's Canteen.* For trivia buffs, estimates of Dagmar's bustline ranged from 39 to 42.

In a typical bit of repartee, Jerry Lester would listen to one of Dagmar's twisted elocution lessons. "A mushroom," she would explain, "is a place where people make love." At other times she would read ridiculous poetry full of malapropisms and double-entendres, or push her shoulders back so that her low-cut gown threatened to overflow, while spouting dialogue in her eternally innocent voice. Although Dagmar held the sexual spotlight, Lester had a few swift quips of his own. "What do you give a man who has everything?" he was asked. Lester blurted, "Penicillin."

OSCAR LEVANT There is a thin line between genius and insanity; Oscar Levant erased that line.

He was well read, erudite, and witty, but a quivering bag of phobias, hypochondrias, and superstitions: when he was offered a room on the thirteenth floor of a hotel in Buffalo, he ran screaming from the place, and never visited the city again.

He was an exceptionally gifted pianist, who idolized George Gershwin and became that composer's definitive interpreter. Yet he could remark to his face: "George, if you had to do it all over, would you still fall in love with yourself?"

Jerry Lester (with Dagmar)

Apologizing for his casual dress when he had no time to change, saying, "I'm sorry but my regular attire is white tie and straitjacket," Levant was painfully close to the truth. On his own interview show on a local Los Angeles TV station (Channel 13) in 1958, he had the audience wondering whether he would crack up right on the air, and when. He would tremble, appear unshaven and unkempt, looking as if he were about to expire, yet his comments were as sardonic as ever, sparing no one—least of all himself.

Oscar's musical background was awesome: on radio's *Information Please,* he could identify the most obscure classical number after the first three bars, give the composer's name, credits, and genealogy, and recollect where and by whom the piece was performed for the first time.

A musical prodigy, an urbane raconteur, an acidulous martinet, impossible to live with, and a sufferer from terminal triskaidekaphobia—we will never see another Oscar Levant.

He was born on December 27, 1906, in Pittsburgh, where his father was a watch repairman. Oscar played piano in his teens at a ballet school, later in clubs and hotels; he composed about forty tunes, the most popular of which was "Lady, Play Your Mandolin," for shows. His ambition was to give piano concerts, but he was offered only bread-and-butter jobs.

His musical erudition got him his wish via the back door of a radio quiz show. Someone talked him into going on *Information Please* as a musical expert in 1938; he stayed on for six years, and suddenly there were offers for concert tours and records. His rendering of *Rhapsody in Blue* became Columbia's all-time best-selling classical album. The movies beckoned and Oscar moved to Hollywood, where he composed for and appeared in

many films, playing more or less himself. Two of his biggest films were *An American in Paris* (1951) and *The Band Wagon* (1953). He appeared on a Hollywood panel show on television, and on the Jack Paar show in the early 1950s.

He married showgirl Barbara Smith in 1932; his second marriage, in 1939 to June Gale, produced three daughters.

When he didn't like a woman, he told her, "Madam, I'll memorize your name, and then throw my head away." When another girl at a party asked if he remembered her, he said, "I make it a point not to remember you." Asked if he was for integration, he replied, "I'm for disintegration—personal disintegration."

After years of psychoanalysis and treatment for real and imagined nervous disorders, Oscar found release from all tensions in 1972.

SAM LEVENSON A teacher by profession, Sam Levenson is a raconteur with a gentle, folksy approach: most of his anecdotes are reminiscences about a childhood on the Lower East Side. His family may have been poor by materialistic standards, but there was never any lack of love or parental discipline—and Levenson's message is that this was the right way, while today's reverse situtation is the wrong one.

"Sure my mother had an automatic garbage disposal—she would detect unerringly when you planned to go out, and put the garbage bag in your hand to take out with you."

"Today you send a kid to his room for punishment—where he has a TV set and a stereo. In my day, I would have considered it a reward."

Levenson was born on December 28, 1911, the last of a Russian-Jewish tailor's eight children. He became a teacher, but

Sam Levenson

in 1940 at a teachers' meeting in a Catskills hotel he acted as emcee and led the orchestra; after that, he was asked more and more to tell his stories on campuses and at various functions. Later he did this successfully in early television, appearing on the shows of Jack Benny, Ed Sullivan, Milton Berle, and others.

His popularity made him attractive to book publishers, and Levenson has authored a number of books, including *Sex and the Single Child* and *In One Era and Out the Other*.

JERRY LEWIS His spasmodic screen idiocy has delighted countless millions of children, and many of their parents. Jerry Lewis has been simultaneously one of the world's most revered and most vilified comedians.

Joseph Levitch was born on March 16, 1926, to a New Jersey show business family. His performing debut came at age five when he sang "Brother Can You Spare a Dime?" on the Borscht Circuit. Lewis was the class clown until he dropped out in the tenth grade.

He remained the clown, but with little success, and supported himself as a bellhop, soda jerk, and whatnot. When he teamed up with Dean Martin, they caught on, and their salaries jumped twentyfold to several thousand a week.

Producer Hal Wallis caught the team at New York's Copacabana, and overnight Martin and Lewis became top movie stars. Beginning with *My Friend Irma* (1949) and ending with *Hollywood or Bust* (1956), they made 16 consecutive box office winners, before their noisy breakup. Both stars went on to achieve a large measure of commercial success on their own.

There has been a storm of critical disagreement over Lewis, nearly matching the Lenny Bruce conflict for intensity. Perhaps owing to their prejudice against Americans who they feel are faithfully portrayed by Lewis' pathological depravity, European critics have exalted him as the equal of Chaplin and Tati. American critics recognize the sheer bad taste in many of his films, which tend to be random collections of superficial gags.

Another possible reason for Jerry Lewis' popularity with the overseas critics, particularly the French, may be that he fitted in neatly with a theory formulated by the French new-wave film devotees. This theory held that the most successful films are invariably made not by craftsmen working for a studio, but by "auteurs"—those individuals who have complete artistic control over a film, acting as producers, directors, writers, and performers. Among the celebrated "auteurs" revered by this clique were Chaplin, Hitchcock, and Welles; when Jerry Lewis came along, doing his own directing, writing, and performing in films like *The Bellboy* (1960), the adherents of the "auteur" theory hailed him as their new messiah.

In the United States, though, the public couldn't care less about what nomenclature Lewis qualified for, demanding that they be entertained with something more than facial contortions and over-contrived gag situations, and his films were less than total successes. There were *The Nutty Professor* (1963), *Who's Minding the Store?* (1963), *The Disorderly Orderly* (1964), and so on. After a while, Lewis slowed down his production pace, and became better known for occasional appearances in Las Vegas and similar resorts, as well as for his annual Labor Day telethons for a charitable cause that he has championed for many years.

JOE E. LEWIS Joe E. Lewis was almost a cult figure among sophisticated nightclub patrons in most of America's big cities, and he was equally popular at gambling casinos. His gravelly voice rasped out witticisms about, primarily, "booze, babes, and bangtails," which also characterized his lifestyle.

Lewis was born on January 12, 1902, to a Russian immigrant family. Aged fifteen, he dropped out of high school and enlisted in the Marines. After being discharged when his true age was discovered, Lewis turned as a last resort to the Chicago burlesque scene.

During Prohibition, Lewis emerged as a nightclub star at the Green Mill, in Chicago. Another club, the New Rendezvous Cafe, which like the Green Mill was run by mobsters, lured or blackmailed Lewis away. Lewis began receiving death

Jerry Lewis

Joe E. Lewis

threats from Machine Gun Jack McGurn, who promised that he would not live to open at the rival club. Lewis ignored the threats and opened his new engagement.

Immediately, three hoodlums barged into his hotel room, and knifed his face and tongue savagely before leaving him for dead. Lewis made a slow, painful recovery. On the day he left the hospital he went after his assailant with a revolver, but was apprehended by police for carrying concealed firearms.

This attempted murder became the central incident in a film about the comedian, *The Joker Is Wild*, in which Lewis was portrayed by Frank Sinatra. The attack also damaged his vocal cords irrevocably, leaving Lewis with his trademark, the raspy voice. His damaged voice did not impair his career—quite the opposite. It suited his humor perfectly, and Lewis skyrocketed in 1940 when he opened his first of 26 consecutive years at the famed Copacabana, playing there 33 weeks in 1940 while creating a sensation.

During the next three decades Lewis commanded fees frequently as high as $10,000 a week, with underworld figures and members of society among his admirers. An inveterate spender and gambler, he had his friends at one time pay him an allowance and invest the remainder of his earnings for him.

Lewis' comedy was as suggestive as was permissible before mixed audiences; the situation was unlike today's "anything goes" nightclub comedy. However, he did not use four-letter words onstage.

His comedy was self-deprecatory, drawing on his own vices—excessive smoking, drinking, and gambling. This humble attitude, which the average guy in the audience could identify with, plus his selfless philanthropy won Lewis universal affection. He was repeatedly honored by the Friars Club. Many thousands from all walks of life went to New York City's Riverside Chapel to pay their last respects to him on June 8, 1971.

ROBERT Q. LEWIS He looks solemn and studious, on the surface, but has a quick wit that is more reactive than creative; as a result, he is an ideal moderator, and has almost continuously been on radio and television since the 1940s.

Born in New York in 1924, Robert Q. Lewis took acting lessons and got into radio as a disc jockey, working his way up to acting as substitute host for Arthur Godfrey. He also did a lot of emceeing and standup comedy around town, and landed in early television, where at first he had his own show. Later, he was on numerous quiz and panel shows.

Lewis has also appeared in about a half-dozen films, including *Good Neighbor Sam* (1964) and *How to Succeed in Business Without Really Trying* (1967).

BEATRICE LILLIE When the definitive history of American theater is written, Beatrice Lillie's career will merit an appreciative chapter. She is one of the perennial Great Ladies of the theater, turning in memorable performances through several decades, except that in her case the style has been comic. She has also appeared in numerous films, including *Around the World in Eighty Days* (1963) and *Thoroughly Modern Willie*, (1967) and written an autobiography, *Every Other Inch a Lady*.

Ms. Lillie was born in Toronto on May 29, 1898. A child singer and teenage actress, she was introduced to American theatergoers in *Andre Charlot's Revue of 1924*. Among her many other milestones have been *This Year of Grace* in 1929 with Noel Coward, *The Show Is On* in 1936 with Bert Lahr, *Inside U.S.A.* in

Beatrice Lillie (right) as Madame Arcati in High Spirits, *the musical version of* Blithe Spirit

1948, her 1952 Broadway solo hit called *An Evening with Beatrice Lillie,* and a 1957 revival of the *Ziegfeld Follies.* Devotees of Broadway theater tell us that her foibles with a Ouija board as medium Madame Arcati in *High Spirits* (1964) was one of the funniest acts ever to convulse a sophisticated New York opening night audience.

No lesser chronicler of show business history than Joey Adams relates that Lillie didn't need a prepared script. On one occasion she was confronted by a bore who noted, "What lovely pearls! Are they real?" She nodded. But the woman persisted, "Of course, you can always tell by biting them. Mind if I try?" Lillie assented, "Gladly, but remember you can't tell real pearls with false teeth."

MAX LINDER Charlie Chaplin owes a debt to him, and so does Charley Chase. He was the first screen comedian of any stature, and the first to derive comedy on film not from crude pratfalls, but from socially embarrassing situations. Always impeccably attired, he was a jaunty boulevardier embroiled in romantic peccadillos and affairs of honor, in which a subtle twist or misunderstanding was all he needed.

Born Gabriel Levielle in St. Loubés, Bordeaux, France, in 1882, he studied at the Bordeaux Conservatory and acted at the Theatre des Arts there. Acquiring confidence in his craft, he joined the Ambigu company in Paris. To augment his meager theatrical salary, he took on a side job in 1905 with the Pathé Brothers, who were among the earliest European film producers. He adopted the name Max Linder because at that time it was considered in poor taste for a legitimate actor to appear in the new, lowly medium.

By 1914 he appeared in the astonishing total of more than four hundred films; early movie comedies, however, never exceeded a reel in length, or about 15 minutes' running time at silent speed. Linder then entered the armed forces during World War I.

In the United States, meanwhile, the Essanay Company had just lost Charlie Chaplin to Mutual, and was looking for a replacement. Recollecting that Chaplin himself had acknowledged his liking for Linder, Essanay brought him over—but did not give him enough artistic freedom and his films were only moderately successful. Two years later, he was back in France, making *Le Petit Café*. Profits from that venture permitted him to return to America where he started his own company, producing three full-length features still considered comedy classics by film connoisseurs: *Seven Year's Bad Luck,* in which a valet breaks a full-length mirror, but fearing his supersti-

tions master's wrath, attempts to conceal the deed by replacing the mirror image with himself; *Be My Wife;* and *The Three Must-Get-Theres,* a gentle takeoff on Linder's friend Douglas Fairbanks.

Linder began to show signs of being depressed and artistically drained. Returning to France, he made one film for Abel Gance, then went to Vienna to appear in a circus film. On October 31, 1925, he was found dead, a suicide at forty-three.

RICH LITTLE Many comic impersonators become so identified with their subjects that they are ruined for any other kind of work. JFK's death practically finished off Vaughn Meader, and Nixon's resignation did irreparable damage to David Frye's career. Rich Little is more secure—he impersonates over one hundred fifty celebrities, including John Wayne, Groucho Marx, James Stewart, Frank Sinatra, Humphrey Bogart, and Boris Karloff.

His humor is strictly for laughs, avoiding stinging barbs and social significance. "I guess I'm chicken," Little says. "But whenever I do political impersonations and satire I go for the joke, putting politics aside. I'm by no means a Will Rogers or a Mort Sahl with an underlying message."

Little was born in Ottawa, Canada, in 1938. It all began for him in high school when he started imitating teachers to entertain his classmates. After graduating from high school he became a radio disc jockey, and on the side worked as an impressionist for $10 a night. Before long he was Canada's favorite political satirist. On Toronto radio one afternoon he did such a convincing impersonation of Elvis Presley that a thousand Presley fans swarmed over the radio station.

Rich Little

Little's big break came in 1964 when Judy Garland booked him for her show, establishing him in America. Since then he has guested on *That Girl, The Flying Nun, This Is Tom Jones,* the *Ed Sullivan Show,* and the *Merv Griffin* and *Johnny Carson* shows, and starred in the series *Love on a Rooftop* along with *Laugh-In*'s sock-it-to-me girl Judy Carne. Network executives gave Little his own show in 1976.

MARY LIVINGSTON,

see JACK BENNY

HAROLD LLOYD He is usually regarded as one of the top four film comedians—along with Chaplin, Keaton, and Langdon. With Lloyd, however, comedy did not come spontaneously, so he worked harder at it, enduring years of obscurity in the minor leagues of film before graduating to his own production unit and feature-length pictures.

He lacked Chaplin's surefire common touch, Keaton's inner fire, and Langdon's expressive subtlety. He compensated for it by energetically pushing the action with all sorts of physical derring-do, and is remembered best for the films in which he hung onto the side of a building or rode in a runaway bus for about half the running time.

Lloyd was born in Burchard, Nebraska, on April 20, 1893, and became thrilled with theater at an early age, picking up odd jobs with passing troupes. In his teens he acted in small parts, which gave him the experience to be hired in the early days of the movies as a $3-per-day extra. He teamed up with another eager youngster, Hal Roach, in 1914, and they began producing one-reel comedy shorts at a steady clip, with at least moderate success.

During these lean years, Lloyd tried two characters: Lonesome Luke, a sort of reverse Chaplin (what was too loose on Charlie's tramp, Lloyd made too tight, and presto!), and Willie Work, an all-purpose loafer. Neither was an inspired creation. In 1917, however, Lloyd tried a new approach, an earnest young man wearing glasses, trying to get ahead against stupendous obstacles.

Although Lloyd never got around to finding a name for him, referring to him only as "the glasses character," he embodied his best filmic qualities, and audiences liked him immediately. The glasses, minus lenses so as to avoid unwanted glare in the camera, became an enduring, instantly recognizable trademark. Lloyd was the only one of Hollywood's top stars who could walk down any thoroughfare without being recognized—he just had to remove his glasses. The glasses character went through a couple of years of one-reelers, then two-reelers, and finally, starting in 1921, full-length features.

In 1923 Harold Lloyd married his leading lady Mildred Davis, and bought a lavish mansion in Beverly Hills; he had "arrived" that year with the film still considered the supreme classic of daredevil comedy, *Safety Last.*

He made a halfhearted attempt to continue making his kind of comedy in the 1930s with sound, but the results convinced him that the days of slapstick comedy were over. He semiretired in 1938, coming back only in 1947 for a film (*Mad Wednesday*), and in the 1960s for a couple of compilations of his best moments. He died on March 8, 1971.

LUM and ABNER The two small-town bachelors had the most leisurely pace, the folksiest humor, the most relaxed style. They had guests like ZaSu Pitts, Andy Devine, and Cliff Arquette, and chatted

Harold Lloyd

about inconsequential matters, all taking place in the mythical town of Pine Ridge, Arkansas.

Sounds like a small-time local program, but Lum and Abner had one of the biggest followings in network radio, staying on the air for a full 23 years—far longer than many prestigious shows. A small Arkansas town actually petitioned Congress to have its name officially changed to Pine Ridge.

Lum was Chester Lauck, and Abner was Norman Goff, from Mema, Arizona, who met when Chester was a bank clerk and Norman a grocery wholesaler in Hot Springs. They hit it off, and their friendly banter was first heard over a local station in 1931. The response was overwhelming and it was almost immediately transferred onto the network.

In 1954 Norman retired after undergoing a cancer operation, and Chester turned to the oil business.

Here's how it went:

LUM: Abner, you hold the nail in place and I'll whack it with a hammer.

ABNER: No, no, why don't you hold the nail and I'll whack it.

LUM: Well, it looks like we've got an oversupply of whackers.

ABNER: Remember the time you were putting up the screens with your cousin Wilbur? You hit him, and he let out such a beller all the fellas down at the sawmill knocked off for lunch.

LUM: Well, all right, this time I'll keep my eyes open. Here goes!

ABNER: Ouch! Oh, you idiot, why don't you watch what you're doing!

LUM: Why, Abner Peabody, I never touched that hand you're holding the nail with.

ABNER: I know! You hit the one I had in my pocket!

WILLIE LUMP LUMP,

see RED SKELTON

AUBREY LYLES,

see MILLER and LYLES

PAUL LYNDE

QUIZ MASTER PETER MARSHALL: Why are motorcyclists always wearing leather?

PAUL LYNDE: Because chiffon wrinkles so easily.

When Paul Lynde delivers a punchline like this, he minces it with such an air of fastidiousness and prissiness that the audience of the long-running quiz show, *Hollywood Squares,* screams with delight. His grimaces of pained exasperation have kept him a permanent centerpiece of this show for more than a decade, and he is one of the few performers who does not consider being a quiz show panelist demeaning.

A native of Mount Vernon, Ohio, where he was born on June 13, 1926, Lynde made an uneventful entry into show business via nightclub routines and revues, (including *New Faces of 1952*) but was suddenly propelled into fame when he portrayed the unwilling small-town host to a rock star in the Broadway musical *Bye Bye Birdie* in 1960. The *Ed Sullivan Show* claimed him next, and after that he served as a regular on the Martha Raye, Red Buttons, and Perry Como showcases. On his own, he didn't do so well: he made three pilots for each of the major networks that were rejected; the fourth try, for ABC, was aired in 1972 but was shelved because of low ratings. He appeared in several films of no distinction.

But the quiz format, where he can come up with unexpected and suggestive quips, suits him perfectly. He admits that most of the "ad libs" are in fact carefully prepared; he feels it is more important to keep the audience entertained than to adhere to a strict code of spontaneity.

In his youth, Paul claims to have had a crush on a girl who married another, which shattered him. He has remained a bachelor.

Paul Lynde

MOMS MABLEY Moms Mabley was a raspy voiced toothless ribald raconteur who came on stage as an impoverished, archaic woman in raggedy clothes and oversized shoes, regardless of whether in real life she was a young woman ("I got old when I was twenty") or an old rich woman (she drove a Rolls-Royce and wore furs offstage). Her wild, wily comments on life that practically became folklore ("An old man can't do nothin' for me except to bring me a message from a young man") made her a favorite among urban black communities for over half a century, but she did not gain national fame until the 1960s when racial barriers were crumbling.

Born Loretta Mary Aiken in Brevard, North Carolina in 1897, she began her vaudeville career at sixteen, having already borne her first child. Miss Mabley later explained, "I was pretty, but didn't want to become a prostitute, so I chose show business."

Joking, dancing, and singing animatedly through her shows, she worked the chief black vaudeville circuit, Theater Owners Booking Association, at $12.50 a week. She performed alongside such legendary greats as Duke Ellington, Bessie Smith, Louis Armstrong, and an act called ButterBeans and Suzie.

ButterBeans and Suzie recognized her talent, and in 1927 brought her to New York. Soon, she became exceedingly popular, playing important spots such as Harlem's Apollo Theater and Chicago's Regal Theater. Despite her obvious potential, for decades Miss Mabley was not given a crack at the big time. "I don't care if you could stand up on your eyebrows, if you was colored you never

Moms Mabley (with Slappy White)

got no work at all," except on the black circuits, she explained.

In the 1960s, when black performers began receiving much fairer treatment, Miss Mabley finally achieved national prominence. She made her television debut in 1967 on a Harry Belafonte special, and appeared with such hosts as Flip Wilson, Bill Cosby, the Smothers Brothers, Mike Douglas, and Merv Griffin. She also began recording during this period, and her first effort, *Moms Mabley—The Funniest Woman in the World,* was certified gold, a million-seller. Subsequent albums included *Moms Mabley at the U.S.* and *Moms Mabley at the Geneva Convention.*

She had appeared in two films, in bit roles: the 1933 screen adaptation of the Eugene O'Neill classic, *The Emperor Jones,* and a forgotten production called *Mom's Boarding House.* In 1974, at seventy-six, Moms Mabley became a bona fide movie star. Her vehicle was *Amazing Grace*, a comedic exposé of political corruption whose message, according to Miss Mabley, is that "black people ought to become involved in politics, but only with good people." During the filming she was stricken with a severe heart attack and restricted to her hospital bed, but harnessed her strength and determination to hoist herself out of bed after only three weeks to complete the film.

Moms Mabley died on May 23, 1975.

During her funeral Dick Gregory lamented, "had she been white, she would have been known fifty years ago."

THE MAD RUSSIAN,

see BERT GORDON

MARCEL MARCEAU The internationally recognized master of pantomime was born in Strasbourg, France, in 1922. One of his idols was Charlie Chaplin, and his decision to study pantomime came partly from watching the little tramp.

In 1946 Marceau appeared in the title role of Jean-Louis Barrault's production of *Baptiste*, sections of which, performed by Barrault himself, were used in the film *Children of Paradise*. In 1947 Marceau made his solo debut in Paris, and the following year he won the Deburau Prize for the pantomime *Mort avant l'Aube*.

After that, his pantomime, featuring the character Bip, was presented many times everywhere in the civilized world. He regularly tours the United States at least once every two years.

Marceau is married to the former actress Huguette, and they have two sons.

RICHARD MARTIN,

see CHEECH and CHONG

CHARLES MARKS,

see SMITH and DALE

DICK MARTIN,

see ROWAN and MARTIN

STEVE MARTIN One of those "overnight" successes that happened after more than a decade of obscurity, Steve Martin is one of the most original screwball zanies in television since Ernie Kovacs and Jonathan Winters. He does things that appear childish, like appearing on the show in an impeccable white suit but with an arrow sticking out of his head. He delights in non sequiturs: "My grandmother told me to be kind, courteous, oblong and to have my knees removed." He does the simplest kind of reversals: "Is it all right to yell 'Movie!' in a firehouse?" He says things that are totally amoral, for shock value: "I shot my girlfriend last night, because I was too lazy to drive her home." And he says things that are simply funny, in a weird sort of way: "I gave my cat a bath, but, boy, did that fur stick to my tongue!"

But the total impression, which has made him one of the hottest "cult" comedians since Lenny Bruce, is one of a rather likable guy who is bewildered by some of the absurdities of life (an image with which nearly anyone can easily associate) and is taking it out on the world in jest. By the late 1970s, he has reached the stage where he can pack a huge auditorium at $25 a ticket for a one-man performance anywhere in the country.

Born in Waco, Texas, in 1945, he moved to the Los Angeles area with his parents at an early age, and grew up near Disneyland. There he got his first after-school job at the age of ten, and stayed on for the next eight years, hawking souvenirs and becoming fascinated with show biz. He patterned himself in the beginning after vaudevillian Wally Boag, who performed regularly at Disneyland. In time, Steve developed an act involving a bit of magic, a few regular (non-weird) jokes, and playing his banjo.

By 1967 Steve was enrolled in a television writing course at UCLA, earning his tuition on the nightclub route. His

Steve Martin

first break came when he was hired for the *Smothers Brothers Comedy Hour* as a gag writer. From there he went on to write material for Pat Paulsen, Glen Campbell, John Denver, Sonny and Cher and others. Leaving the rather comfortable job to try earning a living as a performer only, he served a few depressing years' apprenticeship as a comic traveling with a rock show. He found that his comedy did not go over, because "Chaos in the midst of chaos is not funny; as a comedian, you can only succeed if you create chaos in the midst of *order*!" He hit Las Vegas, and even did a tour of the Playboy Club circuit, failing miserably in both cases.

Finally, he hit the big time when he added a touch of the bizarre to his routines, and with this he landed a guest shot on the *Tonight Show* in 1973: "Now you know why Johnny Carson moved his show from New York City—to be closer to me!" He also claimed his first idea, upon being invited on the show, was to kidnap Johnny and hold him as a hostage, demanding "$100,000 in cash, a getaway car, and having the letter ·M removed from all dictionaries."

The national exposure helped, and soon Steve began appearing on *Dinah!,* the *Merv Griffin Show,* the *Dick Cavett Show* and (speaking of going from the sublime to the ridiculous!) even on *The Gong Show.* His first regular appearance was a four-week stint on the *Johnny Cash Show* in 1976.

As he developed his performing style, Steve Martin slowly became something of a spokesman for the everyman of the 1980s: somewhat cool and cynical, seeing himself as a victim of a world that is often cruel and oppressive, and convinced that it is all right to be as silly as you want to be, as long as that's your bag—an embodiment of the phrase "Let it all hang out," the motto of the new age of the self. Per-

haps the most perspicacious evaluation appeared in an article in *Rolling Stone* magazine: "Basically, Steve Martin has one joke—and he's it."

THE MARX BROTHERS An ill-prepared schoolboy made the classic reply: "The five continents are the following four: America, Europe, and Asia." In reverse, it can be said that the three Marx brothers are actually four: Chico, Harpo, Groucho, Gummo, and Zeppo.

However, they boil down to three because Gummo, who was the first of the family to break into show business with Groucho in 1907, never returned to the act after service in World War I, and has never been seen on film; and Zeppo, who usually played juvenile leads in the early films, was so completely overshadowed by the insane antics of his brothers that he was hardly noticed. He wisely gave up the uneven struggle in 1933, becoming an agent.

But the three other Marxes created unforgettable loonies in a baker's dozen of films made between 1929 and 1949, which have become classics of wild, non-sequitur humor. Groucho, the plot instigator and most genuinely original funnyman, affected a moustache, a cigar, bobbing bushy eyebrows, and a rather apelike gait; he was also famous for leering sexual innuendoes nearly always addressed to some haughty dowager type, preferably Margaret Dumont, a perfect female foil for the brothers.

Chico spoke with a thick Italian accent, and derived humor from constant misunderstandings created by this artificial ethnic barrier in conversations with Groucho. He could also play the piano in a uniquely comic style.

Harpo took his name from his fondness for playing the harp. He affected the

The Marx Brothers (Chico, Groucho, Harpo, Zeppo)

strangest disguise, that of a mute with unruly hair, who communicated with the others by means of honks, whistles, and pantomime that would have driven anyone to distraction, but which Chico always managed to interpret.

In real life, they were as different from their screen characters as they were from each other. Chico, the eldest, was Leonard, born in 1891; he devoted most of his life to the pursuit of women and gambling. Harpo was born in 1893, and his

eal name was Adolph. He led a rather
quiet life with his family.

Julius was the next in line, born in
1895. He acquired the name Groucho
because as a youth he was pensive. He
was the best educated of the quintet, and

became a devoted student of humor.
When the team broke up, he launched a
successful television career in his own
right, and it is unlikely that anyone will
duplicate his feat of remaining consistently funny for 11 seasons on a program

229

(*You Bet Your Life,* 1950–60) in which most jokes were ad libs exchanged with guests.

The next brother was Milton, born in 1897 and nicknamed Gummo, because he liked to wear shoes with soft soles. After his ten-year stint with the family act in vaudeville, he went into the clothing business.

The last one was Herbert, alias Zeppo, born in 1901, the only one of the brothers handsome enough to play juvenile leads. He left the screen to be an agent.

The Marx Brothers' approach to comedy was to deal a joyous kick in the rear to all social conventions, and to tangle up gleefully all lines of communication. From early youth they honed their wits on the tough audiences of provincial vaudeville, where they traveled for about fifteen years before they settled on Broadway, and then for five years on New York audiences, before they went to Hollywood.

The first to tour the circuits were Gummo and Groucho, given some material by their uncle Al Shean in 1907. The others joined the act later.

By the time they reached the zenith of vaudeville, the Palace, they commanded a fee of $10,000 a week.

In 1924 they put many of their best routines together, creating a show *I'll Say She Is,* which scored on Broadway. Two shows later, Paramount put them in their first film, *The Cocoanuts,* in 1929. This was followed by *Animal Crackers* (1930), *Monkey Business* (1931), *Horse Feathers* (1932), and *Duck Soup* (1933).

In 1935 they switched to MGM, where at first they did well with *A Night at the Opera* (1936) and *A Day at the Races* (1937); but later on, the big studio watered down their antics with extraneous plot elements, and besides, their material was losing its freshness by then. After their last feeble effort in 1949, they went their separate ways.

Chico died on October 14, 1961; Harpo on September 28, 1964; Gummo on April 21, 1977; Groucho on August 19, 1977.

But their routines live on. Like this nonsense between Chico and Groucho.

CHICO: I come up to see the Captain's bridge.

GROUCHO: I'm sorry, but he keeps it in a glass of water while he's eating. Would you like to see where the Captain sleeps?

CHICO Aw, I already saw that. That'sa the bunk.

GROUCHO: You're just wasting your breath, and that's no great loss, either. Some sailor you are!

CHICO: You bet I'm a fine sailor. My father was a-partners with Columbus.

GROUCHO: Columbus has been dead four hundred years.

CHICO: You see! That'sa what my mother said about my father!

GROUCHO: Now look, let me explain to you about Columbus. Take a look at this globe here.

CHICO: That'sa Columbus Circle.

GROUCHO: We'll skip that. Columbus sailed from Spain to India looking for a shortcut.

CHICO: Oh, you mean-a strawberry shortcut?

GROUCHO: I don't know. When I woke up, there was the nurse taking care of me.

CHICO: What's the matter? Couldn't the nurse take care of herself?

GROUCHO: You bet she could, but I found that out too late. All right, let's pretend this conversation never took place. Let's get back to Columbus. He sailed on this vessel—

CHICO: On his what?

GROUCHO: Vessel, vessel. Don't you know what a vessel is?

CHICO: Sure I know vessel! (*He whistles.*)

JACKIE MASON This funny nightclub monologist and TV variety show favorite had quite a self-deprecating streak. "The way you look at me, I think you're waiting for the comedian to show up," he might start.

He might mention something about his background: although born in Sheboygan, Wisconsin, he moved with his family to the Lower East Side in New York at an early age, when his father, an Orthodox rabbi of Russian ancestry, took a job there. It was a tough neighborhood: "We played cops and robbers with real cops, and hopscotch with real Scotch."

Yacov Moshe Maza was born June 9, 1930. He got a BA degree from City College of New York and studied for the rabbinate. At twenty-five he was assigned to a congregation in North Carolina. Diffident, he tried warming up the people by telling a few jokes. They went over so well that an agent offered to book him in nightclubs, but Jackie couldn't accept while his father was alive.

When the elder Maza died, in 1957, Jackie accepted the job of social director at a Catskills hotel, calling himself Jacob Masler. A booking in a Hollywood restaurant resulted in an offer to appear on Steve Allen's show. After that he got many offers, including repeated guest spots on Ed Sullivan's program. By way of apology for his thick Jewish accent, he disarmed the audience by saying, "You'd be surprised how many people think I'm Jewish."

Here's a typical Mason routine:

I'm still recovering from a shock. I was nearly drafted. It's not that I mind fighting for my country, but they called me at a ridiculous time: in the middle of a war! Now, I'm not a conscientious objector or anything like that, it's just that I'm afraid. Not of guns; guns don't bother me at all—but bullets!

You may notice I don't do much on the stage. Did you ever see Sammy Davis, Jr.? He comes on, tells a joke or two, dances, sings, does a tap routine . . . it's because he doesn't know what to do. If one thing doesn't work, he'll figure he'll try another. Not me. I've got too much class. I don't have to do all that. I just stand there.

BILL MAULDIN Among the few things that made service in World War II bearable to the average G.I., one of the brightest spots was the weekly cartoon in *Stars and Stripes* with those battle-weary soldiers, Willie and Joe. No full-page editorial could capture the exact feelings of the GI, mired in the mud of New Guinea or some other forlorn location, better than a brief cynical exchange between Willie and Joe: "The sergeant sez he needs a coupla guys wot owe him no money for a little routine patrol."

Or, "Must be a tough objective. The ol' man sez we're gonna have th' honor of liberating it."

Bill Mauldin knew how the soldiers felt because he was one of them. He knew how they felt about officers: in one of his most famous cartoons, a lieutenant is admiring a beautiful view from a mountaintop, then turns to his adjutant with the question: "Is there one for enlisted men?"

William Henry Mauldin was born on October 29, 1921, in Mountain Park, New Mexico, and was just the right age to be one of the first draftees to see service in World War II. He started doing his drawings of Willie and Joe to amuse the boys in his barracks, but soon had a full-time job with the army paper. In 1945 he won the Pulitzer Prize for his help in uplifting GI morale. Later, his characters turned up in a Broadway play and then in a movie, *Up Front*.

Mauldin acted in a couple of films, but by 1958 he was back with his first love, journalism, accepting a position as cartoonist for the *St. Louis Post–Dispatch*.

He continued to cover the GI front in Korea and Vietnam, but his main thrust was now political.

In 1942, he married Norma Humphries, and they had two sons.

In 1947 he married Natalie Evans, and they had four more sons.

ELAINE MAY,

see NICHOLS and MAY

CHARLIE McCARTHY,

see EDGAR BERGEN and CHARLIE MC-CARTHY

PAUL McCULLOGH,

see CLARK and MCCULLOUGH

Fibber McGee and Molly

FIBBER McGEE and MOLLY We hear the sound of a closet door opening, to Molly's dismay, and everything, *including* the kitchen sink, tumbles out in a prolonged cacophony of sound effects, ending with the soft tinkle of a bell. When chaos subsides, Fibber McGee avows, "Gotta straighten out the closet one of these days!"

This closet routine was a regular obligatory event that broke up the audience for weeks and years. Equally durable was the entire show, *Fibber McGee and Molly,* which had a perennial berth in radio's "top 10" tallies.

Jim Jordan (born 1897) and Marian Driscoll (born 1898) were introduced at choir practice, in their hometown, Peoria, Illinois and fell in love. Financial instability prevented their betrothal, Jim's weekly drugstore salary was only $8, and Marian's piano teaching didn't fill the gap. When Jim was hired to a more lucrative job as letter carrier in 1918, they were married.

The couple began performing at small local functions, and were discovered for vaudeville. They moved on to radio, where, as the O'Henry Twins, they were hired for a weekly singing broadcast in 1926.

The Jordans teamed up with cartoonist Don Quinn in 1931 for a creative brainstorming session that resulted in their NBC radio series *The Smackouts.* Jordan, a grocery store owner, was perpetually *smack out* of everything except long-winded anecdotes.

The Smackouts ran until 1935 when the Jordans, again in collaboration with Don Quinn, dreamed up *Fibber McGee and Molly.* The show's format stressed free-wheeling comedy; it sacrificed the concept of a unified plot in favor of exploiting its goldmine of unforgettable characters, who visited Fibber and Molly each day at their famous address, 79 Wistful Vista. They included Mayor La Trivia (played by comedian Gale Gordon), Doc Gamble, Mrs. Wearybottom, The Oldtimer (played by Cliff Arquette), Beulah, and Gildersleeve (played by Hal Peary). The last two were so beloved that separate radio programs were created for them, called *Beulah* and *The Great Gildersleeve*.

Beginning with *This Way Please* in 1937, Fibber and Molly made four films. Their last, in 1944, was named after Molly's trademark expression, *Heavenly Days*. Molly's other catch phrase was her oath, "Dat rat that dat-ratted!"

The 1950s were the beginning of the end; Molly had a heart attack in 1953, and their show went off the air in 1957 after 22 years. In 1959 a television revival was attempted, with Bob Sweeney and Cathy Lewis playing the title roles, but the show was canceled the same year. Molly succumbed to cancer in April 1961. Jim Jordan settled into a career as a real estate trader and married Gretchen Stewart.

Frank J. McIntyre

FRANK J. McINTYRE A jolly fat man, Frank McIntyre came into show business via journalism. He was born in Ann Arbor on February 25, 1880, studying at the University of Michigan where he was on the staff of the school paper and performed in amateur theatricals. After graduation, he became drama critic at the Ann Arbor *Daily Argus*. In 1901 he was covering the preparation of a play, *The Honorable John Grisby,* which called for the part of a fat sheriff; producer Frank Keenan cast him in it and opened the play in Rome, New York.

After that, McIntyre became a member of Keith's stock company in Philadelphia; soon he was the town's favorite comedian. His comedy was derived from his rotundity; he originated the line "We who are about to diet salute you." He came into his own in the show *The Traveling Salesman,* which ran two years in New York and two more seasons on the road between 1908 and 1911. When radio arrived, he played the character of Cap'n Henry for years, and appeared on a few variety shows.

He had only a minuscule career in the movies, and died just as television was coming in, on June 8, 1949.

CAULIFLOWER McPUGG

see RED SKELTON

VAUGHN MEADER Vaughn Meader's is a brilliant, albeit brief chapter in the history of comedy. His album of impersonations of President Kennedy tickled the nation's funnybone, and became the biggest selling comedy album of all time.

A Bostonian born in 1937 with perfect pitch (very useful for impersonations)

Vaughn Meader

and a striking resemblance to JFK, Vaughn Meader in *The First Family* album revived a valuable genre of American comedy—healthy, *friendly* political satire. The public responded by buying an unprecedented 5 million copies of the album. One cut has JFK speaking at a press conference:

Q. What do you plan to do about medical care for the aged?
A. Try to stay young.
Q. Do you think the U.S. will ever have a Jewish president?
A. Well, let me say this, I ah, don't see why a member of the Jewish faith should not have a chance for the office. I know that I as a Catholic could never vote for him, but other than that . . .

Meader had a moment of wealth and glory, making countless television appearances. But his inability to integrate successfully non–JFK material into his act precipitated his rapid downfall. When JFK was assassinated in November 1963, Meader was a twenty-six-year-old with half a million in the bank, but he began to slide and a disastrous comeback attempt propelled him into heavy drinking and dissipation of his entire fortune.

Next in line for Meader were witchcraft, LSD consciousness expansion, Eastern philosophies and religions, Yippie activism, and then reclusive meditation in a tepee among the California redwoods. He bottomed out when forced to excavate for food scraps in LA garbage cans, and got mugged and knocked unconscious in a dirty Chicago gutter.

There have been reports of further comeback attempts, including a pious comedy album about Christ's Second Coming. Whatever, Vaughn Meader was a talent of great magnitude, and we await *his* second coming.

BETTE MIDLER It could be argued that her comic stance of irreverence occasionally degenerates into sleaze, but Bette Midler is the first to admit it: "Trash with flash and sleaze with ease—that's my act. . . . I'm the last of the tacky women, but now I'm getting some class, ain't I? Gar-bahge, that's what I do." One aspect of this would be her barbs directed against such public figures as Linda Lovelace and Richard Nixon. "If Dick Nixon would only do to Pat what he's done to our country———."

Her parents are from New Jersey, but she was born in Hawaii in 1944. Appropriately, her first significant job was as an extra in the 1965 film, *Hawaii*. She moved to New York to conquer Broadway, but managed only a small part in *Fiddler on the Roof*. It was in the Continental Baths, New York's favorite gay hangout, that she began singing her nostalgic songs, flaunting her bawdy humor, and gaining wider recognition. Before long there were hit records (like her remake of The Andrews Sisters' "Boogie Woogie Bugle Boy") and concert appearances in such establishments as New York's Philharmonic Hall.

Whether or not you like this controversial talent (and many do not—with a passion), there is no denying that she is a truly professional comedienne, a master of the trade's many skills and techniques. And her act is never a "downer"; it is geared for fun and merriment. She has an enlivening effect on an audience, especially when she's in love. "I'm good when I'm in love," reveals Bette, "I get hot on stage, too. I try to be in love all the time, I keep my eyes open."

MIKE and MEYER,

see WEBER and FIELDS

Bette Midler

JACKIE MILES A hilariously lugubrious comic storyteller, Jackie Miles spoke haltingly as if he were about to choke up with diffidence; this tended to heighten the overall comic effect, because he was a diminutive pipsqueak, meek and self-effacing: "I had a good day yesterday—I wasn't robbed."

Like Myron Cohen, he drew his inspiration from the rich ethnic fount of New York City's garment center—an area which, according to him, "starts around Seventh Avenue at Twenty-first Street, and stretches up to the Catskill Mountains in the summer, and to Miami in winter."

His archetypical garment center character is "J. Schwartz, New York," pushy and overbearing, with chutzpah enough to rent a whole floor in a Miami Beach hotel even when broke.

Jackie Miles was born in Kiev, Russia, in 1913 but grew up in New York. He started as a commercial artist, but soon turned to gag writing for some of the top personalities on the nightclub circuits, including Harry Richman and Joe E. Lewis.

Finally, he decided to try out delivering the material himself, and became the favorite of the upstate New York resort areas, eventually getting national TV exposure and appearing in Las Vegas. He was a regular on Jackie Gleason's show.

When he died on April 24, 1968, he was still in his prime.

GEORGE MILLER Another one of the new crop of comedians, George Miller was born in 1951 in Seattle. In high school he took a writing course, and discovered he could put down things that made others laugh. He took odd jobs and hustled at pool to pay his rent, meanwhile working for no pay at The Comedy Store,

the workshop for young comics on Los Angeles' Sunset Strip, polishing his routines and testing new jokes.

He finally got his chance to appear on a local TV comedy program in 1975; this was followed, in 1976, by an appearance on Johnny Carson's *Tonight Show.* Both Carson and the audience liked his fresh style—he looked like a kid trying to act adult, surprised that he was getting laughs. After that, he began getting more offers. He seems to be on the way up. With material like this:

I have two hangups: women and cars. I don't know anything about either. I once drove from New York to L.A. with the emergency brake on. I always speed up on the curves; I know it's dangerous so I want to get of there fast.

I grew up in Seattle. I felt sorry for my mom—she had to hold two jobs because she was putting my father through prison. Then we moved to California. I slept through the 1971 earthquake and, when I woke up, Mom complained, "You spoiled the whole earthquake for me."

MILLER and LYLES A black comedy/dancing team composed of Flournoy E. Miller and Aubrey Lyles, they gained their greatest fame from writing the book for the all-black musical *Shuffle Along* and supplying the comedy for it. (Noble Sissle and Eubie Blake did the musical side.)

Miller and Lyles had met at Fisk University in Tennessee, where they appeared in the college theatricals. Appearing in blackface makeup, as was the custom of the day even for black performers, they specialized in Southern small-town humor interspersed with a dance sequence or two, and a famous fight scene that was later imitated by other vaudevillians.

They next appeared as a team in Chicago at the Pekin Theater, then toured English music halls, and finally, back in the States, traveled the (white) Keith vaudeville circuit—a distinction achieved by only a few black artists.

After the huge success of *Shuffle Along,* which ran more than five hundred performances in New York and then toured around the country for years, they were associated with *Runnin' Wild, Great Temptation,* and other shows. In the 1930s Miller became one of the writers on the *Amos 'n' Andy* radio show.

Miller alone assisted on the film *Stormy Weather* in 1943, and on *Harlem on the Prairie.*

A commentary on the racial barriers of the times is the story of Miller and Lyles getting a call from WGN Radio in Chicago with an offer to perform their act, which had been gaining notoriety, over the airwaves. When they came in person to talk over the details, the project was quickly dropped; apparently, the station owners thought they were a blackface white act. Blackface was acceptable, but black skin was not. Then two white performers who used blackface took the Miller and Lyles routine nearly verbatim and WGN signed them up. They became known as Amos 'n' Andy. Miller and Lyles originated such Amos 'n' Andy trademarks as "I'se regusted" and "It all depends on the sitch-ation yo' is in."

Miller and Lyles also came up with a routine called "indefinite talk," which became a staple of the black vaudeville circuits. In it, the listener never allows the person who talks to finish a sentence but anticipates with an answer:

LYLE: What's wrong with your car, is it . . .

MILLER: It ain't that, but I think maybe . . .

LYLE: Oh, I know it couldn't be that, what you need is that . . .

MILLER: I just got one of them last week!

LYLE: No, I mean the one that costs about . . .

MILLER: Is yo' crazy, I can't afford that much!

Lyles died in 1933, Miller in 1971.

MITCHELL and DURANT Frank Mitchell and Jack Durant were burlesque and vaudeville old-timers who could best be described as the forerunners of The Three Stooges type of comedy. According to a contemporary review, "they scratched, bit, kicked, punched and gouged each other with a cheerful disregard of personal safety"—with Durant generally the one who got the business.

They started as acrobats, breaking into vaudeville and burlesque with their roughhouse act: with a little refining, it got them into the 1929 edition of *George White's Scandals* and several other shows on Broadway, after which Hollywood beckoned. During the thirties they made films like *She Learned About Sailors* (1934) and *The Singing Kid* (1936).

They split in 1938. Mitchell continued on films, while Durant went on stage—replacing, for example, Gene Kelly in *Pal Joey*—and to nightclubs, where he did comedy monologues.

MONTGOMERY and STONE One of the best blackface song-and-dance teams around the turn of the century making the transition from vaudeville to musical comedy, Montgomery and Stone were the forerunners of Moran and Mack and Amos 'n' Andy.

David Craig Montgomery was born in St. Joseph, Missouri, on April 21, 1870; Fred A. Stone in Valmouth, Colorado,

Stone (left) and Montgomery (right)

on August 19, 1873. Montgomery joined Haverly's Minstrels at the age of sixteen, Stone went with a traveling wagon show at twelve. They first met in 1887 in St. Joseph; Stone was so impressed that seven years later, when by chance their paths crossed again in Galveston, he was persuaded to join the Haverly troupe. But the minstrel era was over, and they found themselves stranded in New Orleans.

Mongomery and Stone created their own act, making their debut as partners in 1895. For the next twenty-two years they traveled the Keith circuit and appeared together in Charles Dillingham musical comedies until Montgomery died (April 20, 1917). Stone stayed in show business but never again took a partner, although he survived his friend by more than four decades (died March 6, 1959). He did, however, put his daughter Dorothy into his act in 1925, his second daughter Paula in 1930. He was one of the few performers outside of Will Rogers who did a routine with a lariat.

TITUS MOODY,

see FRED ALLEN

MARY TYLER MOORE Mary Tyler Moore has revived a lost art, that of the attractive clown, the comedienne who can win laughter, applause, and a place in our heart without being a blockhead and a nincompoop. In this image she joined the ranks of the most successful women in the history of television, including Lucille Ball and Carol Burnett, and her *Mary Tyler Moore Show* was a favorite for years until she decided to discontinue it in 1977.

She was born on December 29, 1936, in Brooklyn. Her early years in show business were spent as a professional dancer, but a natural flair for acting, especially in comic roles, changed her direction. Ms. Moore appeared in several films, including *X-15* (1962), *Thoroughly Modern Millie* (1967), *Don't Just Stand There* (1968), *What's So Bad About Feeling Good?* (1968), and *Change of Habit* (1969). Her television credits include spots on *Steve Canyon* (1958), *Richard Diamond*, *77 Sunset Strip*, and *Hawaiian Eye,* and her unforgettable stint on the *Dick Van Dyke Show* (1961–66) for which she won two Emmys.

It wasn't as easy as a paragraph of credits sounds. After the dizzy success of the *Dick Van Dyke Show,* she reached the depths of despair. Her film career had flopped, and a Broadway musical she appeared in, *Breakfast at Tiffany's,* did worse. Her pregnancy ended in miscarriage, and she was greeted with the news that she is a diabetic. After years of working her way up, Mary Tyler Moore was lower than ever, and calling her propects bleak would have been generous. "I was at the lowest point possible when I got a call from Dick Van Dyke,"

she recalls, "and he asked me to appear on his TV special, *Dick Van Dyke and the Other Woman.* My appearance on that special stirred new interest in me, and CBS offered me my own show."

The *Mary Tyler Moore Show* featured Ms. Moore as a single woman working in the newsroom of a small-time television station. At first chauvinistic in dealing with Mary, the coworkers come to accept her as an equal—with limitations. The show was a goldmine of comic actors and actresses, including Ed Asner, Ted Knight, Gavin MacLeod, Betty White, and Georgia Engel.

TIM MOORE When Freeman Gosden and Charles Correll conceived *Amos 'n' Andy* for radio, the two chief characters did most of the work. Gradually, the supporting character of the Kingfish became more prominent because his scheming could create better comedy situations; the straight man, Amos, was largely subdued.

Once the series got on TV (1951–66) with black actors, the importance of The Kingfish was further increased, owing to the superb acting job of Tim Moore. He made Kingfish such a thoroughgoing, unregenerate rascal that conniving was not just an art with him, but an all-consuming passion, lifetime hobby, and way of life. As a result of this portrayal, for the last few years the long-running (nearly forty years) series could justifiably have been renamed "The Kingfish Show." Moore managed to make even his bald head glisten more raffishly while engaged in some lowly skulduggery.

Tim Moore was a veteran of the TOBA circuit, where his specialty was—of all things—playing a blackface Scot in kilts. He appeared many times at the Apollo, and was the featured comic in black revues and musicals.

Mary Tyler Moore (left) with Julie Andrews and Carol Channing

Victor Moore

VICTOR MOORE In 1932, George S. Kaufman and Morrie Ryskind wrote a play about the plight of that most neglected of all government officials, the Vice President of the United States. They got George and Ira Gershwin to supply the songs; now they needed someone to play the bumbling, fumbling, faltering nonentity who, after being elected to the ill-defined post, keeps trying to find a description of his duties in the Yellow Pages, cannot discover where his office is or if indeed he has one, and keeps asking strangers and pageboys what he is supposed to do.

At last they settled on Victor Moore, a theatrical pro who had specialized in well meaning bumblers for years. What resulted was pyrotechnics: 441 performances, critical acclaim, the first musical ever to be awarded the Pulitzer Prize—and top of the heap for Moore at the age of fifty-six. The play *Of Thee I Sing* (1932) actually focused attention on the lack of clear duties for the Vice President, and led to reforms.

Moore was at his brilliant best—so much so that the same role was specially written for him into another play in 1940, *Louisiana Purchase,* which was made as a film the following year. He also made about thirty other films, including *Make Way for Tomorrow* (1937) and *Duffy's Tavern* (1945).

Victor Moore was married to a fellow vaudevillian, Emma Littlefield, with whom he toured for years in an act titled *Change Your Act—Or Back to the Woods.* He was born in Hammonton, New Jersey, on February 24, 1876. His first stage appearance was in a nonspeaking part in *Babes in the Woods* in Boston at seventeen. His last was the role of a plumber who walked into Marilyn Monroe's bathroom as she was taking a bubble bath, when he was eighty-three: he didn't say a word. He died in 1962.

MORAN and MACK Also known as Two Black Crows, this duo did a blackface act in vaudeville. They became radio stars before Amos 'n' Andy, with a similar approach: Moran was the faster-talking straight man; Mack delivered the punchlines with an air of frustration and worry, after an appropriate pause for reflection.

MORAN: You say you grow olives on your farm from peas? How do you do that?
MACK: Well, you put peas into vinegar, and when they swell up, you call them olives and sell them.
MORAN: Why did you sell all your white horses?
MACK: We found they ate more than the black horses.
MORAN: Why, that's silly. Why should the white horses eat more than the black horses?
MACK: We tried to figure it out every which way, too, and never could find out why. Except maybe it could be because we had more white horses.

Eight records with material like this, made by Columbia between 1927 and 1929, sold 7 million copies between them, so obviously Moran and Mack were doing something right.

Moran was George Searcy, born in Elwood, Kansas, in 1881; Mack was Charles Emmett Sellers, born in White Cloud, Kansas, in 1887. They served their apprenticeship with Neil O'Brien's Minstrels. Mack broke into vaudeville with partner John Swor and appeared with him in *The Passing Show of 1916,* then did another show, *Maid in America,* alone; in his third one, *Over the Top,* he met Moran and the two Kansans formed a team.

They hit all the top New York revues with their blackface act, and by 1928 were on radio with their own show; the year after that, they made a film that used one of Mack's pet catch phrases for a title: *Why Bring That Up?* (1929). There was a breakup after that and Mack rejoined old partner Swor for another film, *Anybody's War* (1931); but in 1933 Mack Sennett reunited them for their last joint effort, *Hypnotized.*

Mack died soon after on January 11, 1934, in Arizona. Moran did the act with others, appeared in a couple of films, did more radio, USO shows during World War II, and other theatrical work—but with none of the success of the old team. He died in California on August 1, 1949.

MANTAN MORELAND

MANTAN MORELAND Mantan Moreland was one of the veteran black comedians who served his apprenticeship in vaudeville and graduated to the movies. He appeared regularly at the Apollo Theater in Harlem, the black equivalent of the Palace in the vaudeville hierarchy. In the movies, he is probably best remembered for supplying the stereotyped ethnic comedy relief in the Charlie Chan series, once Stepin Fetchit left it. He also appeared in *Cabin in the Sky* (1943) and other films in the late thirties and during the forties.

Here's a sample of Moreland's material:

They wanted me to get a lifetime membership in the NAACP for $250. I said, "Suppose I give you two bucks and take it a month at a time? After all, what if they suddenly decide to integrate and I'd be a member for nothing!"

You know for years I thought people mistook me for Roy Rogers' horse. I thought they were calling me "Trigger."

HENRY MORGAN

HENRY MORGAN The most mordant wit of our time next to Fred Allen, Henry Morgan may not have been the first to kid his own sponsor (Ed Wynn did it years before), but he was the first to make such savagely caustic fun of the product that he was regularly fired from his radio and TV jobs.

Here's how to lose a sponsor, Morgan style:

The Eversharp Injector Razor saves you a lot of time. It changes blades automatically, push-push, click-click, so you have a lot of time on your hands—and that can lead to trouble.

August 3, 1946: a man named Walladacker shaved with a Schick and saved 40 seconds. Being 40 seconds ahead, he went into a saloon on his way to work and ordered a drink. One drink led to another, he forgot to go to work, got fired, his wife left him, he took to crime. Now in Atlanta penitentiary.

A man named Fuzzledink shaved with a Schick and saved a minute and a half. He decided to kill the time while waiting for his train by reading a newspaper. What he read made him so mad the blood rushed to his head; he felt dizzy, stumbled on the track, the train killed him.

Another man, named Platzwither, saved two minutes shaving with a Schick. Being two minutes early coming down, he caught his wife flirting with the delivery man. Took out a gun and killed them both. He was electrocuted Friday.

So you see, friends, don't rush out and buy a Schick right away. Think it over.

Born in New York City on March 31, 1915, Henry Lerner Van Ost grew up with early radio, and that became his consuming ambition. At seventeen he joined WMCA in New York as a pageboy; a few months later, he rose to the position of announcer. From there, he went to progressively smaller towns where he could be a bigger fish: WCAU in Philadelphia, WEBC in Duluth, Minnesota (where he held the lofty title of program director), then two years at WNAC, Boston; finally, back in New York with WOR, he was given a fifteen minute show of his own, *Here's Morgan*, in 1937.

After an interruption for World War II, he repeated the quarter-hour format on WJZ in New York in 1945; later, it was extended to a half hour. By the following year, the ABC network gave him a half-hour show Sunday evenings, sponsored by Schick, and featuring a fine cast of supporting comics (Arnold Stang, Florence Halop, Art Carney, and Fred Allen's own Minerva Pious).

Fired for product sacrilege, Morgan tried the stage (*The Man Who Came to Dinner,* 1947) and the movies (*So This Is New York,* 1949), but neither medium offered him the freedom to debunk popular concepts and satirize the contemporary scene. He settled for a virtually permanent seat on the panel of television's *I've Got a Secret* program from 1953 on, and for one season, in 1959, he hosted a late-night talk show on a local New York City station.

In 1946 he wed Isobel Gibbs, a clear case of holy acrimony: one of the bitterest divorce wrangles in show business left him somewhat misogynistic in 1953. For many years a summer resident of Truro, Massachusetts, he contributes articles to a local paper.

HOWARD MORRIS Pint-sized Howard Morris leaped into national fame as the mischievous, impish sidekick of Sid Caesar on the celebrated *Your Show of Shows*. He could be relied upon to do something unexpected—like holding onto Caesar's leg as Sid limped around the room in a heated argument with Imogene Coca.

After the show went off the air, he demonstrated his versatility by branching into directing (some *Dick Van Dyke Show* episodes), acting in films (*Boys' Night Out,* 1962), and even producing (film *Who's Minding the Mint?,* 1967).

ZERO MOSTEL Zero Mostel is a master of primitive, mindless slapstick comedy, who has lectured at Harvard on the philosophy of comedy. He has also mastered the more subtle forms of comedy, as well as comic and dramatic acting. Mostel calls himself a painter who makes a living as a comedian-actor.

In order to support his hobby of painting, Mostel began doing comedy in Greenwich Village nightclubs—just a stone's throw and a subway ride away from his birthplace, Brooklyn (born on February 28, 1915). This son of a kosher slaughterhouse superintendent/sacramental wine manufacturer (an orthodox rabbi), was born Samuel Joel Mostel, and nicknamed Zero because such were deemed his chances of success. But he was a hit in those early nightclub engagements, with bits of comedy like his Charles Boyer impression: "Let me run through your hair, Hedy—barefoot." From there it was all uphill, with starring roles on Broadway, solo appearances in major theaters, radio, and television, and such films as *The Hot Rock* (1972). He was uproariously funny in *The Producers* (1968) as an over-the-hill Broadway producer trying to make a fortune by designing a play that will fail.

Mostel has won Tony awards for his Broadway roles as Tevye in *Fiddler on the Roof* (1964), the Roman slave Pseudolos in *A Funny Thing Happened on the Way to the Forum* (1962), and the lead-man-

turned-rhinoceros in Ionesco's *Rhinoceros* (1961).

The House Un-American Activities Committee got him blacklisted for a time, but Mostel wasn't destroyed, he made it back. The experience may have influenced his theory of comedy, as expressed in those Harvard lectures: "Comedy is rebellion against that kind of piety which we may call false piety . . . against hypocrisy, against pretense, falsehood, humbug, bunk, and fraud, against false promises and base deceivers . . . against all evils masquerading as true and good and worthy of respect."

He died on September 17, 1977.

BARON MUNCHHAUSEN,

see JACK PEARL

JAN MURRAY As a kid, Murray Janofsky amused his bedridden mother with jokes. He became one of the outstanding nightclub monologists in the New York area by the time World War II broke out. His fast-clip delivery was second only to Bob Hope's. "You have to laugh faster," he'd say to his audiences in 1942, "I'm 1-A." But the laugh was on him; he was drafted. Later he became an all-purpose emcee and panelist.

He was born in the Bronx, New York, on October 4, 1917. He quit high school ("I was voted the dropout most likely to succeed") to take a Borscht Belt job at $3 a week plus room and board. Years later, he was to regret his lack of schooling and finally got his high school diploma ("How old am I? How old could I be—I just finished high school in 1962!").

His first regular job was as resident comedian at Leon and Eddie's in New York City. Then came the war and USO service, and upon discharge Jan went into radio (*Hildegarde's Show*, 1947) and tried

Jan Murray

musical comedy (*Music in My Heart*, 1947). But he succeeded best as a versatile master of ceremonies on early television: he could ad lib, he enjoyed helping contestants get over their mike fright, and he neither patronized nor embarrassed them. He hosted a succession of quiz and audience participation shows in

247

Zero Mostel

the 1950s—*Songs for Sale, Go Lucky, Meet Your Match, A Dollar a Second, Treasure Hunt, Charge Account,* and others ("We gave away a little more than our Foreign Aid program. But, of course, the government doesn't have the sponsors we had").

Murray was much sought after as a panel member on various celebrity shows, and that is where he can still be found in the late 1970s. Meanwhile, he continues to play nightclubs, adding Las Vegas and Miami to the New York niteries where he had his start.

In addition, he has made a few films: *The Busy Body* (1966), *Thunder Alley, Who Killed Teddy Bear?* (1965), and *Tarzan and the Great River* ("The director wanted me to look young. I used so much makeup that Max Factor went up three points on the stock market.").

He's been married twice ("Sorry I'm late. That stupid wife of mine! She didn't shovel the snow from the driveway this morning. Forgot to put on the snow tires. And halfway to New York I realized she hadn't dressed me.").

N

BOB NEWHART Veteran of several TV series, with his own *Bob Newhart Show* a network fixture, Bob Newhart is a master of the imaginary one-way phone dialogue ("dialogue" because he responds to an imaginary person on the other end), and occasionally uncorks one on his show. But for the full treatment listen to one of his vintage LPs.

He was born George Robert Newhart on September 5, 1929, in Chicago. He studied law, started out to be an accountant ("because I *looked* like an accountant"), but got bored and cut a comedy album, *The Button-Down Mind of Bob Newhart* (1960). This album, the first of several chart toppers for Newhart, contains such precious moments as a Madison Avenue type placing a call to Abraham Lincoln: "Hi ya, sweetheart, how's everything going? How was Gettysburg? Abe, listen, I got your note, what seems to be the problem? You're thinking of shaving it off? Abe, you're kidding, aren't you? Don't you see that that's part of the image? It's right, with a shawl, and a stovepipe hat . . ."

His first TV series came in 1966, an award-winning (Emmy and Peabody) artistic gem that lost out in the ratings race. In his recent, long-running series, Newhart is more of a straight man than a jokester as the phlegmatic psychologist, Dr. Hartley. He and his writers haven't run dry; this is fidelity to his role. Newhart explains, "I never use a joke for the sake of a laugh. If it doesn't belong to the character I am playing, I won't use it.

He has made several movie appearances, notably the Major Major Major in *Catch-22*. Other film credits include *Cool Millions* (1968), *On a Clear Day You Can See Forever*, and *Cold Turkey* (1971).

Newhart's routines are monologues in

Bob Newhart

which he is either talking to someone on the phone or addressing an imaginary audience—as does this bus driving instructor:

Okay, now, do you see that little old lady running up behind you out of the rearview mirror? Now, let's see how you handle it? . . . Well, that was all right, but you pulled out of the stop too soon. She gave up all the way down the block there. You see, what you want to do is wait and sort of hesitate, so that they still hope they catch you. Now, let's try it again. . . . Much better this time. Class, did you notice how he slammed that door right in her face this time? . . . Oh, good, the way you blocked both lanes of traffic while taking on passengers . . . . All right now, you see this woman with the packages? What do you do when she puts her fare in and starts going back to the seats? . . . Yes, that's right. The gas, then the brakes—gas again—brakes again—Okay, that was fine. You see how she's sprawled all over the floor now, all the packages scattered? All right now, for homework we'll be mispronouncing names of streets. Class dismissed.

NICHOLS and MAY The most inspired improvisational duo of recent decades has been Mike Nichols and Elaine May. Their singular Nichols-and-Mayhem was well received in nightclubs, radio, TV, and records. Comedy suffered a real loss when they split up in 1961, but the field of directing made a rich gain.

Nichols was born in Berlin, Germany, on November 6, 1931. His real name is Michael Igor Peschowsky; his father was a Russian émigré. He was a premedical student at the University of Chicago when the acting bug bit him, and he went to New York to study at the Actors' Studio with Lee Strasberg. Elaine May was born in Philadelphia on April 21, 1932, the daughter of a Yiddish theater actor who helped his daughter get into radio and theater performing at an early age.

Nichols and May met at the University of Chicago and found they performed well as a team. They joined a Chicago improvisational theater group before deciding to test their skills in the nightclubs of New York. Their nightclub act contained a few regular routines (although even these varied since they never wrote down any lines on paper); the rest was sheer improvisation. They would take two lines shouted up randomly from spectators in the audience, and improvise a short play beginning and ending with those two lines—and they would match the style of any author requested by the audience. They were known for their strictly unsentimental, sardonic humor, which satirized love in all its forms.

As the duo became increasingly popular, offers to make guest appearances began pouring in. They accepted some, appearing on the shows of Jack Paar, Dinah Shore, Steve Allen, and Perry Como. They had a best-selling comedy album in the late 1950s, a big success in its era.

Their sharply satirical humor caused problems. They were censored right out of the 1960 Emmy Awards program because their sketch knocked home permanent waves, and because they portrayed television as sponsor controlled. (That Emmy broadcast was sponsored by a home permanents manufacturer.)

Nichols and May ultimately disbanded to specialize in writing and directing. "We just got bored," Nichols explained. Both have become accomplished directors, especially Nichols, whose films include *Who's Afraid of Virginia Woolf?* (1966), *The Graduate* (1967), *Catch-22* (1970), and *Carnal Knowledge* (1971). May acted in and directed *A New Leaf* (1970).

Nichols and May

Here's how Nichols and May parodied the kind of people who, at a party, pretend they know everyone and are on intimate first-name terms with them:

NICHOLS: And then there's Albert Einstein's theory.

MAY: Oh, you mean Al. A great dancer. Love his hair.

NICHOLS: But of course he had to leave Germany because of Adolf Hitler.

MAY: Oh, that Dolphie, he was a riot, I used to call him Cuddles.

NICHOLS: Good God!

MAY: Oh, Him—a close personal friend of mine!

MABEL NORMAND Staten Island's major contribution to cinema was a hoydenish bundle of natural comedy talent yclept Mabel Normand. Her movie career is inextricably entwined with that of Mack Sennett: she was his best female discovery, and the widespread fame she gained was largely because he had the good sense to let her have her own way when acting in and *directing* comedies.

Mabel stuck with Sennett through thick and thin, and while most of the talent he discovered left him for greener pastures (he was a tight-fisted Irishman), she never deserted. There was also a love affair between them, which never reached the orange blossom stage—tragically for both personally, and unhappily for the cinema, as it was felt that Mabel had a lot more comedy in her if only she had not wasted her health while on the rebound from Sennett.

Mabel was born on November 10, 1895, in Providence, and was working as a model in New York when she came to Biograph looking for extra work. There she was noticed by Sennett, who was impressed by her irrepressible sense of humor and smitten by her good looks.

When he was given the job of heading Keystone, Sennett made her his first leading lady.

She was impish, frisky, and imaginative, and despite a frail five-foot, ninety-five-pound frame was willing to throw herself with abandon into any physical gag set up by the Keystone horde of madmen. This agility, combined with an expressive, pretty face with big brown eyes, made her the queen of film comedy virtually overnight.

In his memoirs, Sennett credits her with film comedy milestone: originating the custard pie bit, and throwing the first one at Ben Turpin's cross-eyed face. This was belated gallantry by Mack, who late in life apparently regretted losing Mabel's love owing to his philandering ways. And the story must be discredited because Turpin did not join Sennett until 1917, whereas the first pie definitely established was thrown in June 1913 in a Keystone film *A Voice from the Deep,* and the recipient was Fatty Arbuckle. Possibly Sennett was mistaken about the receiver but not about the originator of the gag, because Mabel threw that historic pie; that distinction, at least, belongs to her.

Mabel also holds the unique record of directing Chaplin in more pictures than any other director. Chaplin started directing himself within a few months of arriving on the Keystone lot, and thereafter never let anyone else direct him. While learning the trade, however, he was directed by Mabel in six one-reelers. She was his frequent costar at Keystone, and in 1914 appeared with him and with most of the Keystone menagerie in the first full-length film comedy ever made, *Tillie's Punctured Romance.*

It turned out to be a prophetic title, as her own real-life romance with Sennett was punctured, and Mabel went off on a wild spree. Sennett lured her back later

Mabel Normand

for another full-length comedy, *Mickey* (1918). But the embers of romance were cold, and Mabel's health was precarious: she had to use drugs to keep up the frenzied pace.

As the madcap decade of the 1920s was drawing to a close, Mabel, a shadow of her former self, dragged herself all over Europe and America looking for thrills she could no longer enjoy. In 1922 a pall of suspicion was cast over her, as she had

been one of the last persons to have visited William Desmond Taylor, an actor-director who was killed by a shot in the back. Although officially cleared, she had to lie low for a couple of years as distributors would not accept her films.

She made a few films later, and got married (to actor Lew Cody) but mostly for appearances' sake. On February 23, 1930, Mabel was dead from tuberculosis.

MRS. NUSSBAUM The character of the slightly muddle-headed, malaprop-prone Jewish housewife on Fred Allen's radio program was created by Minerva Pious, one of the most accomplished dialectitians in radio.

FRED ALLEN: Aah, Mrs. Nussbaum!

MINERVA PIOUS: You ekspected maybe Talooraloora Bankhead?

ALLEN: Mrs. Nussbaum, what do you think about this cold wave?

PIOUS: Mine husband Pierre is havink a cold all week. I think maybe he'll be goink to the Meyer Brothers Clinic if I can't cure him soon.

ALLEN: Well, have you tried some remedies?

PIOUS: First, one doctor is tellink him to eat froots. So, I give him lemons, oranges, tambourines . . . then Pierre's throwink them out the window. Someone else is sayink wegetables, so next I give him spinach, turnips, rutabagels . . . then Pierre is throwink them out the window. So another doctor says complete rest. Pierre is sittink around the house all day, eskink me to do this, to do that, now I'm throwink out de window Pierre. Dank you.

Minerva Pious was born in Odessa, Russia, in 1909, and came to the United States with her family at the age of three, settling in Bridgeport, Connecticut. She joined Allen's radio program as a complete amateur in 1933, and stayed with him until the end of the show's long run, in 1949.

Occasionally she handled chores on other shows, where her sharp ear for accents was needed: thus, she played the role of a Park Avenue debutante on the *Kate Smith Hour,* and made guest appearances with Al Jolson, *Easy Aces, Duffy's Tavern,* the *Philip Morris Playhouse,* and others.

On Sammy Kaye's show, she did another Jewish character, Gypsy Rose Rabinowitz.

She appeared in one film with Fred Allen (*It's in the Bag*, 1945) and in several other films on her own. In 1963 she appeared with another archetypal Jewish mama, Gertrude Berg, in a Broadway show, *Dear Me, the Sky is Falling.*

JACK OAKIE This master of the double-take and possessor of an all-American good-natured country-hick puss mugged his way through dozens of campus comedies and early musicals in Hollywood. He is perhaps best remembered for his hilarious takeoff on Italian dictator Mussolini in Charlie Chaplin's film, *The Great Dictator* (1940).

More typical of Oakie's style was the key role of an American bumpkin in *Million Dollar Legs* (1932), where he managed to hold his own against such comedy talent as W.C. Fields and Lyda Roberti.

Born Lewis Delaney Offield in Sedalia, Missouri, in 1903, he went to school in Oklahoma and thus picked up his stage name. He started in vaudeville and quickly made it to Broadway, where he appeared with the visiting Mistinguette in

Jack Oakie

Innocent Eyes in 1924. A couple more musical comedies followed, with Lulu McConnell, and this led to an appearance in Paramount's silent film, *Finders Keepers,* with Laura La Plante, in 1927. He remained one of the busiest supporting actors in Hollywood, although he did take time out for many network variety shows on radio, and emceed his own show, *Jack Oakie's College,* in the late 1930s.

Oakie married Venita Varden in 1936 and divorced her two years later; his second marriage was to Victoria Horne. He died on January 23, 1978.

OLSEN and JOHNSON Ole Olsen and Chic Johnson (actually, John Sigvard Olsen, born in Peru, Indiana, in 1892, and Harold Ogden Johnson, born in Chicago in 1891, both of Swedish ancestry) comprised an anything-goes act that emerged from vaudeville's dying embers to shine on Broadway and in the movies. They proved that rambunctious, nonsensical buffooonery did not perish with vaudeville by outdrawing the great dramas, and everything else in Broadway theater.

Olsen and Johnson met in 1914. After months of vain attempts to find work, out of desperation they made their debut in a Chicago nightclub, univited, unannounced, and unwelcome. Their surprise act was a hit, and soon they began working the Pantages circuit for $250 a week between them. When they graduated to the Keith–Orpheum circuit, the apex of vaudeville, their salary increased tenfold.

The duo first appeared on the Broadway stage in *Take a Chance,* in 1933, but their masterpiece of mayhem was *Hellzapoppin,* which ran from September 22, 1938, through December 17, 1941, for 1,404 performances—one of the longest runs in the history of Broadway comedy.

Hellzapoppin was a conglomeration of their old vaudeville skits, as legions of caustic critics hastened to point out, but theatergoers ignored them and enjoyed some of the most chaotic comedy ever created. During *Hellzapoppin* the audience had bananas, beans, "pottie-seats," eggs, and live chickens hurled at them; loud shots exploded; planted hecklers raised a rumpus; a ticket scalper cavorted up and down the aisles with tickets for a rival show; a clown tried to extricate himself from a straitjacket for the show's duration; an elderly woman, outraged that her dress had been lifted by a trick gust of air from under the stage, attacked the entire cast with her umbrella (this actually happened accidentally, and was so funny that it was incorporated into the show); a woman persisted in bellowing "Oscar! Oscar!" (it was Chic Johnson's wife); the audience was bombarded by rubber snakes and spiders; and a whirling madness of cacophonous pandemonium and blatant boorishness engulfed the theater. Only one thing resounded above the deafening din—a continuous roaring laughter from the audience. In the midst of it all, Olsen and Johnson executed their gags with seasoned professionalism.

This was comedy at its intellectual low point—it was devoid of anything remotely resembling intellect. Yet New York's intellectual elite paid its way night after night to become submerged in the mindless merriment of *Hellzapoppin*. "In our act," Chic Johnson once explained, "it's either a belly laugh or nothing." They avoided finesse, social significance, and reason like the plague.

The partnership of Olsen and Johnson spanned 47 years. Subsequently, they appeared on Broadway in several thinly disguised remakes of *Hellzapoppin,* in-

Olsen (left) and Johnson (with Lew Lehr, center)

cluding *Laffing Room Only* (1945), and *Funzapoppin* (1949).

Their film efforts included *All Over Town* (1937), and *Hellzapoppin,* (1941) (a stultified adaptation from the show). Unfortunately, the comedy of Olsen and Johnson never really emerged in film as it did on stage, because Hollywood "creative men" insisted on confining their freewheeling, disconnected humor within traditional plot structures and love triangles.

Chic Johnson died on February 28, 1962, his partner passed away in 1965.

JACK OSTERMAN At the age of fifteen, Jack Osterman tried to enter show biz via Tin Pan Alley by composing a song "We're Glad We've Got You, Mr. Wilson," which he thought was surefire: it was patriotic, topical, and thanked President Wilson for keeping us out of World War I. Within days, Wilson declared war on Germany; Jack figured that if the President would go so far just to stop his song from being published, he was probably not meant for a songwriting career, and switched to comedy.

His real name was J.J. Rosenthal, and

259

he was born on April 8, 1902, in Toledo, Ohio. Show business came natural to him: his father was a press agent, his mother was the actress Kathryn Osterman. He left school as a teenager to join a road company of *Oh Boy,* and later scored in *Parlor, Bedroom and Bath.* He is best remembered as a permanent master of ceremonies at the Winter Garden with a reputation for quick ad libs and topical one-liners.

His style and delivery were akin to the rapid-fire barrage of gags that Bob Hope later made his own. He occasionally sang in an individualistic style, with exaggeration and clowning.

Osterman married an ex-Ziegfeld girl, Mary Dolores Daly.

Barbers have to charge more now [during the Depression]: the faces are longer.

You ask why I haven't gone on radio yet. I don't like germs—how do I know who spoke into the microphone last?

Some of these radio performers are getting spoiled. The Boswell Sisters' apartment caught on fire last night. One of them got on the phone and asked the hotel manager what to do. He asked, "Why didn't you yell for help?" The answer was, "We couldn't. There's no mike in our room."

A bank president and a theater owner were old chums. There was a run on the bank, and the bank president called his friend. "There's a thousand people milling around outside. I need your help to avert panic." The theater owner replied, "All right, I'm sending over ten of my best ushers."

Have I been at the Palace? What for, I've got a radio.

You may have noticed that lately I have stopped making fun of producers. I'd rather be working than right.

Bing Crosby introduced me to the girl who became my wife. But I still tune him in occasionally on the radio. I went with her for a few months, then I asked her to marry me. She gave the wrong answer: she said yes.

I finally met [radio crooner] Russ Columbo. I said "Hi Russ." He replied, "One—two—hello, Jack—three—four—how are you?"

I needed a specialty song for my act, so I wired [songwriter] Lew Brown: SEND SONG. IF GOOD I'LL SEND CHECK. He wired back: SEND CHECK. IF GOOD I'LL SEND SONG.

JACK PAAR One reason that Jack Paar's tenure at the helm of the high-rated NBC *Tonight Show* (which during this time was renamed the *Jack Paar Show)* was so successful was that much of the audience watched it as a cliff-hanger: Paar had such an intimate, insinuating way with his remarks that it was only a question of time before some guest would get really offended, a slightly risqué joke would turn definitely off-color, or Jack himself, for all his brass a sensitive man, would break out crying.

He was shrewd enough to take slurs made against his show and to use them offensively:

The only people who stay up to watch my show are insomniacs or married people who are staying together only on account of the children.

The show is sometimes so interesting you forget that you're not being entertained.

I don't really do anything, and have no talent. Having finally discovered that, I decided to get out of show business, but I can't because I'm a star.

Born on May 1, 1918, in Canton, Ohio, Paar got his first job at eighteen on WIBM Radio in Jackson, Michigan, as a part-time announcer. This was followed by similar jobs in Indianapolis, Youngstown, Cleveland, Pittsburgh, and Buffalo. In 1942 he was drafted, and soon was in the Special Services entertaining GIs with antiofficer barbs.

An unspectacular Hollywood period after the war brought him back to radio in 1947 as summer replacement for Jack Benny.

Jack Paar

In the early years of television, he substituted occasionally for Walter Cronkite and Arthur Godfrey, then came on as a guest on the *Ed Sullivan Show,* and took on four daytime shows as master of ceremonies. There he established such a rapport with his puppy-like friendliness and candor that in 1957 he was offered the prestigious post on the *Tonight Show,* vacated by its original host, Steve Allen.

Paar put such an intensely personal stamp on the show that it was given his name a year later: unlike the polished but impersonal Allen, Paar gave a complete public airing to all his private quibbles, feuds, and love-hate relationships, and the public ate it up night after night for five years.

Then he slowed down to a weekly half-hour variety show and finally semi-retired to run his own television station in Maine. He was married twice, the second time to Miriam Wagner, with whom he had a daughter.

PARKYAKARKUS,

see EDDIE CANTOR

JACK PEARL Jack Pearl was not so much a dialect comedian as he was a language mangler. A burlesque and vaudeville veteran, he developed a character borrowed straight from *Grimm's Fairy Tales,* Baron Munchhausen, the teller of tall—and, in Jack Pearl's case, downright grotesque—stories. The peculiar twist that got big boffos and assured him a long run in radio was his doubting friend Charlie (played by Cliff Hall on radio), who would pooh-pooh each nonsense story, whereupon Baron Munchhausen would come out with the payoff line, in an accent you could slice cheese with:

"Vass you dere, Sharlie?"

This would get loud guffaws. Perhaps those were simpler times.

Pearl had been a member of Gus Edwards' "School Days" act and toured in vaudeville, including the Palace in New York. For a time he was teamed up with Ben Bard, and with Bard he made one of the earliest experimental sound short films for Lee De Forest, in 1922. Afterward the partners split, and Pearl went into musical comedy.

Early in 1932, he made his first radio appearance with the Baron Munchhausen character, on Ed Sullivan's radio show. It clicked and became an immediate success when he got his own show the following year. He also made a film out of it.

Here's how it went:

JACK PEARL: Aw, zis is awful. I am zick from ze cold.

CLIFF HALL: You are what? I can't quite understand you.

PEARL: Zat's funny. Lots of beeple dake me for an American. I was zaying I am zick from ze cold.

HALL: How did you catch it?

PEARL: I didn't catch it, it caught me. I zink I got it by drinking from a damp glass. It was draft beer.

HALL: That's silly. You can't catch a cold from draft beer.

PEARL: Vass you dere, Sharlie?

MR. PEEPERS,

see WALLY COX

JOE PENNER Joe Penner achieved fame on the stage and screen, but it was minor compared with his career in radio comedy. There, Penner became a national celebrity, and his catch phrases like "Wanna buy a duck?" and "Don't ever dooo that!" were known to everyone who had a radio.

Born in Hungary in 1905, Penner came with his family to Detroit as a child, making his show business debut there in amateur contests. He soon became a professional—a mind reader's assistant. One night a top-billed comedian didn't show up. After much pleading, Penner was allowed to fill in for him, and this launched his career, although it got off to a slow start. After years of struggling in carnivals, vaudeville, and burlesque, Penner made the big time in 1926 when the *Greenwich Village Follies* inked him for $375 weekly. Then came a series of shorts for Warner Brothers Vitaphone in the early years of sound film.

In 1933 Penner guested on Rudy Vallee's radio show, and was hailed as a major new talent. A month later he had his own program and became one of the nation's favorite radio personalities in an era when radio stars were really important. His radio fame was in great measure built upon a few ingenious gags that involved his famous catch phrases, like "Wanna buy a duck?" and "You naaasty man!" He had a collection of hundreds of ducks, many of them live, sent by his listeners.

Joe Penner died in his sleep of a heart attack on January 9, 1941; he was only thirty-five years old.

JOE PENNER: Let's stop here. Hmm, look what that sign says: The Fractured Arms Hotel. Sleep here and we'll give you a break.

MAD RUSSIAN: How do you do. We cater to high-class elite . . .

PENNER: That's fine. I'm Joe Penner.

RUSSIAN: . . . and we also cater to riffraff.

PENNER: I want a room with a bath.

RUSSIAN: I'll give you a room.

PENNER: How about a bath?

RUSSIAN: What do you think this is—a summer resort? Listen—our rooms are clean enough to eat in.

PENNER: How about sleeping in them?

RUSSIAN: That I wouldn't recommend.

ZASU PITTS The flustered, feather-brained, helpless types were her specialty and she portrayed them to perfection in several hundred films.

Born in Parsons, Kansas, on January 3, 1900, she got her odd first name from two aunts named EliZA and SUsan. When the family moved to California ZaSu found work in the movies as a teenager and never left. Her first role was supporting Mary Pickford in *The Little Princess* in 1917, and after that she did about fifty more silents.

In 1931 she teamed up with Thelma Todd for 17 shorts, which established her in the sound medium. Among her sound features were *Meet the Baron* with Jack Pearl, *Mrs. Wiggs of Cabbage Patch* (1934), with W.C. Fields, and *Ruggler of Red Gap* (1935).

In the 1940s ZaSu Pitts tried Broadway, appearing in productions like *Ramshackle Inn* (1944). In the 1950s, still a comedy foil, she appeared on the *Gale Storm Show* on television.

She was married to John Woodall. She died in 1963.

GEORGIE PRICE "They tell me dice is a dirty game—but it sure cleaned me!" Such quick thrusts, usually with a self-deprecating flavor, were the trademark of George E. (hence "Georgie") Price, a musical comedy favorite of the 1920s.

Born in New York City on January 5, 1900, he got a lucky break at the age of seven when he attended a party for a neighborhood boy and did imitations of show business personalities of his day, such as Raymond Hitchcock and George M. Cohan. Unknown to him, one of the adults at the party was Gus Edwards; two days later, Georgie was trying out his imitations on audiences at one of Edwards' famous kiddie shows. He stayed

Joe Penner

with Edwards for eight years, usually doing a two-act with a girl known only as "Cuddles," who in her teens changed her stage name to Lila Lee and became a partner of Eddie Cantor.

At eighteen, Georgie joined the Keith vaudeville circuit, and a year later signed a contract with the Shuberts. He founded the American Guild of Variety Artists. Among his theatrical credits were *Ziegfeld Midnight Frolics* (1916), *Cinderella on Broadway* (1920), and *A Night in Paris* (1926).

Georgie Price married Mildred Page, an actress from Minneapolis. He died on May 10, 1964.

ROGER PRICE Looking a little like an absent-minded professor, bespectacled Roger Price made an original contribution to American humor by inventing the "droodle"—a drawing which is as simple to do as a doodle, but which represents a clever idea. For example, he would draw four squares (two black, two white) and call it "Chessboard for Beginners." Or a black circle with only two white triangular patches opposite each other might be entitled "Outside World as Seen by Very Small Man Living in a Beer Can."

First published in 1951, *Droodles* caught on as something of a fad, and for the next few years Price appeared with them in clubs, had his own show on television, contributed to several newspapers and periodicals, and published other books, such as *In One Head and Out the Other* (1952), where he propounds the philosophy of avoidism (Descartes said: "I think, therefore I am." Roger Price's avoidist says: "I won't therefore I ain't gonna.").

Later, Price, who was born in Charleston, West Virginia, in 1920, published a humorous periodical of his own (*Crump*).

Finally, in the 1960s he joined the publishing house of Stern and Sloan, issuing a series of what may be called "Non-books", such as a collection of elephant jokes, more droodles, and so on.

RICHARD PRYOR Richard Pryor is among the most fertile contemporary comic minds. In addition to rich artistic and commercial success in nightclubs and on record albums, he helped write such films as *Blazing Saddles* and *Lady Sings the Blues* (1972), and has numerous television writing credits.

Born in Peoria, Illinois, in 1940, Pryor was a junior high school dropout. He took on a succession of odd jobs, including shoeshine boy, janitor, and nightclub piano player. On occasion he added bits of comedy and impressions to his piano playing, and finally he decided to concentrate exclusively on comedy.

Pryor found himself in New York City with a total of thirty-three cents in his pocket, drifted into the Wha? Coffee House, and got a booking. There he was spotted by TV producers, invited on the *Ed Sullivan Show*, and launched into "the big time."

He has since won an Emmy for TV comedy-variety writing, for his brilliant contributions to Lily Tomlin's 1973 special, *Lily*. He has also written for the *Flip Wilson Show*, and for *Sanford and Son*. He wrote the poignant Piano Man character for *Lady Sings the Blues*, injected the essential black humor into *Blazing Saddles*, and added his distinctive touch to several other films, including *Uptown Saturday Night* and *The Mack*.

That Nigger's Crazy and *. . . Is It Something I Said?* are two of his popular recordings. In them Pryor uses the language of the street, and of the black community, for some very funny mono-

Roger Price

logues, on race, sex, money, and what-not.

Here's a bit of the Pryor touch:

I went to jail to find justice, and that's what I found—*just us*!

Do you know why money is green? Because the Jews pick it before it's ripe!

B.S. PULLY It's the voice that immediately identifies "Big Jule" the crap shooter in *Guys and Dolls*. It sounds like Charles Boyer and Joe E. Lewis having a conversation with a foghorn. Even as a child in Newark, New Jersey, B. S. had gravel in his throat, and he made the

other kids laugh just by reciting state capitals. He enjoyed making them laugh (it was better than having to fight with them over his initials, which stand for Bernard Shaw), and so he took every opportunity to perform.

He started out as a performing busboy on the Borscht Circuit, took jobs in circuses, carnivals, and burlesque. His resemblance to tough-guy-type Victor McLaglen got him some heavy parts in Hollywood, where he did 37 pictures, mostly grade B programmers. His most famous role came by accident. Never dreaming of trying for the legitimate Broadway theater, he met comedian Gene Baylos on a New York street one day, and agreed to accompany him to an audition held for the upcoming production of *Guys and Dolls*. Sitting in the audience, he suddenly saw an acquaintance and uttered two fateful words: "Hello pal!" On the spot, George S. Kaufman signed him for the part of Big Jule. He repeated the role in many productions of the play as well as in the film, and it became his springboard to the Miami and Las Vegas nightspots. He gained added publicity when his earthy nightclub routine got him arrested in Boston.

The huge success of *Guys and Dolls* enabled him to settle in style in Miami, but underneath it he remained true to type: "Since I went legit I get more subpoenas and owe more money. Now that we hobnob with the high and mighty, my wife wanted me to go get some culture. She recommended a book, and I started reading it. That was 17 years ago, and I only have 1,300 pages to go." His wife was the former vaudeville star Hope Carter; they were married in 1943.

B. S. Pully died on January 6, 1972, aged sixty-one.

Here's a sample of Pully's offcolor material:

A guy checks in at the hospital. Soon all the nurses snicker behind his back: he's got "Shorty" tattooed on his thing. So none of them want to accept any of his invitations. Finally a new nurse comes in, very cute young thing, and goes into his room. Stays there ten minutes, twenty minutes, half an hour— finally emerges smiling from ear to ear. The other nurses are surprised: "How can you have fun with 'Shorty'?" The new kid says, "Oh, when he got excited it read: 'Shorty's Pizzeria free delivery, call BUtterfield 8- . . .' "

Richard Pryor

MARTHA RAYE She has an infectious, raucous laugh; her comedy is a bit on the wild, high-decibel side; and she has a mouth big enough for a twenty mule team to drive through. She is a genuine trouper, and made a number of trips to entertain GIs overseas despite danger, illness, and her own marital problems.

Martha Raye reached the zenith of her career when she played the indestructible Annabelle in Charlie Chaplin's *Monsieur Verdoux* (1947). She remains in memory as the only bright spot in this otherwise grim, un-Chaplinesque film, and her restrained clowning as the nitwit who escapes being murdered by being to naive to suspect it is nothing short of admirable.

Margie Yvonne Reed picked up her rowdy, knockabout style of comedy from her parents, who toured vaudeville as Reed and Hooper. She was born on August 27, 1916, in Butte, Montana, and joined the act with her brother Bud when they were still children. Since audiences like them, the act went under the name of Margie and Bud from then on.

When the act got stranded in Cleveland one year, Margie, then fifteen, took a job with the Paul Ash orchestra as a singer, and took the name Martha Raye. For a year she sang in Chicago, then in New York at various clubs, and finally in Los Angeles. At the Trocadero there, her aggressive belting of songs attracted the attention of film talent scouts who saw her comic potential, and she accepted a contract offer from Paramount.

After playing the comic sidekick or female supporting role in several undistinguished films (*Waikiki Wedding,* 1937, was one) she was noticed by one of the

Martha Raye (with Bob Hope)

studio executives, who wanted to change her image to a glamour star on the basis of her statuesque figure. Audiences refused to accept her that way, and the studio dropped her. Chaplin's good taste rescued her from oblivion.

Just then television was coming into national prominence, and here Martha made her biggest hit: after appearing on vitually every variety show on the tube, most regularly with Steve Allen, she got her own show for four years, and has remained busy in the medium, with time out for five trips to Vietnam, ever since.

Martha Raye married six times, was divorced ditto.

CARL REINER With an unerring sense of situation comedy, Carl Reiner has helped to create some of the funniest moments in television, including many savagely satirical sketches on the Sid Caesar–Imogene Coca program and on the top-ranking *Dick Van Dyke Show,* in addition to serving as straight man for Mel Brooks' "2,000-year-Old Man" character. He is equally adept at writing, performing, and directing comedy.

Born March 20, 1922, in New York, he enrolled in the WPA's Dramatic Workshop during the 1930s. During World War II, he toured with Maurice Evans' GI troupe in the South Pacific, and after the war, with the road company of *Call Me Mister.*

Then came 1949 and *Your Show of Shows,* and Reiner found his niche. He stayed with Caesar as sidekick and writer for nine years, then started writing screen plays, and acting in films, such as *The Gazebo* (1960). His autobiographical novel, *Enter Laughing* (1958), was made into a very funny movie, which he wrote, produced, and directed. In 1961 he was back on television with the award-

winning *Dick Van Dyke Show,* playing to perfection a neurotic TV comedian who employs Van Dyke, though his behind-the-screen contribution to the show as writer and director was even bigger.

He married Estelle Lebost in 1943; they have three children, one of whom, Rob, has been a big star in own right in the long-time TV hit, *All in the Family.*

DON RICKLES The master of the insult, the curt jester, the merchant of malice, has never met a man he didn't dislike. In top show business circles they say you haven't really made it until you've been insulted by Don Rickles—it's a coveted status symbol. Dean Martin says, "The more he loves you, the more Rickles will insult you. I hope he insults me forever!"

This paradox is accurate. Rickles himself admits that "my style is to insult the people *I like,* and then only to a degree. . . . I've got almost a sixth sense that releases a triphammer in my mind warning me when I go too far. . . . The presence of anger in an insult destroys the humor."

Rickles was born in New York on May 8, 1926, where he was brought up as an orthodox Jew; he remains very religious today. After a slow start in show business, he became a favorite in major nightclubs during the late 1950s, which opened the door to appearances on major TV talk shows, which in turn enabled Rickles to attain the widespread popularity (or notoriety) that is still his.

To the casual observer, his insults are merely a device to incite laughter. But Rickles has a definite purpose in mind. "I try to make people laugh at negative qualities. Like bigotry—the dumb stereotypes ascribed to certain races and people. Like every Irish guy always has a

Don Rickles

bottle in his hand, every Jewish guy is a money-hungry millionaire, every Italian is a gangster, and no black guy likes to work. If I can make people laugh at these things, I can help them see how foolish it all is. In my own little way I'm trying to wash away all the baloney and hostility we carry around.

Rickles has hosted the *Tonight Show* many times in recent years, insulting everyone with impartiality. He has appeared in minor roles in about a half-dozen films, including a very funny bit in *Enter Laughing* (1967). After both 1968 and 1973 versions of his own show folded, he starred in *C.P.O. Sharkey* (1976).

Here's Rickles's razor-sharp touch:

Looking at you, madam, I understand why we read about some women being cut up and stuffed in trunks.

If you had lived, sir, you'd have been a very sick man!

Look, if you want to trade insults, let me go and check in my brains, and then we start out even!

THE RITZ BROTHERS For sheer verve and nerve, The Ritz Brothers surpassed at times even Olsen and Johnson and The Marx Brothers. In one film, they play a trio of lion tamers trying to break into the movies: "When you think of animals, think of us," they tell the director. And they did throw themselves into their act with a sort of animal ferocity that made this a perfect line for them. As one critic put it, "Subtle, they're not. New, they're not. But funny!"

Unlike the Marxes, who played entirely different characters, The Ritz Brothers, who started in vaudeville as precision dancers, usually did things in unison or in a well executed joint effort. They spoofed well known acts and personalities; they did a takeoff on monster movies, bur-

lesqued Snow White, and The Three Musketeers. One of their best remembered routines is "The Man in the Middle is the Funny One," in which each tries to get in the middle between the two others.

In real life, most comedy connoisseurs agree, Harry (born 1908) was the genuine funnyman, an inspiration to many, including Sid Caesar; the others were Al (born 1903) and Jimmy (born 1906). There was also a fourth brother, George, who never joined the act but put it together and managed it; plus a sister, Gertrude. Their real family name was Joachim, and they hailed from Newark, New Jersey.

When they were first being booked by an agent, he wanted them to shorten their name; they saw a passing Ritz Crackers truck, and that was it. They started out at Fox's Folly in 1925, and played a major hotel at Coney Island that year. They were a hit, and Earl Carroll put them in several editions of the *Vanities* and other shows.

In 1934, they made a film short for Educational Pictures, and that got them an offer from Twentieth Century–Fox, where they were placed in several light-weight musicals. Later, they made films for Columbia and Universal. Among their film credits were *Sing, Baby, Sing* (1936), *One in a Million* (1937), and *Kentucky Moonshine* (1938).

After ten years in Hollywood, The Ritz Brothers opted for the nightclub route, staying in it until December 22, 1965, when Al died during the course of an engagement at the Roosevelt Hotel in New Orleans. They never replaced him, and later Harry and Jimmy appeared a few times as a duo.

They were seen on television many times, starting with an appearance on NBC's *All Star Revue* in 1952.

Some dream stuff from the Ritz Brothers:

Ritz Brothers (Al, Jimmy, Harry)

JIMMY: I had a lovely dream last night. I went to Coney Island, and all the rides were free, and you could have all the hot dogs you wanted, and I had a great time!

HARRY: I also had a nice dream last night, oddly enough. I dreamed I was just getting ready to retire in my hotel room when there was a knock, and in walked Marilyn Monroe and Jayne Mansfield. They said they were lonely and so the three of us had a grand time.

JIMMY: Three of you? You mean you had those two lovely broads there and you didn't think of inviting me over?

HARRY: I did, I did! I called your house but your wife said you had gone to Coney Island!

Joan Rivers

JOAN RIVERS A master of pejorative humor, Joan Rivers has written for everything and everybody from *Candid Camera* to Zsa Zsa Gabor. Although both network television and the nation's top nightclubs have applauded her appearances, Ms. Rivers considers herself first a writer, second a performer.

Born Joan Molinsky in Brooklyn in 1935, she recalls being an unhappy, obese child. To take her mind off being fat, her parents launched her on a show business career. Even in show biz, she couldn't escape being a fat girl: "It was Christmas time and they put me in the school Christmas play. The first part I ever had was the three Magi. I got to do a solo: "I three kings of the Orient am . . .' "

At Barnard College, Ms. Rivers acted in plays by Jean-Paul Sartre, edited the newspaper, had pieces published in the literary magazine, and won various scholastic honors. She gradually worked her way back to show business, but found it hard to rise from its seamy side—real dives and strip joints. "My agent had a business card with the two masks on it—both tragedy."

The dry spell ended, and an acclaimed guest appearance on Johnny Carson's *Tonight Show* signaled Joan Rivers' attainment of stardom. She has appeared many times on the *Tonight Show*, plus *Hollywood Squares*, and has made a few films.

Here's Joan:

My figure is a disaster area. On our wedding night my husband said, "Can I help you with the buttons?" I said, "What buttons? I'm naked!" As to my sex appeal—I was stood up by Bigfoot!

When I was little, I had to beg a boy to play doctor with me. He finally agreed, and sent me a bill.

LYDA ROBERTI With a weak heart, Lyda Roberti died at the age of twenty-eight. What a tragic end for one of the most endearing comediennes Broadway and the movies have ever known! A pert, vivacious blonde from Poland, she had both charm and looks, yet was always ready to be kidded about them, as well as about her accent.

Her broad burlesque of femmes fatales in the W.C. Fields film, *Million Dollar Legs* (1932), where she plays Mata Machree, the superspy whom no man can resist ("Resisting Done Every Day from Two to Five") is a memorable comic highlight. Appearing in a stunning gown, she tells the assembled resisters: "I know what you think—" adding with a pretty pout, "—you beasts!" With a vacuous smile, she watches them knock each other senseless fighting over her; when they are all lying around unconscious, she whoops, "Terreefeec!" and walks out. Trying to inspire one fellow to a supreme effort during an athletic event, she writhes and wriggles for him, then pants, "I done all I can do—een publeec."

Born in Warsaw, Poland, on May 20, 1909, she sang in cafés as a child, and came to America as a teenager. Lou Holtz saw her, liked her, and took her as a partner into the Broadway musical *You Said It* when she was only twenty-one. This appearance caused Fields to ask for her for *Million Dollar Legs,* and led to about a dozen film appearances, in *George White's Scandals* (1935) and *Big Broadcast of 1936* among others, as well as to more roles on Broadway.

According to Patsy Kelly, Lyda suffered from shortness of breath and had to rest frequently during the making of their last film together, but didn't want to worry the rest of the crew so she hid it as

Lyda Roberti (with Joe Penner)

best she could. A few months later, on March 12, 1938, she was dead from heart failure. She was married to Hugh Ernst (since 1935).

ROCHESTER In April 1937, Jack Benny needed a Pullman porter for a single appearance on his radio program. For $50 he hired well known vaudeville and movie performer Eddie Anderson, and his writers gave him the name of Rochester Van Jones.

Twenty-one years later, Rochester (he never got his second name back after that one show) suffered a heart attack while rehearsing for the Jack Benny television show, and decided to quit. His foghorn voice and inimitable way of playing up Benny's foibles assured him a permanent niche in the pantheon of comedy.

His main role on the show was to point out in various ways just how stingy Benny was:

ROCHESTER: Boss, you'd better buy another tube of toothpaste. The last one's run out.

BENNY: What are you talking about? There must be another squeeze in it.

ROCHESTER: Look, I didn't mind when you had me squeeze it with a nutcracker day before yesterday. I didn't mind when you sent me down to the Union Station yesterday and had me put it in front of the train. But this is it. I refuse. I won't do it!

BENNY: Rochester!

ROCHESTER: All right, all right! But that's the last time I'm asking Don Wilson to sit on it.

Eddie Anderson was born on September 18, 1905, in Oakland, California. His father was a minstrel, his mother was a circus aerialist; with such a background,

vaudeville was an almost inevitable vocation. But young Eddie almost didn't make it: on getting his first job hawking papers on a street corner in San Francisco, he was so intent on outshouting the competition that he suffered permanent damage to his vocal cords.

Nothing daunted, he got into show business anyway, and turned the cracked voice into a comedy asset. By 1919 he made it into the chorus of *Struttin' Along,* and joined an all-black revue starring Edith Sterling. For touring vaudeville, including the Roxy on Broadway and the Apollo in Harlem, he formed an act, "The Three Black Aces," with his brother Cornelius and another performer. After some appearances in Los Angeles nightclubs, Eddie started getting roles in films: his first was *What Price Hollywood?* in 1932.

The trio then enjoyed a 2½-year run at the Cotton Club in Harlem. When they broke up, Eddie returned to the movies, with occasional radio stints, and that is how he came to do the small bit on Benny's show.

In all, he was in about sixty films, including *Three Men on a Horse* (1936), *Gone With the Wind* (1939), and, with Benny, *Man About Town* (1939), *Love Thy Neighbor* (1940), *Buck Benny Rides Again* (1940), and *The Meanest Man in the World* (1943).

He died on February 28, 1977.

WILL ROGERS In his heyday, Will Rogers was known as the most brilliant American humorist since Mark Twain. He was one of the most likable and well liked men of his time, endearing himself to the American public in the *Ziegfeld Follies,* on radio, in film, and in print as a newspaper columnist. He was born in Oolagah, Oklahoma on November 4, 1878.

As a boy, America's knowledgeable wit-to-be despised education with a passion, preferring to weave patterns with his lariat (which he later twirled to stardom). He spun his lariat with awesome expertise in Wild West shows the world over, and finally in the *Ziegfeld Follies.*

Rogers gradually added spoken comedy to his stage routines. His political cracks deflated the corruptness and pretensions of politicians. He was suspicious of politicians (especially Republicans), the rich, lawyers, missionaries, and bankers. As the guest of honor at a banker's convention, he opened his speech by saying, "You're as fine a group of gentlemen as ever foreclosed on a widow. I'm honored to be with you Shylocks." More than anything, Rogers was a critic of war, although sullenly resigned to the fact that it would never be done away with.

Rogers made several silent films for Hal Roach, proving that he could manage well even without verbal wisecracks. Besides the usual Western stunts like bronco-busting and roping, Rogers did accurate impersonations of the day's top stars. In all, he appeared in more than two dozen silent films including *Water Water Everywhere* (1919), *Scratch My Back* (1920), and *Connecticut Yankee in King Arthur's Court* (1921), and in a number of talkies.

He died in an airplane crash on August 15, 1935.

Here are a few of Rogers' deflating wisecracks:

We are a nation that runs in spite of and not on account of our government.

Russia is so much bigger than us that we'd rattle around inside it like an idea in Congress.

Cairo's a great place. I was the only tourist there who never went to see the Sphinx. I've seen Cal Coolidge.

When you ain't nothing else, you are an artist. It's the one thing you can claim to be and nobody can prove you ain't.

SLAPSEY MAXEY ROSENBLOOM

Damon Runyon created many a book character out of a real personality; in this case, he created a real Runyonesque character out of a boxer. As a sports reporter, Runyon had to cover many Rosenbloom bouts—Rosembloom had 410 between 1921 and 1934—and gave the fighter the nickname "Slapsey Maxey," encouraging him to enter show business.

In keeping with his mentor's advice, Rosenbloom capitalized on his alleged dopiness, and stuck to Runyonesque roles. He would deliberately mangle his syntax ("I almost had conclusion of the brain") or make fun of his background ("I was kept in third grade for two years. You see, my father was still in fourth grade, and it would have been impolite to pass him.").

Much of this was close to the truth; Rosebloom was born in a poor section of New York City in 1903, and wound up in reform school in his early teens. A street tough, he did well in boxing, and in 1921 won the New York State championship in three weights. From 1930 to 1934 he was light heavyweight champion.

Slapsey Maxey was in the road company of *Guys and Dolls,* and had a role in the hit musical on television too. He appeared in more than a dozen films, including *Louisiana Purchase* (1941), *Irish Eyes Are Smiling* (1944), *Skipalong Rosenbloom* (1951), and *Abbott and Costello Meet the Keystone Kops* (1955).

ROWAN and MARTIN

Slapstick, social commentary, Gracie Allen–type confusion, all this and much more transpired regularly on *Laugh-In,* often within the space of a mere 60 seconds. The breathlessly paced program won the race to the Emmy awards six times, and was the vehicle through which Dan Rowan and Dick Martin contributed a lunatic chapter to the history of television comedy.

Dan Rowan was born in Beggs, Oklahoma, in 1922. His experiences before *Laugh-In* include two tries at screenwriting, a stint in the service, ending when he landed a single-engine P-40 on a dry riverbed, and a job selling cars for Madman Muntz.

Dick Martin was born in Detroit in 1928. He spent a decade bartending while attempting to break into show business. At one point he earned $50 a week selling jokes to the *Duffy's Tavern* radio program.

Rowan and Martin met at a party in 1952 and formed a comedy act that opened at Hymie's Barbecue in Albuquerque. Then came a series of minor L.A. nightclubs, and no pay. The team's first-year gross was $6,000. In 1969 it exceeded $1 million.

Their professional writing backgrounds notwithstanding, Rowan and Martin discovered that they achieved the funniest results through improvisation, using the universal moron–straight man combination that they later employed so effectively on *Laugh-In.* Rowan would make a logical, mundane statement, which was mangled by the sex-maniac mentality of Martin, who claimed membership in Bridegrooms Anonymous. "Whenever the marriage urge hits me, they send over a woman in hair curlers and a housecoat to burn my morning toast for me."

Their big break was discovery by Walter Winchell, which led indirectly to more prestigious bookings, and then to a movie contract. Their initial film outing, the 1957 *Once upon a Horse,* flopped com-

Rowan (left) and Martin

mercially, and they were forced back into the nightclub and casino lounge circuits for several years, until Dean Martin witnessed their act and invited them on his NBC-TV show. Then they were selected as Martin's summer replacement.

Laugh-In first aired in January 1968, and immediately became a ratings giant. The program was an unparalleled rapid fire gag machine, cutting from skit to joke to pun to some other form of insanity every 12 seconds, on the average.

A typical minute might have seen George Wallace portrayed as a presidential candidate opposed to letting freedom and liberty fall into the wrong hands . . . Goldie Hawn flashing a sign bearing the message, VIRTUE IS ITS OWN PUNISHMENT . . . Dick Gregory producing a submachine gun from a violin case, concertizing with it as if holding a real violin . . ."The Pope is so distressed by The Pill that he has Excedrin Headache number 9!" . . . ad infinitum.

One evening Sammy Davis, Jr., wafted around the stage chanting, "Here come the judge. Here come the judge." It became the most quoted comedy catchphrase since "Wanna buy a duck?" There was also "Sock it to me," a running gag in which a person saying this would get a bucket of water or a pie in the face; Arte Johnson's dirty old man propositioning old maid Ruth Buzzi; and Goldie Hawn tripping over her tongue.

ANNA RUSSELL There didn't seem to be much of a market for spoofing operas and classic—that is, until, Anna Russell held a recital at New York's Town Hall in 1948. Introducing herself as "the former leading soprano of Ellis Island Opera Company," she gave credit to her teacher, "Dr. Schachtel Streichhoelzer, who taught me everything I know—including

singing." She then launched into advice to singers who want to make it in the classical field.

She recommended a lied named "Schlumpf" for the singer of tremendous artistry but no voice, and an aria, "Ah Lover?" from *The Prince of Philadelphia* for the loud singer with no brains who cannot count the tempi. She has held recitals in dozens of towns and countries, made several records (*Anna Russell Sings?*, 1952) and carved out her own special niche in the realm of comedy.

Born Claudia Russell-Brown on December 27, 1911, in London, Ontario, Canada, she attended the Royal College of Music in London (England), and became a regularly featured singer on BBC Radio. Her voice did not qualify her to become the best in her profession; since she possesses a sense of humor, she decided instead to become the worst— and in that she had succeeded magnificently.

NIPSEY RUSSELL Even before Dick Gregory and Godfrey Cambridge made black humor fashionable on TV, Nipsey Russell had been poking fun at racial relations at the Baby Grand, a Harlem nightclub where he appeared regularly for two decades since 1948. Being a well educated man, he kidded in a gentle way, as often as not using a bit of poetry. He is one of the few working comedians who can quote fluently from classical literature at the drop of a hat.

"The American motto seems to be: When you're white, you're right; when you're brown, stick around; but when you're black, get way, way back!" he might say. Or he would tell how he stopped at a roadside inn near Washington, D.C., and was refused service: "I told the proprietor: 'But I'm the diplomatic representative from Ghana. But it didn't do me any good. He said, 'I don't care who you are, you ain't Ghana eat here!' "

Surprisingly, he can view racial discrimination with tolerant amusement even though he was born right in the heart of Dixie, Alabama, well before integration was even heard of (1920). By the age of six he was a performer, but he did not simply stay in show business. He finished high school and entered a college in Cincinnati, earning a B.A. in English. He also spent four years in the army during World War II, emerging as a captain. That's where he found out that "the whole battle of bigotry is won and lost in words," and decided to do something about it.

Russell's television credits include guest shots on *Arthur Godfrey, The Tonight Show, Car 54 Where are You?* and many panel and game shows.

He made it so big on TV with material like this:

When I finally got ready to leave the South, I went to the bus station, bought a ticket, and then, having to wait with nothing else to do, I put a penny in the weighing machine. Back came a ticket which said, "You weigh 150 pounds, you're black, and you're on your way to Chicago." I couldn't believe it, so I waited a few minutes, and put in another penny. Same card, same text. Now I was determined. I went to a store that sold makeup, painted my face as an Indian, and disguised myself with an Indian headdress. Then I sneaked back to the bus station and weighed myself again. The card said, "You still weigh 150 pounds, you're still black, and by screwing around you missed your bus to Chicago."

S

MORT SAHL When Mort Sahl came on the scene in the 1950s, he was something new and fresh in American comedy: a college type acutely aware of political and social issues of the day, who poked fun at issues not just to make people laugh, but also to make them change things for the better.

On the American Medical Association: "The AMA opposes chiropractors and witch doctors, and any other cure that's quick or inexpensive."

On religion: "I don't see why some Catholics are for capital punishment. Look at the very big mistake they made once."

On psychoanalysis: "I'm against it because it turns you against your folks. When you watch an Arthur Miller play, you know someone's going to hit his father before the end of the second act."

On folk singers: "They wear shirts open to the navel but they have no navel. That's the ultimate rejection of Mother."

On materialistic culture: "If you have enough healthy interests like automobiles, razors, pantyhose, you will have no further need for human relationship, and that will solve many social problems."

Mort Sahl was born on May 11, 1927, in Montreal, but his family returned to their regular home in New York when he was four. He started to work as a clerk, but it didn't appeal to him, and he spent years trying to break into nightclubs with routines that had convulsed his office colleagues around the water cooler.

Finally a 1953 appearance at San Francisco's hungry i night club clicked. He became a frequent guest on TV variety and talk shows, and cut about a dozen record albums, including *Mort Sahl,*

Mort Sahl

Iconoclast. Since much of his humor was derived from headlines of the day, he kept changing this act.

Sahl married a girl he went to college with, divorced her, and married her again. He succumbed to some materialistic attitudes he had once ranted against, buying several cars, hi-fi sets, and similar status symbols to celebrate his affluence. He is now seen infrequently in nightclubs and on an occasional interview show.

CHIC SALE Charles Sales was one of the country's best cracker barrel monologists. Well known in vaudeville's top houses—he played the Palace many times—he had a fanatically adoring public in the rural areas. For a couple of generations of Midwesterners, "chic sale" was the outhouse—a homespun tribute to a favorite character. (His monologue, "The Specialist," consisted of hilarious advice on how to construct an outhouse.)

He was responsible for popularizing the term "wisecrack." In 1906 he introduced a town "smarty" into his act, who always said, "I'll tell you a riddle and a couple of wisecracks before I run back to the poolroom." Soon the term caught on and was incorporated into dictionaries.

All his other characters were rural types (country teacher, caretaker) who would talk about ordinary subjects. A special favorite was "the old man playing the tuby."

Born in Huron, South Dakota, on August 25, 1885, Chic Sale served his apprenticeship in small-town vaudeville. In 1917, after appearing throughout the major vaudeville circuits for years, he made it to the Broadway musical stage in the *Passing Show of 1917* and in the *Ziegfeld Midnight Frolic of 1919.* The Shuberts liked his style, and he was one of their featured stars in the 1920s.

When sound came, he made about a dozen movies, using many of his characters. Among them were *When a Feller Needs a Friend* and *Stranger in Town* (both in 1932). For a lark, he wrote a book about one of these characters, *The Specialist;* surprisingly, it sold very well in the otherwise non bookish rustic areas.

Chic Sale died in Los Angeles on November 7, 1936.

SAM 'n' HENRY

see AMOS 'n' ANDY

SAN FERNANDO RED

see RED SKELTON

JIMMY SAVO A happy-looking, rotund little fellow, Jimmy Savo specialized in pantomime sketches and interpretations of popular songs, earning himself a unique niche in the American theater. He could convulse audiences with a frantic facial exertion in "River, Stay 'Way From My Door" or a hysterical rendition of "Swiss Lullaby." His mimic routines were unusual, like "Swedish girl going to church meeting a bull in the field," or "The timid young man whose first visit to the beach is disrupted by the question of whether he should go into the water." He was one of the first performers to have a successful one-man show on Broadway—*Mum's the Word,* in 1940.

He was a native of New York, where he was born in 1896, the son of an Italian shoemaker—which is why, as he later claimed, he wanted to give his "awl" to show business. At fourteen, he made his debut at the Bowery Theater as a straight singer. Making no headway, he switched to juggling, and started adding bits of mummery to his act. When that clicked, he joined the vaudeville circuits. He had

Jimmy Savo

a bit part in *Listen, Lester* on Broadway in 1918, but did not graduate to Broadway musical comedy until 1924—he joined the *Vogues* of that year with another ex-juggler, Fred Allen.

For the next two decades, he stuck pretty much to Broadway. He appeared in a number of productions, including *Earl Carroll's Vanities* (1930), *The Boys from Syracuse* (1938), and *Wine, Women and Song* (1942). He also made two brief trips to Hollywood. In his second and best film, *Merry-Go-Round of 1938,* as he pridefully announced, he "appeared in 211 of its 291 scenes but spoke only one of its 2,454 lines of dialogue!"

When a young lady reporter, Nina Vecchi, came to interview him, he told her, "I know how we can get your paper to give me a good write up. I'll marry you!" And he proceeded to do just that.

In 1946, he lost a leg due to a cancerous tumor, but not his good humor; within a year, he was giving benefit performances for amputee veterans. That year he also wrote a book about his experiences acquiring a genuine Italian castle as a private retreat. He died on September 1960 at the age of sixty-four.

AL SCHACHT Combining sports with humor is a particularly American characteristic; appropriately, it was brought into being in conjunction with that particularly American sport, baseball. It was a major source of inspiration for the humorous stories of Ring Lardner, and one of America's funniest authors, Damon Runyon, started out as a baseball correspondent for a daily paper. Comedian Joe E. Brown was thought to have been good enough to qualify for major league play, had he chosen a sports career rather than comedy. In the early days of the Brooklyn Dodgers, when the family outing at Ebbets Field was a major entertainment outlet for many Brooklynites, the management used to hire well known stage clowns, among them the great Emmett Kelly, to warm up the audience with pantomime.

Al Schacht was a baseball player who at first added a few funny gestures to his plays now and then. They became so popular that he eventually became the clown prince of baseball, doing lengthy pregame routines—and appearing, in the days before mass media like TV, before more people on a single day than most stage comedians at that time saw in a whole season.

MOSES SCHANFIELD

see WEBER and FIELDS

RONNIE SCHELL One of the new faces on TV variety shows, like Merv Griffin's, Ronnie is a veteran of the nightclub circuit, having done all the best niteries from the hungry i in San Francisco to Miami and Las Vegas/Lake Tahoe. His first job was at the Taylor Supper Club in his native Denver, Colorado.

He is personable, amiable, and has a straightforward style in which he kids many things, especially his youthful appearance (he looks as if he's in his early twenties but is actually in his late thirties).

Here's how his act goes:

I almost got the big role in *A Star Is Born*—but Fredric March beat me to it. So I tried to star in a porno film, but my part wasn't big enough. You know it's sad: now that it's all right to sow wild oats, I keep having crop failures! Well, I knew I was getting old when I realized I was watching *Charlie's Angels* hoping to get a peek at Charlie!

JOE SCHENCK

see VAN and SCHENCK

LONNIE SCHORR Lonnie is one of the newcomers to the business, from Zebulon, North Carolina. His material, seen occasionally on TV talk shows, is drawn from his army life, his hernia operation, and the contrasts between his life in the South and his new environment:

In New York, people always look down. Either they just don't like to say "hi there" to each other, or it must be on account of the dogs.

GEORGE SEARCY

see MORAN and MACK

CHARLES EMMETT SELLERS

see MORAN and MACK

PETER SELLERS Peter Sellers is a self-proclaimed star of "stage, screen, and alimony." He is known to movie audiences as one of the zaniest actors of his era, who is able to transform himself, mind, voice, and demeanor, into any insane character dreamed up by the screenplay scribes of Hollywood or England.

After seven years' worth of playing in properties that were insufficiently ridiculous for his style, Sellers was propelled back into the limelight in 1975 by *The Return of the Pink Panther* playing the befuddled, foolishly vainglorious, monomaniacally persistent detective Clouseau.

Sellers was born in Southsea, England, on September 8, 1925. His parents were active in British vaudeville, and Sellers claims they first brought him on stage at the ripe old age of two days. During World War II he was a blackmarket whiz in trafficking liquor and petroleum, and accumulated at least a million francs. On the side, he was a drummer.

Sellers won entree into show business through an ingeniously conceived and executed ruse. He phoned a top BBC producer twice, perfectly impersonating a different BBC star on each occasion, giving rave reviews of a certain Peter Sellers. The producer eagerly asked how to reach him. "You *are* in touch," Sellers revealed, "I'm Sellers." His *Goon Show* became a top radio comedy program in England, and he became a favorite of American comedy devotees (as well as millions of everyday filmgoers) with such films as *The Pink Panther* (1964), *What's New, Pussycat?*, *There's a Girl in My*

Peter Sellers

Soup (1970), and *The Magic Christian* (1970).

One of his best characterizations appeared in *Dr. Strangelove* (1965), where he plays a magnificently deranged (as well as physically crippled) German scientist who is used by the U. S. government as an expert on nuclear war. It was a dream role for a ham of Sellers' caliber, and he made the most of it, supplying off-beat comic relief to this otherwis rather grim film fantasy about nuclea brinkmanship.

Sellers is a car freak who once owne 62 of them within a year. That is h number two passion. As for number on "I always wanted to be a character-act comedian—and always will be until drop."

LARRY SEMON In his heyday, Larry Semon enjoyed a popularity as big as that of anyone from Mack Sennett's renowned laugh factory. In 1923 he proudly announced he signed a $3 million contract to make just six films—the highest amount ever offered a comedian. Five years later he was dead, after artistic failure and bankruptcy. His wife, the former costar Dorothy Dwan, said he died of a broken heart.

This strange little man with the pinched, weasel-like face made more than one hundred one- and two-reel comedies for Vitagraph, all furiously paced and frenetically funny, in the purest slapstick tradition. He was adept at staging absurd chases in which every conveyance imaginable was used, and tin lizzies bit the dust by the hundreds.

Semon set a pace so strenuous that he could not keep it up; also, he was at fault for sticking with the same formula right into the 1920s, by which time other comedians (Chaplin, Keaton, et al.) developed new comedy techniques that weaned audiences away from the simple, unmotivated mayhem of the Sennett school, once so successful. Whatever the reason, as soon as he switched to feature length in 1924, his films failed dismally. Even today, with wholesale revivals of classic comedy films on campuses and on TV, virtually none of Larry Semon's output is seen.

He was born on July 16, 1889, in West Point, Mississippi, the son of a magician. An art student, he started making a living as a cartoonist for a New York paper. In 1916 he heard that Vitagraph, one of the busiest New York–based film companies, was looking for a comedian to replace their former star, John Bunny, who had died the year before. Semon was hired and started producing one-reelers at the rate of two per month.

Larry Semon

He was the first to use Oliver Hardy regularly—as the villain. In 1919 he changed his formula to one two-reeler per month; and from 1920 to 1923, he made one two-reeler every two months. In 1923 he signed a big contract with a distributor and formed his own company, Chadwick Productions, to make feature comedies for them.

When the features failed, he seemed to have no further reason to live, and on October 6, 1928, he died.

MACK SENNETT Comedy didn't find a home in movies until Mack Sennett built an asylum for it named Keystone. He directed the madness, and once in a while acted, either as a rube or as a heavy-handed villain.

His acting was, to be charitable, mediocre. But, even if he couldn't be funny himself, he knew who was funny when he saw them—and earned his place among cinema's immortals by bringing to films Mabel Normand, Fatty Arbuckle, Charlie Chaplin, Harry Langdon, Ben Turpin, and Ford Sterling.

Above all, he discovered that cops can be screamingly funny—if they are so insanely dedicated to their sworn duty that the pursuit of crooks becomes a sort of athletic event orchestrated with the precision of a ballet performance. Serious students of the Sennett period have been amazed to discover how little actual footage was devoted to the Keystone Kops, compared to the total output of the studio, and how disproportionate was their notoriety. Obviously, Sennett hit the funnybone at just the right spot.

This talent seemed to be uniquely his

Mack Sennett

When Bing Crosby was still known mostly from radio, he gave him several short comedies to romp in, wisely letting him sing a lot; when W. C. Fields was facing an uncertain future in sound films, he let him make shorts his own way, recognizing instinctively that Fields knew what he was doing. Some of Sennett's top stars, such as Ford Sterling, were always directed by others, while Chaplin was allowed to direct his own films after only a few weeks of apprenticeship.

Michael Sinnott was born in Richmond, Ontario, Canada, in 1880, and gained experience in burlesque and in Frank Sheridan's touring company. In between, he had menial jobs in factories. In 1908 someone told him it was possible to make $5 for a day's work at the Biograph Studios in New York, and he signed on as a rustic type.

Developing a fascination for the mechanics of comedy, he turned to directing. By 1912 he was ready to go independent, and with two partners formed the Keystone Company, which was to make films in the newly discovered film mecca, Hollywood. By the time Keystone broke up, five years later, he was responsible for nearly a thousand single-and double-reel comedies. He also broke new ground in 1914 by making the first full-length comedy, for which he recruited a formidable Broadway star, Marie Dressler.

Like anyone else, he had flaws, which didn't matter much in the first flush of creative frenzy, but as films became big business, these flaws began to work against him.

One was tight-fistedness. Sennett brought most of his stars out of total obscurity, when they were happy to take the few dollars a day he was offering; perhaps he felt they owed him a debt of thanks, and didn't think of giving them raises proportionate to their importance to the studio. Anyway, he lost the cream of the crop almost as fast as he developed them: he let Chaplin go because he thought $150 a week was enough for him, while a rival studio offered him $1,250 a week.

Then there was the unhappy love affair with Mabel Normand. He cheated on her, and she left in a huff. He tried to compensate by building her a studio at his own expense and making feature-length films with her, but it nearly broke him financially, and she did not reconcile with him as a lover.

In the 1920s, no longer able to finance his own ventures, he worked for other studios. They did not permit him the leeway he enjoyed at Keystone, and his later efforts show the strain. Also, the art of comedy had progressed, while Sennett continued to trust his own formula, which was fast becoming primitive compared to the more sophisticated work of artists like Keaton, Chaplin, and Lloyd.

When the coming of sound restricted the actors' freedom of movement, slapstick comedy was in deep trouble, and so was Sennett. His shorts, with Andy Clyde and others, were unsuccessful; by 1935 he was bankrupt. His type of comedy could now be seen only in Walt Disney cartoons, where there were no physical limitations. The mighty force he had unleashed rolled right past him. His last gasp was a compilation of his best footage in a 1949 nostalgia trip *Down Memory Lane,* but it got a lukewarm reception from the public.

Sennett did become the proud owner of a special Academy Award (in 1937) for his lasting contribution to comedy techniques. He never married. He died in his home town in Canada in 1960.

AL SHEAN

see GALLAGHER and SHEAN

JEAN SHEPHERD Apostle of Americana, troubadour of trivia, and philosopher without portfolio, Jean Shepherd has an uncanny talent for weaving a spellbinding anecdote out of the commonplace.

Not long ago, in a shabby motel in New England, I sat down on a cold, rainy dawn to a bowl of soggy Wheaties and found myself suddenly, and for no reason, thinking of Rochelle Hudson. Rochelle Hudson!

I swished my plastic spoon around the bottom of the bowl to scoop up the last few spongy flakes, and it was at that instant that I *knew*. It was the bowl *itself* that had caused Rochelle Hudson to make an unscheduled guest appearance!

I stared hard at it. It was unmistakable, a bowl of remarkably aggressive ugliness, made of a distinctive type of dark green glass, embossed with swollen lumps and sworls representing the fruits of the vine and the abundance of Nature. A bowl that had but one meaning. I peered at it long and hard. Yes, there was no mistake. It was genuine—a mint-condition, vintage Movie Dish Night Premium Gift Bowl.

Spinning out tales like this over the radio in the early fifties, making each reminiscence sound important and thrilling or mysterious by a hushed, intimate delivery, dramatic pauses, and a flair for implying tension, Jean Shepherd attracted a devoted coterie of followers. Far more than a disc jockey, he became a chronicler of the ordinary, and a guru to a generation of insomniacs.

Born on July 26, 1923, in Hammond, Indiana, he majored in psychology at Indiana State, and got his first job on a radio station in Cincinnati in 1949.

The program moved to Philadelphia, and later to New York, where he started in 1955. Soon he put out several albums of humorous miscellany, appeared on Broadway, and by the late 1960s was making a series of narrations for thirty-minute films of American scenes for television. Titled *Jean Shepherd's America,* the series has been shown several times on the PBS stations.

ALLAN SHERMAN For years, Allan Sherman wrote comedy material for others, including Jackie Gleason, Joe E. Lewis, and Jerry Lester. He created the TV show *I've Got a Secret,* and produced several others.

Then came an event that Sherman described as "I became an overnight success after 18 years." He recorded an LP of takeoffs on well known songs, entitled *My Son the Folk Singer.* To the amazement of everyone—most of all, Sherman—it zoomed into the stratosphere with 1½ million copies sold.

The song "Matilda" became "My Zelda" ("She stole my money and run with the tailor"). "Frère Jacques" became "Sarah Jackman," and "Water Boy" became "Seltzer Boy." One of Sherman's singles, "Hello Muddah, Hello Faddah," also went the million-seller route, as did his second LP album, *My Son the Celebrity.*

Sherman now had to do the sons on TV and in nightclubs, but he continued writing. He invented the "Pornophone," a service supplying obscene calls to girls too homely to get them otherwise, and similar ideas, mostly through *Playboy* magazine and such media. In 1973 he wrote the book, *The Rape of the APE* (American Puritan Ethic), a hilarious account of the sexual revolution.

Sherman died in 1973.

HERB SHRINER He would probably have been content to remain "Harmonica Herb," featured on the radio program

Allan Sherman

Hoosier Hop in his native Indiana. On one show, however, his lip gave out, and to cover up his embarrassment he started talking.

The laughter of the audience encouraged him. Later, in the Army during World War II, he used more humor and less harmonica to help fellow GI's endure military life. Then came the offer to do a seven-minute stint of his best Army jokes in a Broadway musical show, *Inside U.S.A.* (1948). Audience reaction forced the producers to reshuffle the schedule and permit him to do 25 to 30 minutes instead of seven—almost unprecedented in the annals of musical comedy.

Suddenly a hot property, Shriner found himself on television (*Herb Shriner Show*) and in the movies (*Main Street to Broadway*), doing overseas tours, acting as quizmaster (*Two for the Money*), and recording albums of humorous monologues (*Herb Shriner on Stage*).

Throughout this, he remained consistently low-key, his homespun humor deriving basically from a country boy's "gee whiz" attitude. A favorite ploy was to follow up a tall tale with the apology, " 's possible!" He reminisced about Indiana and his youth, mourning that "things ain't what they used to be; in fact, at our house, they never was!" Here's more of his homey style:

Hoosiers are congenitally inquisitive. That means nosy, in a nice sort of way.

I've played the harmonica ever since I was big enough to defend myself.

In the Service, I was just as happy as if I was alive.

We used to buy things by mail order. You looked things up in the Sears Roebuck catalogue, and when you got back to the house, you wrote them and ordered it.

Had a friend back home who started drinking.

They were afraid he was going to turn out to be a bum, so they put him in politics where it wouldn't be noticed. They made him a dogcatcher. For a while he had trouble because he didn't know what he was supposed to catch them at. We had more dogs around town after he became dogcatcher than before. He was probably catching them a bit too late!

Herb Shriner was born on May 29, 1918, in Toledo, Ohio, but grew up in Indiana (as advertised). He played the harmonica on a Fort Wayne station, toured small midwestern theaters with a harmonica quintet, appeared solo in Chicago's Oriental Theater, and appeared on network radio. Then came *Inside U.S.A.*

Shriner married Eileen McDermott in 1949. He died in 1970.

PHIL SILVERS Like Harold Lloyd, he wore horn-rimmed glasses, and like Eddie Cantor, he is known for fathering five daughters and no sons, but at this point Phil Silvers ceases to resemble any other comedian. Beginning in the baggy-pants burlesque tradition, and later on the Broadway stage, in nightclubs, films, and television, over the course of half a century, he has developed a unique performing personality, that of a lovable con man full of tricks, schemes, and plots who would rather connive than eat.

Silvers plays the traditional buffoon, but his buffoonery is distinctive for being intelligently mapped out instead of being propelled on a random road of banana peels and pratfalls. He is capable of enacting a script expertly when necessary, but is at his best when given free rein to ad lib. He has the gift of brilliant spontaneity, whether employing words or mimicry.

Silvers' birthplace is Brooklyn, where he appeared on May 11, 1912. He is of Russian immigrant stock, and his rea

Phil Silvers

family name is Silversmith. His school-days came to an end at age twelve when he became a member of Gus Edwards' famous children's vaudeville troupe. His golden soprano voice took him straight to the Palace, but tragedy struck before his sixteenth birthday—his voice changed. He was forced to select a new trade—comedy.

He took to the burlesque wheels, but worked his way up to a Broadway musical by 1938, and then to Hollywood in the 1940s. His entry into television in 1955 with the durable Sergeant Bilko character was on a show originally called *You'll Never Get Rich;* it assured him undying fame.

Silvers married in 1945 but the union was of short duration. He made several USO tours during World War II. His film credits include the tour de force *Top Banana* (1954), *It's a Mad, Mad, Mad, Mad World* (1963), and *Buona Sera, Mrs. Campbell* (1969), and he was very funny as a "flesh peddler" in *A Funny Thing Happened on the Way to the Forum.* In the 1970s he was still appearing in various media.

RED SKELTON The most gifted of America's pantomime clowns, Red Skelton was also the creator of a legion of comic characters portrayed on radio and television, such as San Fernando Red the crooked politician, Clem Kadiddlehopper the country bumpkin, Willie Lump Lump the nasty tramp, Freddie the Freeloader the lovable bum, and Cauliflower McPugg the punchy ex-prizefighter.

McPUGG: You know, I'm worried about some boys at the gym. When they take a break, they step out on the balcony for a breath of fresh air.
GUEST: Well, what's wrong with that?
McPUGG: There ain't no balcony in the gym! —Answer the phone, will ya?
GUEST: But there is no phone here, McPugg, either!

There was also Sheriff Deadeye, the chicken of the West, and (on radio, especially) the Mean Widdle Kid, a sort of male counterpart to Fanny Brice's bratty Baby Snooks.

In addition to all this, Red also made use of a "straight" personality, that of himself as a shy, inept young man, in his films.

He was born Richard Skelton in Vincennes, Indiana, on July 18, 1913, but his hair condemned him to the nickname "Red" from childhood. His father was a circus clown, but died soon after the son was born. Perhaps by becoming a clown, collecting memorabilia of clowns, and ultimately even painting portraits of them, Red was in a way searching for the absent father.

Red started in circuses and vaudeville stock companies, including even a medicine show and a group of minstrels singing on the then-still-running Mississippi riverboats. Teaming up with a Kansas City usherette, Edna Stillwell (whom he later married), Red toured the circuits with her. During a six-month stay at Loew's Montreal Theater, he devised the classic dunking routine—about a doughnut dunker who knows that dunking in public is bad manners but contrives to dunk anyway. It was a big hit and got him a booking at the Paramount in New York City in the summer of 1937.

There he tried out some vocal characterizations on the national radio audience via the *Rudy Vallee Show,* and again was a success.

In 1938, RKO was filming the story of the Borscht Belt, titled *Having Wonderful Time.* Although everyone knows the Catskill resorts were virtually 100 percent

Red Skelton

Jewish, the logic for which Hollywood is so famous dictated that the roles be played by such 100 percent non-Jews as Ginger Rogers, Douglas Fairbanks, Jr., Lucille Ball, and Red—who got to do his dunking routine. The historically inaccurate film was a big break for Skelton, who was favorably noticed and stayed around for about thirty-five films from then until 1965. They included *Whistling in Brooklyn* (1944) and *The Fuller Brush Man* (1948).

While in the film capital, Red got on network radio with a show consistently rated near the top. Ditto for his television show, which made its debut in 1953 and ran an incredible 18 seasons, outlasting and outrating all competing comedians.

Just as incredibly, when the *Red Skelton Show* was cancelled in 1971, it was not because of failure to garner an audience—it was still among the top ten shows—but because of "demographics." It seems that the audience for Red's show averaged around thirty-five years of age, whereas the sponsors were looking for an audience averaging in the twenties.

Skelton divorced Edna in 1943, and married starlet Georgia Davis in 1945. They were divorced in 1971.

Since the demise of his TV show he has been semiretired. He did hundreds of pantomime sketches on his show, virtually the only American comedian to do this consistently. His "An Old Man Watching a Parade" is a classic.

SMITH and DALE

PATIENT: What are your office hours?

DOCTOR: Twelve to 3, 3 to 6, 6 to 9, 9 to 12, and 12 to 3.

PATIENT: You give good odds. You must be a horse doctor.

DOCTOR: Stick out your tongue. Hmmm! I've seen better tongues hanging in a delicatessen.

The immortal Doctor Kronkheit routine (of which the above is a fragment) was originated in 1908, and was still featured in the repertoire of Smith and Dale in the 1960s. They performed the legendary sketch tens of thousands of times, making it one of the most performed and most durable live comedy routines of modern times. The lines are strictly run-of-the-mill antiques, but a magical chemistry flowed between Smith and Dale when they performed the routine. Smith knew that their doctor sketch

Smith (right) and Dale

was just like any of a thousand others, and he couldn't account for its unparalleled longevity. "I just don't know," he said, "I've asked myself the question a thousand times—what keeps that doctor alive forever?"

Joe Sultzer (Smith) and Charles Marks (Dale) were both born in New York, on February 16, 1884, and September 6, 1881, respectively. When they first teamed up in 1898, Smith and Dale worked New York's old beerhall circuit, from Chinatown to Fourteenth Street. The duo danced, sang, and supplemented their income by tending bar and waiting on tables. In 1902 they joined two other comics to form the Avon Comedy Four, a vaudeville favorite for many years. Smith and Dale later acted in films, guested on the radio programs of Al Jolson and Kate Smith (among many others), and were a big hit when reunited on television. Their credits include appearances on Broadway in *The Passing Show of 1919* (ditto 1920 and 1921) and film shorts with corny titles like *La Schnapps, Inc.* (1930) and *S. S. Malaria* (1930).

The play and later film, *The Sunshine Boys,* was loosely based on their lives, but they never broke up their act, as portrayed. Charles Marks passed away in 1971.

THE SMOTHERS BROTHERS The Smothers Brothers belong to that rare breed of comedian, whose ranks include Henry Morgan, Dick Gregory, and the late Lenny Bruce, that is determined to tell it like it is—even if it means inviting destruction at the hands of the powers that be. In The Smothers Brothers' case, speaking out meant the axe for their TV variety program.

The brothers were born on New York's Governors Island, where their father, an Army major, was stationed. Thomas Bolyn Smothers was born first, on February 2, 1937; Richard was born on November 20, 1939. Their childhood was a seemingly endless array of stepfathers and elementary schools during which, as Dick recalls, "we ran pretty wild," just as they would later do on the national hookup.

Playing music, mostly folksongs, in trios and quintets was their entree into show business. When the headlining flamenco dancer at San Francisco's Purple Onion nightclub injured his ankle, Tom, Dick, and a third partner had to fill the vacuum. Running out of songs, they resorted to spontaneous repartee. The Smothers Brothers had discovered comedy.

They were soon discovered for television, by Jack Paar's *Tonight Show,* and later appeared on the *Steve Allen Show,* the *Jack Benny Show,* and the *Judy Garland Show.*

Their own first TV show, in 1965, was a disaster. It had an inane script in which Dick was an executive and Tom portrayed his brother's blundering ghost. Their second venture, in 1967, fared much better. *The Smothers Brothers Comedy Hour* won out over even the cowboys of *Bonanza,* with a surprising 36 percent share of the audience.

Success was not smooth for The Smothers Brothers. Their unflinching political and social satire incited first tension, and then full-scale war, between themselves and the network. First individual segments were censored, and ultimately the whole show was killed by CBS. "Objectionable" material included film clips of the Democratic Convention, with Harry Belafonte significantly singing "Lord, Lord, Don't Stop the Carnival." Another no-no was Pete Seeger's antiwar song, "Waist Deep in the Big Muddy."

The Smothers Brothers (Tom and Dick)

The first time the network censors cut an entire routine was when Tom Smothers, helped by Elaine May, satirized them:

ELAINE: I think the word "breast" should be cut out from the dinner scene. I think that "breast" is a relatively tasteless thing to say while you're eating. I wouldn't mind if they were having cocktails or even a late supper, but dinner is a *family* meal.

TOM: (*writing a note*) Take the word "breast" out of the dinner scene.

ELAINE: Tell them to substitute the word "arm." It has the same number of syllables and it's a much more acceptable thing to say at the dinner table.

TOM: But won't that sound funny? "My heart beats wildly in my arm whenever you're near"?

Finally, the ridiculous guardians of public morality decide on "My pulse beats wildly in my wrist whenever you're near." They conclude, "We could write as well as they do."

Although their forbidden comedy was very tame in comparison with what's happening all over the tube today, The Smothers Brothers helped to open the door to free speech and frankness on network television.

MORTIMER SNERD

see EDGAR BERGEN and CHARLIE McCARTHY

BABY SNOOKS

see FANNY BRICE

SKIP STEPHENSON A blond six-footer from Nebraska, Skip is one of the newest faces on the standup comedy circuits, including various TV talk and variety shows. Here's how he sounds when he's on:

I went to parochial school. We called it "parochial" so the other kids wouldn't know we went to Catholic school.

I took a girl to dinner. She said, "I guess I'll have the steak." So I told her, "Better guess again, honey."

COLONEL STOOPNAGLE Colonel Stoopnagle was the alter ego of F. Chase Taylor, a radio disc jockey with a zany, whimsical sense of humor. He loved spoonerisms ("This is Colonel Speaknagle stoopling"), absurd inventions (an upside-down lighthouse for submarines), and screwball logic (he put salt in the pepper shaker and pepper in the salt shaker, so that if a person grabbed the

wrong one, by mistake, it would be all right).

With a fellow announcer, Budd Hulick, he formed a team operating in radio for a number of years as Stoopnagle and Budd. The sheer freedom of their nonsense endeared them to audiences. In the middle of a discussion, Stoopnagle might ask Budd to scratch his back; whereupon the microphone would pick up sounds of scratching for a couple of minutes, and then they would be off on a different tangent. Stoopnagle might announce, "Will the lady who was in the audience last night and sat on a plate of syrup please return the plate, and nothing further will be said about the syrup." Or he might say that he wouldn't touch a certain guy with a ten-foot pole, and that he, Stoopnagle, would like to hire someone whose duty would be to carry around a ten-foot pole, not touching that guy. He took common expressions literally: when he said, "You wouldn't know me from Adam," he went on to describe a specific person named Adam in minute detail to prove that there was a resemblance.

F. Chase Taylor was born on October 4, 1897, in Buffalo, New York, and appeared in amateur theatricals from the age of twelve. He got his first stage laughs when he forgot his lines, and was hooked on comedy.

After graduating from the University of Rochester, he joined the U.S. Naval Reserve, and after discharge got married and became a stockbroker. Comedy remained an absorbing hobby, and by 1925 he was on WMAK Radio in Buffalo with an act called "Nip and Tuck."

The format of nonsense talk that gained him national fame developed by accident. Having lost faith in stocks after the 1929 crash, Taylor joined the staff of WMAK as continuity writer. He was pounding the typewriter on October 10,

1930, when a hurricane cut the CBS feedline to Buffalo, and announcer Budd Hulick told him they had dead air on their hands.

The two men filled the time as best they could. They had no time to discuss what they were going to say: whatever came into their heads went on the air. Taylor's wild imagination went over big with the listeners. WMAK put them on regularly, and the following year they were on the CBS network.

The individualistic Taylor refused sponsorship from several advertisers because they wanted to change *his* format to what *they* thought was funny. ("An individualist," says Stoopnagle, "is a guy who, when in a crowd, is never lonelier than, only more so.")

He married his first wife in 1919, divorced her in 1936, and married ex-newspaper reporter Kay Bell.

Now Stoopnagle and Budd, uncensored:

STOOPNAGLE: I have written a slight play.
BUDD: What, again?
STOOPNAGLE: No, I only wrote it once.
BUDD: What is it about?
STOOPNAGLE: Well, you see, I think our subway guards are too tough, and the mellow-toned radio announcers are too soft. So I arranged for two of them to change jobs, and this is the result:

"Hello there, this is Doormat Brokenwire, of Hope Springs, Eternal, bidding you welcome on our refreshing ride through mother earth to your destination. There are peerless patented plush pillows for your comfort on every seat. Tea and cookies will be served as we pass Fifty-seventh Street."

"Okay, youse guys, now look here: this here program is brung to ya by the Corrugated Butter Company, and if you're gonna listen to it you'd better go out and get some, or you know who'll be looking for ya."

JOE SULTZER

see SMITH and DALE

MACK SWAIN This rotund comic with 22 years of vaudeville and theatrical experience became one of the most familiar faces in early film comedy. For Sennett, Swain's corpulence was a natural butt for humor pertaining to comic villainy, on the one hand, and bumbling incompetence, on the other. Thus, Swain was alternately a grotesque heavy or "Ambrose," a rollicking, overgrown babe in the woods whose wooing of some maiden fair was always thwarted by more agile adversaries.

Despite hundreds of roles, his vogue was over rather quickly, and by the mid-1920s, he was virtually forgotten, when Chaplin chose him for the role of coprospector in *The Gold Rush*. Between them, they created one of the all-time great comedy scenes in the history of film when they were snowbound in a cabin without food. Their pathetic meal out of a boiled shoe, and later their cunning attempts to kill each other with cannibalistic intent, remain comic film highlights today and should live forever.

Mack Swain was born in Salt Lake City, Utah, on February 16, 1876. He died in 1935.

DONALD SWANN

see MICHAEL FLANDERS and DONALD SWANN

JULIUS TANNEN A versatile monologist, Tannen developed a rapid-fire style that sometimes got him billed as "The Human Chatterbox." But he also used a number of dialect characters, such as Cohen in his famous *Cohen at the Telephone* series. He was the originator of the curtain speech that has been wrongly attributed to George M. Cohan: "My mother thanks you, my father thanks you, and I thank you." He played Broadway in 1920 in *Her Family Tree*, and was in three editions of *Earl Carroll's Vanities* between 1925 and 1927. He recorded his *Cohen* routine for Victor in 1927.

Tannen was born in 1881, and turned to the theater at an early age; his good material, knowledge of human nature, and stage presence made him one of the highest paid acts in vaudeville around the turn of the century. In the 1908 season, he wowed London with his standup com-

edy and his specialty sketches, such as "a little boy doing a mind-reading act." Earl Carroll used him as a master of ceremonies, and his glib wit attracted favorable notice in three successive editions of the *Vanities*. Around 1922, he persuaded a stuttering violinist to say a few words into the newfangled contraption called a microphone; in 1937, when Ben Bernie had one of the most successful dance programs on radio, the grateful band leader repaid the debt by having Tannen frequently on his show.

Julius Tannen died on January 3, 1965.

Here's a sample of *Cohen on the Telephone*:

Hello, hello, are you dere? I vant to speak to the landlord. Hello, I'm Cohen . . . no, I ain't goin'—Cohen, Cohen, your tenant Cohen . . . no, not Lieutenant Cohen, your tenant.

Last night the vind blew down the shutter . . . no, I didn't say 'shut up'; shutter. And I vant you to send a carpenter to mend it . . . no, not two men; to mend! Van man to mend . . . oh, never mind, I'll fix it myself.

JACQUES TATI If anyone was entitled to wear Chaplin's mantle after his abandonment of the tramp character, it would have to be Jacques Tati. His films are, for the first of many parallels, always his total creations; they feature a character, played by the film maker himself, who is something of a misfit—but who gamely tries to "fit."

Then there is the startling fact that his films are virtually silents—that is, they have sounds and dialogue, but are so purely oriented to visual comedy that he can afford to use the music and sounds for nothing more than mood setting.

A perfect example of his style is *Mr. Hulot's Holiday* (1953), a comedy created out of the simple fabric of an ordinary, mildly befuddled bachelor taking a seaside vacation. During the entire picture, Tati says only a single word ("Hulot," pronounced through clenched teeth as he is registering at a hotel, pipe in mouth, hands full of luggage). Snatches of conversations, in French, English, and what have you, drift in and out—all meaningless except to the persons absorbed in their own pleasures and pastimes. The film is full of minutely accurate comments about human foibles, annoying habits, and failure to communicate. A loudspeaker at a railroad station erupts with totally unintelligible announcements, and a herd of tourists, like frightened chickens, starts running from platform to platform without having the least idea what the announcer said. Tati's genre is not a comedy of destruction, as most slapstick, but a comedy of observation and recognition.

He is a devastatingly accurate observer, having started out as an imitator in French music halls. Born Jacques Tatischeff, of Russian émigré parents, in Le Pecq, Seine-et-Oise, France, on October 9, 1908, he was first interested in sports, especially rugby. He was good enough to play for a prominent French national team, but he became more popular among the players for his mimicry and imitations of other sports figures. Recognizing his true vocation, he went on the music hall circuit in the early 1930s.

At first Tati drifted into films in order to record some of his routines in shorts. After World War II, he had small roles in two feature films directed by Claude Autant-Lara, and these convinced him he should stay in the medium. He began making feature films in 1947—and, like Chaplin, took time to polish them with loving care, so that there are gaps of several years between them. He also works in French television.

F. CHASE TAYLOR

see COLONEL STOOPNAGLE

THEODORE The darkest side of humor was exploited by one of the strangest phenomena of the mid-1950s, a German immigrant who went simply by the name of Theodore. Weird even by the standards of Greenwich Village in New York City, where his cult flourished for a while, he specialized in the kind of savagely sardonic humor that Ambrose Bierce used to write. In fact, he used some of Bierce's offbeat stories on stage, adapted to his own ferocious, hostile delivery. He made his presentations, often done at mignight in dank cellars, seem like rituals of some sect—and, as a matter of fact, he advocated his own brand of salvation for mankind, quadrupedism (living on all fours).

Think you can take it? Well, brace yourself—here's Theodore:

May I remind you, in a voice cold with loathing, that this is a serious show. I see from your idiotic laughter that I am faced with the usual collection of epileptics, vegetarians, triplets, nail biters . . . you there, giggling person: better get sterilized, or we're headed for a moronic future. Science . . . what is science but an organized system of ignorance? What do we know about the beyond? Do we know what's behind the beyond? I'm afraid some of us don't even know what's beyond the behind. The best thing is not to be born at all—but who's as lucky as that? Look at me: in a few years, I have worked my way from comparative obscurity to utter oblivion. But I'll have you know that in these corduroy pants there beats a passionate heart. You say I'm mad? Yes, but this is a healthy sickness. Don't you realize that if it wasn't for my madness, I would have gone insane long ago?

DANNY THOMAS Danny Thomas is one of the comedians who has done it all; standup comedy in nightclubs, films, starring in and producing TV and radio series, and on and on. He is one of the

Danny Thomas

few comedians to survive on network television for a decade (from 1953 to 1964).

Thomas represents the conservative wing of comedy, being a devout Catholic who advocates "clean entertainment." Walter Winchell once called him a "preacher." The basis of this attitude can be traced back to 1940 when Thomas was virtually destitute; he prayed fervently to St. Jude, patron saint of those without hope. *Help me to find my place in life*, he prayed, *and I will build you a glorious shrine dedicated to the helpless, hopeless and poor*. His prayers were "answered" with uncanny speed as film and nightclub jobs began materializing. Thomas kept his word by building the $2 million St. Jude's children's hospital in Memphis, Tennessee.

This isn't to say that his comedy is antiseptic. Even a Lenny Bruce couldn't have come up with a line like, "I invented the hatpin. But the girls looked pretty silly walking around with holes in their heads, so I invented the hat."

Danny Thomas was born Amos Jacobs on January 6, 1949, in Deerfield, Michigan. Before his successful TV series, *Make Room for Daddy* (1953–64), later renamed the *Danny Thomas Show*, he worked his way up through the nightclub circuit and appeared with Marlene Dietrich's USO troupe on a tour of Europe. An acclaimed 1945 guest spot on radio's *Baby Snooks Show* was a milestone in his career, and was followed by appearances in several films, including *Call Me Mister* (1951) and *The Jazz Singer* (1953).

THE THREE STOOGES When the Three Stooges got into the movies, it was as if Mack Sennett had never left; or, rather, as if the nuthouse of slapstick got new tenants. For sheer uninhibited physi-

The Three Stooges (Moe, Larry, Curly)

cal comedy, using every time-honored trick known to burlesque, circus, and vaudeville, The Three Stooges were the zenith—or the nadir, depending on the viewer's attitude toward knockabout mayhem.

The driving force was Moe Howard (born 1905 in Brooklyn), who ran away from home at the age of nine and somehow made his way to the Midwest where he appeared on Mississippi riverboats. After World War I, he formed a blackface act with brother Samuel, nicknamed Shemp (born 1901 in Brooklyn), and they toured in vaudeville.

In 1923, the brothers joined Ted Healy in his act, and were so helpful that he made them his permanent assistants, and they got billed as Ted Healy and His Stooges. In 1928 they added a third stooge, Larry Fine (born in Philadelphia in 1911). He had started with Gus Edwards and worked in an act called Haney Sisters and Fine; he married one of the sisters. The expanded act appeared first in *Earl Carroll's Vanities* that year.

In 1930 the group was in the film *Soup to Nuts* at Fox, with a fourth stooge, Fred Sanborn. Three years later they made another film, this time at MGM, but without Sanborn and without Shemp— who wanted a separate career. Sanborn was not replaced, then or ever, but Shemp was—by a third Howard brother, Jerry, nicknamed Curly (born 1911 in Brooklyn). The film, *Dancing Lady* (1933), was followed by a dozen or so more, made in quick succession.

Finally, in 1934, Columbia put the trio into a short, *Woman Haters*, without Healy—whose price as a headliner was apparently too high for the struggling studio. The three of them alone went over so well that they stayed at Columbia for the next 24 years, producing nearly 200 two-reelers. The shorts always earned a profit even on original release, and when television revived them, they became spectacularly successful with the kids of another generation—so successful that The Three Stooges, semiretired, found themselves all of a sudden the objects of a worshipful cult.

They were coaxed to come back to films, this time full-length features, and they made another dozen or so in the 1960s—all panned or frostily ignored by the critics, but box office bonanzas.

The personnel changed from time to time. Jerry had a stroke in 1946 and was replaced by Shemp (who had appeared alone in a number of films; he was bartender in *The Bank Dick* with W. C. Fields in 1940). Jerry died in 1952.

Shemp died in 1955, and was replaced by veteran comedian Joe Besser. However, when Besser's wife became ill, he left the act in 1958, the year in which they stopped producing shorts. Thus, for the features and for the many personal appearances caused by TV exposure of the old shorts, Joe de Rita became the third member.

Larry Fine died on January 24, 1975. The final survivor and originator, Moe Howard, died on May 4 of the same year.

Moe will be best remembered for the flawlessly executed assaults and batteries upon his two cohorts—such as the two-handed skull bash, the "select-two-fingers" eye poke, and the traveling multiple face slap.

CAL TINNEY Calvin Lawrence Tinney shared two things with Will Rogers: a homespun sense of humor which more often than not took on the nation's political scene, and the home state of Oklahoma, where Cal was born on February 2, 1908. Where Rogers was the leisurely voice of rural America during

World War I and the 1920s, Cal Tinney took over the same duties during the late 1930s and World War II.

He would kid his long-drawled-out delivery: "I talk so slow so I can get home and catch my own broadcast." But with all his folksy ways, he was ready with a sharp barb when he felt it was deserved. When Westbrook Pegler, the mud-slinging columnist, attacked Charlie Chaplin viciously, Tinney remarked, "We all know that Pegler gets up on the wrong side of his bed every morning. But this morning he must have got up on the wrong side of the gutter."

Cal earned his spurs in journalism, starting as a lowly "legman," since he had not even finished high school, and working his way up to stints on the Paris edition of the *Herald Tribune* and a Shanghai English-language paper. On his return to Oklahoma, he was secretary to a local congressman, and started his own paper. The circulation was low, and he hit on the idea of advertising his paper on the local radio station, where he delivered his own commercials. His capsule comments on the day's news, delivered in a hometown accent, elicited an outpouring of mail that induced Cal to quit the newspaper business to concentrate on radio news commentary. He was on many local and later national radio programs from 1932 on, including *The March of Time* (1932), *Voice of America* (1933), and *Sizing Up the News* (1941–43).

FRANK TINNEY One of the best remembered headliners of vaudeville and Broadway revues, Frank Tinney started in blackface makeup, like so many comedy monologists of his day, but climbed to the top of vaudeville working for Hammerstein, Ziegfeld, and Carroll. He was equally popular in English music halls,

making lengthy visits overseas in 1913, 1919, and 1924. In 1920 he abandoned blackface, but it made little difference as he used no dialect. A master of timing and delivery, he could get big laughs out of shamelessly old chestnuts:

Why is an old maid like a tomater?
Because it is hard to mate 'er!

How about lending me a dollar for a week, old man?
Who's the weak old man you want it for?

The ingenuous approach endeared him to audiences, who could feel superior to him; he came near the top of the pay scale on Broadway, and his 1919 English appearnce, at $2,250 a week, was publicized as the highest salary paid to an American single act there up to that time. His first trip overseas, in 1913, was caused by a bit of a scandal back home; he was accused of beating up Imogene Wilson, a Ziegfeld chorus girl who he thought was two-timing him.

Frank Tinney was born in Philadelphia on March 29, 1878, and as a child was pushed into performing by his ambitious mother. After gaining experience around Philadelphia, he was taken by her to Texas, a territory often bypassed by traveling shows and hence starving for entertainment. In no time at all, he was the biggest name in the Southwest, and then one of Hammerstein's agents convinced him, after offering him five times his Texas pay rate, that he was ready for the big time. His credits in the theater included *Ziegfeld Follies of 1912*, *Tickle Me* (1920), *Music Box Revue* (1923), and *Earl Carroll Vanities* (1926).

Tinney died in Northport, New York, on November 28, 1940.

THELMA TODD The one-time Miss Massachusetts, Thelma Todd was that rarity, a beautiful girl with a natural flair for comedy. Her timing and her rapport with comedians was so good that all the big names wanted her as their leading lady—and her film credits read like a list of filmdom's most beloved laugh-getters.

She was leading lady in the films of Charley Chase, Joe E. Brown, Laurel and Hardy, Buster Keaton, Jimmy Durante, Wheeler and Woolsey, The Marx Brothers, Harry Langdon, and Ed Wynn; and she costarred with Louise Fazenda, ZaSu Pitts, and Patsy Kelly—all in a brief span of seven years.

Born July 29, 1905, in Lawrence, Massachusetts, she wanted to become a teacher, and entered the Miss Massachusetts contest with her teaching certificate earned. However, her winning the pageant in 1926 brought with it the offer of a Paramount contract. She was given small roles in *God Gave Me 20¢* and *Fascinating Youth*, purely because of her looks, but a bigger role with Gary Cooper in *Neveda* (1927) showed that she was a quick study and a good mime. When, that same year, she made a hit in *Rubber Heels*, with Ed Wynn, her comedy future was assured. She played in Harry Langdon two-reelers for Hal Roach, and in films of Charley Chase and Laurel and Hardy on the same lot. During the sound period, she did shorts with ZaSu Pitts and later with Patsy Kelly as partners. She also appeared with the Marx Brothers in *Monkey Business* and *Horsefeathers* (both in 1931).

Thelma Todd married Pasquale Di Cecco in 1932 and divorced him in 1934. She died on December 16, 1935.

LILY TOMLIN Lily Tomlin is best remembered for her refusal to accept half a million dollars to play Ernestine in a commercial.

Ernestine is a nasal, frustrated, cantankerous, and slyly libidinous telephone operator, who takes perverse pleasure in calling up her victims ("One ringy-dingy, two ringy-dingies") in behalf of the telephone company, using the most grating, insolent manners to reduce the poor souls to gibbering idiocy. "This is the Telephone Company," she'll begin in a menacing manner. "We're not subject to state, local, or federal regulations. We are omnipotent."

Or: "We handle 84 billion calls a year from everyone, including presidents and the Pope. We don't need the business of scum like you, who owes us $18.34 for your last month's bill."

The real telephone company, its corporate dignity undermined by Lily's insidious jibes, tried to get her to do the Ernestine character in commercials for Ma Bell, where her lines would be under their control. But despite the huge fee, Lily declined—or, rather, as Miss Tomlin told the press, Ernestine declined: the character was too strong and mean and tough to be subjected to commercialism.

Tomlin has other characters: Edith Ann, the obnoxious brat; Tess, the bagwoman who sees flying saucers; Lupe, the world's oldest beautician. But when she does Ernestine, it seems almost a demonic possession rather than a comic characterization. It won her a Grammy for the album *This Is a Recording*.

Lily Tomlin is Mary Jean Tomlin, born in 1939 in Detroit. After high school, she entered Wayne State University as a pre-med student, appearing in her spare time in Unstabled, a cabaret-type nightclub in Detroit, with characteristically weird routines, such as tapdancing in bare feet (by taping the taps on the bottom of her feet). She first auditioned for TV in 1966 and appeared on the *Garry Moore Show*, but nothing really

Lily Tomlin

happened to her career until her 1969 appearance on Rowan and Martin's *Laugh-In*. The minute Ernestine came to life there ("Is this the party to whom I am speaking?"), she was in for a three-year stay.

After that came various specials, and an appearance in one of the sleeper hit films of 1977, *The Late Show*—which, in turn, led to a one-woman show on Broadway.

Lily's humor holds a mirror to reality, probing and experimenting with the real world:

When you read a lot, you are well read. Now that most people see a lot of TV, can they be called well viewed?

When we talk to God, we're said to be praying. But when God talks to us, we're schizophrenic.

If love is the answer, could you rephrase the question?

Ever wonder why someone doesn't try softer?

Things will get a lot worse before they get worse.

PAUL TRIETSCH

see HOOSIER HOT SHOTS

RUDY TRIETSCH

see HOOSIER HOT SHOTS

SOPHIE TUCKER Sophie Tucker was known as "The Last of the Red Hot Mamas," and her songs and repartee, replete with good-natured sexuality, justified the nickname. Many old-timers remember her singing her trademark song, "Some of These Days," also the title of her autobiography. It was often said that inside her 194-pound body beat the heart of a million-and-one Jewish mothers.

Her singing debut came in her family's Hartford restaurant. Between hours of scrubbing dishes, she would emerge from the kitchen and elicit penny and nickel contributions by singing very sentimental tunes. "Between me and the onions there wasn't a dry eye in the house," she quipped.

After coming of age, Tucker ventured forth from the family restaurant into the real world of vaudeville, where she rose steadily in the ranks. In 1932 the Loew's organization, hurting from a series of poor films and in danger of losing patrons, lured her to their theaters with an offer of $7,500 a week, three times her then current price.

She belonged to the old school of entertainers that included Eddie Cantor, George Jessel, and Al Jolson, known for ignoring finesse and subtlety in favor of bowling over the audience with energy and movement, spiced with sugary sentimentality and unspectacular but fun comedy.

The basic unit of a Sophie Tucker performance was sex—that was what the people came for, and that was what she gave them, openly, honestly, and with unabashed laughter rather than self-conscious snickering.

She was born Sophia Abuza somewhere in Poland, as her family was making their escape from a Russian pogrom, on January 13, 1884. Her father was Jewish, named Kalish, but he stole the passport of a dead Italian soldier, and that's how they were able to make it to America.

In 1900 Sophie sneaked off with a neighbor, Louis Tuck, and they were married. But married life did not come up to her expectations; soon she was on her own, only the stage name "Tucker" remaining to remind her of the escapade.

Her first New York appearance was a

blackface act at the 116th Street Music Hall; she also clicked at Tony Pastor's, a far more prestigious place downtown. Trying out for the *Ziegfeld Follies* in Atlantic City, she was so good that the star of the show, Nora Bayes, felt threatened and had Sophie's numbers trimmed down to just one song. After that, she never tried the *Follies* again, but worked the Keith circuit, hitting the Palace in 1914. Her theatrical credits included *Shubert Gaieties of 1919* and *Earl Carroll's Vanities of 1924*.

During the jazz age, she formed her own combo, which appeared with her from 1917 to 1921, becoming the first star to be backed by jazz on stage. "A tall, thin kid, in horn-rimmed spectacles, solemn as an owl" came to audition for the piano spot in the combo. His name was Ted Shapiro. Sophie told him, "If you're good enough I'll give you a contract."

Forty years later, he was still her accompanist—and still waiting for his contract. He played the piano for her at the Latin Quarter in New York City in October 1965, her last performance. On February 9, 1966, Shapiro learned he would never get his contract, after all.

BEN TURPIN No, Ben Turpin was not born crosseyed. His eyeballs slipped permanently out of alignment when he was holding them offcenter for the role of Happy Hooligan. No, Turpin didn't see double. But those cockeyed eyes were a supreme delight to early filmgoers.

Ben Turpin

317

Born in New Orleans in 1873, Turpin started acting in film comedy in 1907, which makes him one of the very first American motion picture comedians. He quit the world of film to seek his fortune as a clown with a traveling circus, but returned to work in short subjects with the Keystone company.

It didn't take Mack Sennett long to appreciate the potential of Turpin's ludicrous appearance. There were, of course, his improbably askew eyes. There was his short, agile frame, well suited for slapstick and pratfalls. There was his fantastically eloquent Adam's apple, which more than compensated for the absence of sound; any vehement emotion felt by Turpin was punctuated by the jutting out of his Adam's apple. It served him the way brandishing his fists or inflating his chest served a less ridiculous gent. There was his comically high forehead. In fact, his appearance was simply funny. The man was a born clown.

Turpin was reputedly the kind of fellow who would have been chased by men with butterfly nets if other men hadn't been busy chasing him with movie contracts. He pinched pennies to a degree that makes avarice look generous, and shunned filmdom's usual luxurious travel accommodations in favor of hopping a bus. But he had the last laugh in 1929: as dozens of his colleagues faced bankruptcy and poverty, Turpin, who had invested in apartment houses and real estate, became one of the richest people in Hollywood.

His films include *Uncle Tom Without the Cabin* and *The Shriek of Araby*, his hilarious parody of Valentino, the screen's greatest lover. Turpin was an early master of the infant art of film parody, essaying such other subjects as William S. Hart, von Stroheim, and Douglas Fairbanks. This memorable character of primitive yet timeless film comedy was laid to rest in 1940.

TWO BLACK CROWS

see MORAN and MACK

HUBERT UPDYKE

see JIM BACKUS

PETER USTINOV Versatile Peter Ustinov is only a part-time comedian. He is often diverted by his other occupations: writing, acting, directing, producing, cartooning, and mimicking everything from pingpong balls to a singing quartet backed by a full orchestra (the latter being immortalized on a record album).

He was born on April 16, 1921, in London, dropped out of school at age sixteen, and became a professional actor. His multifaceted career has won him Oscars, Tony, Emmys, and Grammys, and his gigantic physique has not proven a stumbling block in winning every award in sight. "The only time I lose weight," Ustinov says, "is when I cook for myself and I keep thinking, *Oh well, I'll wait for the next meal*."

His satirical wit has been said to rival that of George Bernard Shaw. He is especially witty on the subject of women: "In America, ambitious women are finding it so easy to dominate men, they no longer bother to be feminine about it. In France, women are still careful to force the men they control to dominate them."

Ustinov made history in England by doing unscripted radio broadcasts, under the title *In All Directions*. There were no jokes per se; instead, Ustinov reeled off funny observations of human nature and its glorious follies. By this time he was well on his way to becoming one of the finest satirist-raconteurs on either side of the Atlantic.

He has acted in dozens of films in England and the United States, including

Spartacus (1960), for which he won an Oscar, *Romanoff and Juliet* (1961), for which he was also director and writer, and *Topkapi* (1964), a comedy about a gang of crooks out to steal a priceless gem.

Peter Ustinov

V

DICK VAN DYKE Since Dick Van Dyke exploded onto the TV scene in the early sixties, everyone to come in contact with him agrees that he's one of the nicest guys in show business. He apparently lacks the standard feature of stardom that is thrown in at no extra cost—the exaggeratedly inflated ego.

Born on December 13, 1925, in West Plains, Missouri, he grew up on a steady diet of Stan Laurel (years later delivering the eulogy at his funeral), and got his first experience touring with a comic pantomime act called The Merry Mutes. For over a decade he kept trying to break into show business, and was so poor that in order to afford a proper wedding ring and honeymoon, he and his fiancée had to be wed on the *Bride and Groom* radio show.

Van Dyke finally got his break in 1960 when the stage musical *Bye Bye Birdie* (and later the film version) made him a name performer. The next year he had his own hit series on CBS-TV, the *Dick Van Dyke Show*. The show was enhanced by an allstar supporting cast that included Mary Tyler Moore, Morey Amsterdam, and Rose Marie, with occasional appearances by one of America's funniest comic minds, Carl Reiner, who created the show and wrote some of its finest scripts. The show's style, like Van Dyke's per-

onal style as a comedian, was emphati-
cally visual, at times in the slapstick
tradition of early comedy. (This did not
prevent it from being credible and realistic for a sitcom.) Many highlights came
from sight gags and from the excellence
of the cast. Van Dyke comments, "Some
of our funniest shows came from our
worst scripts."

Dick Van Dyke played starring roles in
a number of films, including *Bye Bye
Birdie* (1963), *Mary Poppins* (1964), *Divorce American Style* (1967), *The Comic*
(1970) and *Cold Turkey* (1971).

VAN and SCHENCK Two Brooklynites, Gus Van (1887–1968) and Joe
Schenck (1892–1930), formed what was
generally conceded to be the best two-
man singing team in vaudeville in the
1910s. They presented novelty songs,
many of them written by Van; comic
patter and skits; and a little dancing and
soft shoe. Van often played the piano,
and sang dialect comedy songs.

Although many individuals and teams
have claimed to have the most frequent
appearances at the Palace, vaudeville's
mecca, Van and Schenck must be among
the top contenders, having made it as
often as three or four times a year. They
also played the Chicago Theater in Chicago and Loew's State in New York, and
they were a smash hit in England.

When Schenck died in 1930, Van con-
tinued appearing alone, and in the film
Atlantic City (1944), where a Van and
Schenck routine is presented, he had
Charles Marsh substitute for Schenck.

*Van (right) and Schenck
(with Bert Williams)*

Dick Van Dyke

JIMMY WALKER Jimmy Walker is widely known as the biggest laugh-maker on the CBS comedy *Good Times*, a top ten smash. "J.J."'s pantomime, the deadpan reactions of a comically strange face situated atop a six-foot-tall toothpick frame, and his merry cry of "DYN-O-MITE!" combine for a ratings dynamo.

Jimmy Walker became a popular nightclub comic after nearly seven years of trying. His ghetto-oriented humor (he was raised in one, the South Bronx's Melrose Project) extends to such subjects as politics, riots, schools, venereal disease, TV's pandering to black people, blacks recasting their race's singularities, and what he calls the "black bourgeois." "You know what I mean," Walker says, "the folks who move to Scarsdale so they can have a black picket fence and white jockey sittin' out in front of the house."

Although *Good Times* is an innocuous and carefree show, Walker's comedy originated with a black, combative message.

Don't ask him his age. Walker once told Earl Wilson that "even my mother [a registered nurse] doesn't know."

Here's Jimmy Walker on crime:

The worst thing about crime is that black people have been robbing black people, man. We rob *us*!

Which leads me to the area of nonviolent crime. Now, in violent crime, we're doing damn good. But in nonviolent crime—when was the last time you seen a black embezzler—or a black man getting busted for juggling the bankbooks?

Take your everyday black holdup guy. He ain't got the money to take a cab to work, he's gotta ride the bus, and they don't run so good at night. Then he's gotta wait in that dark

Jimmy Walker

alley, catching rheumatism, suffocating from the wife's stocking he's wearing over his head, and all that just to hit you over the head for a couple of dollars. I mean, what's the use of having a black brother on the Supreme Court if none of us can commit a crime classy enough to get it tried there?

OTTO WARD

see HOOSIER HOT SHOTS

CHARLEY WEAVER

see CLIFF ARQUETTE

DOODLES WEAVER

Did you hear about the owl that married a goat? They had a hoot-'n'-nanny!

Some of the world's oldest puns and quips were exhumed for another reprise by a city slicker (born in Los Angeles, 1914) turned professional hayseed. As a kid, Winstead S. Weaver was nicknamed "Doodles" by his mother, because his freckles and big ears made him look like a doodlebug to her.

These looks made him a natural for rustic rubes, and he capitalized on them in Andy Clyde and The Three Stooges shorts. He also appeared in several features—including *Li'l Abner* (1940), where he played Hannibal Hoops.

One of the pioneer television performers, he was on TV regularly since 1946. He is probably best remembered for his four-year stint with Spike Jones and His City Slickers, where he slaughtered the classic "The Man on the Flying Trapeze" and narrated that most infamous of all horse races, accompanied by Spike Jones' rendition of "William Tell Overture," in which the winner was a nag named Feedlebaum—announced in sepulchral tones over the track loudspeaker. It became something of a national fad, especially among GI's.

In 1951 Doodles got his own show on television, and later he hosted a kiddie program.

STRAIGHT MAN: Hey, Doodles, did you put the cat out?

DOODLES: I didn't even know he was on fire!

STRAIGHT MAN: Hey, Doodles, your hair's getting thin.

DOODLES: Well, who wants fat hair?

'Nuff said. Incidentally, he is the brother of Pat Weaver, ex-president of NBC.

WEBER and FIELDS Joe Weber and Lew Fields celebrated their fiftieth year together as a team in 1932. Thus they were in the business during the entire time in which old-fashioned comedy— i.e., slapstick knockabout, crude ethnic humor, simple puns and quips—was gradually evolving into modern humor— i.e., burlesque, parody, and satire. In fact, Weber and Fields, alert to new trends, helped to shape some of the new ideas—Fields, especially, produced shows and managed theaters, so he knew what pleased the patrons.

One of their innovations was to take a pool table routine, and instead of knocking each other about with cue sticks (every other act was doing this then), they used elements of farce and situation comedy, which up to then had been seen only in the legitimate theater, and served it to vaudeville audiences. Satirizing social customs through the medium of vaudeville, the partners became very popular.

They became prosperous enough to go into the producing and managing end of the business, continuing to present their act as part of the lavish revues they were staging in their own theater.

Their shows had nonsense names: *Cyranose de Bric-a-Brac* (1898), *Fiddle Dee Dee* (1900), *Hoity Toity* (1901), and on to *Twirly Whirly* (1902), *Whoop-Dee-Do* (1903), and whatnot.

Morris Weber (later known as Joe Weber) was born in New York City on August 11, 1867; Moses Schanfield (later known as Lew Fields) was born on January 1, 1867, in the same neighborhood. They were both sons of Jewish immigrants, and teamed up at the age of nine in minstrel shows around New York. In their teens they changed into a knockabout "Dutch" act—meaning they mangled their English, using an exaggerated German accent. In 1895 they acquired Broadway Music Hall and operated it under the name Weber and Fields Theater until 1904. Then they separated, but were reunited for two shows in 1912, and also for a silent movie and a short with Fatty Arbuckle. They made a series of recordings—humorous dialogues on etiquette, baseball, and so on—under still another pseudonym, Mike and Meyer.

In 1918, Weber retired. Fields, however, opened his own theater and ran it until 1930. The ex-partners made a few radio appearances and personal tours together in the 1930s. Fields died on July 20, 1941; Weber followed on May 10, 1942.

Here's a typical Weber and Field routine:

WEBER: Do you have any money?

FIELDS: No.

WEBER: Well, all I have is a nickel—just enough for one beer.

FIELDS: Why don't you have one, then, don't want a drink just now.

Weber (right) and Fields

WEBER: Oh, good. But it wouldn't look good if we both went in and I ordered a beer without offering one to you. Tell you what we do. We'll go into this bar, I'll ask you if you want a beer, and you'll say, "I don't care for any."

FIELDS: Okay, I'll do that

(*Door to saloon opens and closes. Pause. Sounds of altercation. The door opens again and they come out.*)

WEBER: Oh, you idiot! Now see what you've done!

FIELDS: Why, I done just what you told me. When you asked me if I wanted a beer . . .

WEBER: . . . you said, "I don't care if I do." And the bartender gave you the beer, and I had to pay my last nickel!

Talk about inflation—read it and weep.

MAE WEST When the word "sex" was used in public only as the equivalent of "gender," she wrote a play and called it *Sex* (1926), and the word became fraught with a more libidinous meaning. When the subject was only snickered at in burlesque, she brought it on the legitimate stage and kidded the pants off it, so the audience could enjoy open laughter at innuendoes, rather than hiding a secret smirk. Mae West almost single handedly broke the fetters of Victorian morality with which legitimate theater was shackled; in films, she got away with blue murder at a time when censors decreed length of skirts, depth of décolletage, and latitude of language in minutest strictures.

She did it by eschewing blatant sexiness: it is a rare film in which her legs are seen above the knees. But she wrote lines for herself that are unique in suggesting everything but leaving nothing for the censor to latch onto. Until she came along, it was practically impossible for a woman to ridicule sex in any medium of expression; Mae West proved it could be done without lewdness and without debasing herself. There were many women before her who have done things to advance the cause of female liberation, but none who was so far ahead of her time, exposed such a raw nerve, or used such finesse and sophistication to score a resounding victory.

Her dialogue bristled with hidden revelations and intimations: her "Come up and see me some time" was an invitation so unmistakable and yet so untouchable that it became a legend.

Here's one of many suggestive bits that sneaked by the censor:

MAN: (*any of dozens of costars*): Have you ever had your virtue questioned?

MAE WEST: I've never even heard it mentioned.

MAN: Have you ever met a man who could make you happy?

MAE WEST: Sure. Lots of times.

MAN: You haven't got a streak of decency in you.

MAE WEST: I don't show my good points to strangers.

MAN: Do you mind if I get personal?

MAE WEST: Yes, but I don't mind if you get familiar.

MAN: If only I could trust you.

MAE WEST: Hundreds have.

MAN: How did you get that jewel?

MAE WEST: From a patron of the arts

MAN: Weren't you nervous getting such a precious jewel?

MAE WEST: I was calm, and collected.

MAN: My goodness, it certainly is a lovely stone.

MAE WEST: Goodness had nothing to do with it.

Mae West was born August 17, 1893, in Brooklyn. Her mother liked vaudeville and would take her to matinees; by five, Mae was doing imitations, and at the age of seven, she did a song and dance number on the stage of the Royal Theater in downtown Brooklyn. Then she tried child parts in stock companies playing around New York. Her first break in Manhattan came in when she had just turned eighteen, and was already married to actor Frank Wallace. She played in *A la Broadway*, a cabaret at a theater-restaurant; after that, she appeared in many musical shows, vaudeville, and burlesque, in and out of town.

By then, she began to discover that songs and routines written for conventional performers did not fit her style, and she started writing her own material. In addition to *Sex*, she wrote several plays,

Mae West (with Paul Cavanagh and Ivan Lebedeff)

all produced on Broadway, including *The Drag* (one of the earliest dramas featuring homosexuality, 1927), *The Wicked Age* (1927), *Diamond Lil* (1928, probably her best), and *Pleasure Man* (1928). The year after that, she wrote her first book, a novel titled *Babe Gordon*; in 1931, under the title *The Constant Sinner*, it was also presented on Broadway.

During the 1930s, she went to Hollywood and produced a series of films for Paramount, all of which she wrote herself; they were very successful at the box office, particularly because religious zealots and self-appointed guardians of public morals created an uproar, witlessly contributing to her fame. She appeared on radio, and again stirred up a controversy. Her best remembered film is probably, and undeservedly, *My Little Chickadee* (1940), in which she was teamed up with a similarly iconoclastic figure, W. C. Fields. Unfortunately, the film became a contest between two strong performers trying to hog all the good lines, so that neither is funny alone, and they are not funny together.

Mae West continued her career into her eighties, recording suggestive songs (like "A Guy What Takes His Time"), appearing in nightclubs with an act featuring musclemen offering biceps for her appraisal, and doing movies right up to *Sextette*, filmed in 1977. Nothing so great. But back in the 1920s, when having fun with sex was a clandestine male pursuit exclusively, she pioneered in so many ways that women's libbers are indebted to her.

WHEELER and WOOLSEY When two vaudeville veterans meet and execute a slapping routine, it's not exactly a show biz breakthrough; but when Bert Wheeler (1895–1968) and Robert Woolsey

(1889–1938) did it in the Broadway production *Rio Rita* in 1928, it went over so big that it established them as a team. They were asked to repeat it in the film version made at RKO, and stayed together, mostly in films, until Woolsey died.

Albert Jerome Wheeler, of Paterson, New Jersey, started out in Gus Edwards' "School Days" act with George Jessel and other celebrated classmates. At eighteen he married a showgirl, and for eleven years they toured vaudeville together as Bert and Betty Wheeler. In the 1924 *Ziegfeld Follies*, he appeared solo for the first time; for the next few seasons, as well as on radio, he sometimes teamed up with Hank Ladd.

Robert Woolsey got his start in a traveling Gilbert and Sullivan troupe, and came to Broadway for the first time in 1919. He was the star comic in *The Right Girl* (1921) and second banana in *Poppy* (1923), with W. C. Fields. He joined Ziegfeld for the 1926 and 1927 editions of the *Follies*, and then came the fateful *Rio Rita* where Ziegfeld assigned him to work with Wheeler.

After Woolsey's death, Wheeler worked in two more films (*Cowboy Quarterback*, 1939, and *Las Vegas Nights*, 1941), several Broadway productions, including *Laugh Time* and *Harvey* (where he replaced Frank Fay), a TV series (*Brave Eagle*, 1955), and nightclubs and Las Vegas.

In their routines together, Wheeler and Woolsey favored nutty repartees of the type that Abbott and Costello popularized for the next generation. In fact, the latter's "Who's on First" bit had a clear predecessor in Wheeler and Woolsey's map-reading routine:

WHEELER: This is a town of Which where General Diddy died.
WOOLSEY: Diddy?
WHEELER: Yes, he did.

Wheeler (right) and Woolsey

A few more samples:

WHEELER: Do you have any wild duck?
WOOLSEY: No, but if you like we'll bring a tame one and aggravate him for you.
WHEELER: I can't eat this duck you served me. Call the manager.
WOOLSEY: It's no use, he won't eat it, either.
WHEELER: You know, I'm not as big a fool as I used to be.
WOOLSEY: Oh? Did you diet?

WHEELER: This girl says she studied music in Paris for four years but is not a virtuoso.
WOOLSEY: I would think not, after four years in Paris!
WHEELER: She looks like a loose woman to me.
WOOLSEY: Don't worry, she'll be tight before the evening is over.

COP: You broke the law!
WOOLSEY: Well, couldn't you get another one?
COP: I'm giving you a ticket.
WOOLSEY: Can you make it in one of the front rows? My eyes aren't too good.
WOOLSEY: Officer, while we're here, wouldn't you like to buy some insurance from us? You know, people are dying this year who have never died before.

THE WIERE BROTHERS The three brothers Wiere sang, danced, did acrobatics, played instruments, and clowned around. One of their favorites was a routine in which they passed their hats to each other in ways that Brooks Atkinson called "fast, expert, vastly amusing." They were neither as gag-happy as The Marx Brothers nor as wildly slapsticky as The Ritz Brothers: they relied on their skill at sleight-of-hand and nonsense jokes in a smooth, polished, versatile performance.

They came from a European show business family of long lineage: their grandmother was with the Prussian State Opera, their grandfather was an acrobat, their father a comedian, and they also had a singing and dancing sister. They were born wherever engagements took their parents: Harry was born in 1908 in Berlin, Herbert in 1909 in Vienna, and Sylvester in 1910 in Prague.

They formed their act in 1922 in Dresden when their father fell ill. A U.S. tour in 1935 brought them to the French Casino in Chicago where they were such a sensation that they decided to settle permanently in the United States in 1937, especially since comedians found it increasingly difficult to work under the cloud of Nazism in Europe.

In 1938 they opened in New York in *Vaudeville Marches On* at the Majestic Theater, and later appeared at the Radio City Music Hall. Their best routines were filmed for several Hollywood musicals in the 1940s. In the fifties they toured with several shows, including *Roberta* and *Rosalinda*. The latter, repeated on TV's *Producer's Showcase*, led to guest shots on other TV variety programs, and in 1962 they got their own 13-week series, *Oh, Those Bells*. Later, they were regulars on the *Merv Griffin Show* and appeared on *Laugh-In* with Rowan and Martin.

Sylvester died in 1970.

GENE WILDER Gene Wilder is an inspired film comedian whose raw creative powers are just beginning to flourish.

He was born in Milwaukee on June 11, 1936; his father was a chocolate importer. At the University of Iowa he earned his B.A. in theater. Wilder moved to New York to attempt a career as an actor, and his first role was in an off-Broadway production, *Roots*. Moving up to Broadway, he played in *The Complaisant Lover*, and in *One Few Over the Cuck-*

Gene Wilder

oo's Nest, for which the New York Drama Critics nominated him as the season's Best Supporting Actor.

His next stage role was as the minister in *Mother Courage*, starring Anne Bancroft. Of the part Wilder remembers, "I was badly miscast, I was all wrong." But Anne Bancroft was going with Mel Brooks, who invited Wilder to play a part in his upcoming film, *Springtime for Hitler*, and one of history's most inspired comedy teams was born. In three years the film, renamed *The Producers* (1968), was released, with Wilder masterfully playing an infantile, timid accountant who carries around a baby blanket to give him a sense of security.

Before and since *The Producers*, Wilder has been a brilliant character actor. His first film role was as the bewildered undertaker in *Bonnie and Clyde* (1967), and he managed to steal a scene from Warren Beatty. In *Quackser Fortune Has a Cousin in the Bronx*, Wilder played a horse manure dealer whose livelihood is endangered when automobiles begin replacing horse-drawn wagons. In *Start the Revolution Without Me*, he plays eighteenth-century twins. Yes, both of them; one is a Corsican brother, one a peasant. In *Everything You Always Wanted to Know About Sex (But Were Afraid to Ask)*, he appeared as a doctor whose sexual preference is sheep. In *Young Frankenstein*, whose script was a Brooks–Wilder collaboration, he starred as the great grandson of the original mad Dr. Frankenstein. Like father, like great-grandson, and that's where the fun begins.

Wilder admitted, regarding Mel Brooks, that "I'm his protégé, his child, and in certain ways, I'm his monster." But after three films with Brooks, he resolved, "I want to do my own comedy . . . I want pee-in-the-pants comedy, but with something more troubling, more romantic." Being, by this time, a top star, Wilder had no difficulty converting wish to reality. The result was *The Adventures of Sherlock Holmes' Smarter Brother*, written and directed by Wilder, who starred in the title role as Holmes' passionately jealous brother, Sigerson. The potent combination of Wilder, Marty Feldman, Dom DeLuise, Leo McKern, and the rest provided some classic bits of comedy.

Although strongly influenced by Brooks, Wilder, unlike his mentor, adeptly slows down the compulsive laugh-making machinery long enough to inject subtlety and pathos into his work. Personally, he projects a note of sadness, of defenselessness, that really touches an audience.

BERT WILLIAMS "It is no disgrace to be a Negro," Bert Williams once said, "but it is very inconvenient." And at the time this most legendary of all black entertainers was making history breaking into all-white vaudeville, it certainly was.

Egbert Austin Williams was born in Nassau, British West Indies, on November 12, 1874. He came to the United States as a child with his family, and worked at all manner of odd jobs around the theater, which was his consuming passion.

He started to do comedy routines with an older black comedian, George Walker; they remained partners until Walker's death in 1908. Bert used the standard characterization of the shiftless loafer, but with a fine difference: instead of exaggerating he underplayed, used no gestures that traveled more than a few inches, and injected droll pantomime and dry wit. This set him far apart from the usual eye-rolling, spasmodically-shaking stage Negro and he quickly rose to the top rank of black vaudeville.

He became possibly the first black comedian to be preserved for posterity on early Victor recordings in 1901; his songs, again, were different, and instead of dialect minstrel stuff he featured wry social comment: "I'm in the Right Church but the Wrong Pew," and "Come After Breakfast, Bring Along Your Lunch, and Leave Before Suppertime."

One of Bert's 1914 routines, "The Darktown Poker Club," was revived in the 1940s by band-leader-turned-comedy-singer Phil Harris.

Some of Bert's comedy was dangerously close to tears, as is all great comedy. Thus, his classic song "Nobody" is really a depressed Bert trying to cheer himself up by a show of bravado, which fools no one.

Williams' talent was such that he was finally able to bridge the yawning abyss between black and white vaudeville circuits. He became the first, and for a long time the only, black who could be booked through the white circuits (all other black comedy was supplied by whites in blackface). In 1910 he appeared in the *Ziegfeld Follies*; Ziegfeld had to brave the wrath of the industry and deal with a threatened strike by other performers to accomplish this. Williams played a Pullman porter trying to put Leon Errol into a berth—Errol being, naturally, inebriated. The sketch had four prepared lines, all the rest being strictly ad lib; it is a tribute to the professionalism of Williams and Errol that they were able to convulse audiences for more than 20 minutes with ad libbing. Following this triumph, Williams appeared in the *Ziegfeld Follies* of 1911, 1912, 1913, 1914, and on and on.

Williams died suddenly on March 4, 1922.

Here's some of his material:

Where I'm living now is a nice place, but you have to go along a road between two graveyards to get to it. The other night I was coming home rather late, and as I came to the graveyards I happened to notice a transparent looking gentleman sitting on one of the headstones. He started to get up as he saw me coming. I started to run. When I was just about ready to drop, I stopped and sat down, hoping that I had left him far behind. Imagine my shock when I saw him sitting down next to me, and saying, "That was a nice run, the best running I ever saw." I said to him, "I'm glad you liked it. As soon as I get my breath, you'll see some more."

NAT M. WILLS Between about 1890 and World War I, the lovable hobo was a standard character in vaudeville, and many headliners such as Paul Barnes, Lew Bloom, Charles R. Sweet, and W. C. Fields did their act in tramp costume. Nat M. Wills was one of the best of them; his was a happy, congenial tramp, somewhat like Freddie the Freeloader, Red Skelton's lone survivor of the tramp craze. Wills (real name, Edward McGregor) was born in Fredericksburg, Virginia, on July 11, 1873, the son of a minister. From youth he had a great desire to get into the theatrical world. Since he could not afford to buy a ticket, he figured the only way he could ever see a play was by being one of the kids selling candy inside, but those positions were all filled. Nothing daunted, he lay in wait for one of these "candy butchers" behind the old Comique Theater in Washington, beat him up until he was unfit to work, and just happened to offer his services to the management just as they realized their candy seller had not reported for duty. From then on, Wills kept asking at every opportunity to be allowed to do a turn, and got his chance at the Globe when a tramp character in the play *A Block Game* was felled by a beam. Wills substituted at a moment's notice, and liked the audience's reaction so much that he kept the characterization for the rest of his career—stoutly denying that he had anything to do with the falling beam.

At first he worked with a partner, Bony Dave Halpin—so named because he was unbelievably thin—in an act where Halpin was a policeman, and they finished with a dance in which Halpin's expert stepping was parodied by Wills in slap-shoes. Around 1900, Wills started appearing as a single. He was married three times, always to a vaudeville performer: the first was known as Madame Loretto; then May Harrison, who died in 1909; and, last, Nellie McTierney, who performed as La Belle Titcomb. He worked the Keith and Orpheum circuits, and played in the 1913 *Follies*. He was found dead of carbon monoxide poisoning in his garage on December 14, 1917.

Here are some alleged telegrams, 1916 vintage, which the tramp "found in a trash bin":

From a well-behind-the-lines war reporter:
SCANDAL IN PARIS—FRENCH OFFICER FOUND IN BED WITH GERMAN MEASLES.

From an explorer:
BUMPED INTO CLOTHESLINE IN THE DARK—EXPECT TO DISCOVER THE POLE SHORTLY.

From Allied troop commander to headquarters:
GERMAN TROOPS ISSUED LIMBURGER RATIONS. WE FIND THEIR TRENCHES UNAPPROACHABLE.

From foreign correspondent of a small paper:
SAW THE CZAR ATTENDING THE OPERA IN MOSCOW. THE CZARDINE WAS IN THE BOX WITH HIM.

Nat M. Wills was the originator of the "No News" routine, one of the most famous in all vaudeville, in which a master absent from the house for a few days reaches a servant on the telephone, and gets a report that there is "no news—except that you don't have to bring home any dog food—well, because the dog died—he was trying to save the baby from the fire—the one your wife started when she ran off with the chauffeur."

FLIP WILSON *Time* magazine called Flip Wilson "TV's first black superstar." His success saga is a show business classic—years of unapplauded, struggling and then, suddenly, a dizzying ascent to superstardom, leading to one of television's highest-rated variety shows, which stayed on for a couple of seasons.

Clerow Wilson was born in New Jersey on December 8, 1933. His father's occupations were carpentry and inebriation, while his mother abandoned her husband and 24 children (16 survived) during Clerow's seventh year. From then on he endured abject poverty in a long succession of foster homes.

While serving in the U.S. Air Force, as the story goes, he flipped out his company with comic routines, which explains the "Flip". Another version attributes the nickname to his flippant disposition. Wilson's reputation spread, and his superiors sent him on a tour to boost the spirits of military personnel throughout the Pacific. His most popular topic was "The Sex Habits of the Coconut Crab."

Despite this promising beginning, for the next decade Wilson failed to top $1,000 in annual earnings as a comedian. Then suddenly, in 1965, Flip Wilson was "in," and through his guest shots on

Flip Wilson

Johnny Carson's *Tonight Show* and Rowan and Martin's *Laugh-In*, his high-pitched voice became known and imitated.

In 1969 Wilson did an NBC special with Jonathan Winters, to universal acclaim, which resulted in his own variety program, the *Flip Wilson Show*.

Wilson believes that a comic must be, above all, "a good friend," and his own performance is always adapted to this end: "Often I throw in bad jokes just to establish a rapport with my audience. I build bad jokes into my act now and then just to let people know that I'm not perfect, because people don't relate to someone who is perfect. I think the audience must get to know you as a person and think how nice it is to be with a friend each week."

Commenting on the racial question that affects all black entertainers to some extent, Wilson said in 1969, "When people pay to see me, I try to make them laugh. Not deliver a sermon or become a spokesman for this or that. I guess I am involved in civil rights because I am a Negro. But if you are a comedian, your first obligation is to be funny. I'll confess that I tuck a little message here and there in my routines, but it's carefully placed so that it doesn't interfere with the audience's fun."

Most recently Wilson has been doing specials for CBS, recording for his own label, trying his hand at feature film producing, and playing benefit golf tournaments for which he has been honored with the American Cancer Society's Humanitarian of the Year Award. He is aware of his power and feels a responsibility to help the less fortunate. His single record, *Berries in Salinas*, deals with the plight of migrant farm workers.

The role of Reverend Leroy in *Uptown Saturday Night* marked his film debut.

His female impersonation, Geraldine, became the definitive comic gender transposition of the 1960s.

As a kid, I used to have a lemonade stand. The sign said, "All you can drink for a dime." So some kid would come up, plunk down the dime, drink a glass, and then say, "Refill it." I'd say, "That'll be another dime." "How come—your sign says . . ." "Well, you had a glass, didn't you?" "Yeah." "And that's all you can drink for a dime."

Later I got a job at a drive-in theater. I went around with a flashlight after the show, and told the folks who were still parked there the movie was over. I got $25 a week and all I could see.

JONATHAN WINTERS His people-portraits place Jonathan Winters among the most inventive of modern comedians. He is a familiar face to television viewers, and has appeard in such films as *It's A Mad, Mad, Mad, Mad World* (1963), *The Loved One* (1965), and *The Russians Are Coming, The Russians Are Coming* (1966).

Born in Dayton, Ohio, on November 11, 1925, Winters tried his hand at cartooning, disc jockeying, apricot picking, and antiaircraft gunning before gaining his reputation as a comedian at New York's Blue Angel nightclub.

His TV debut was a losing effort on *Arthur Godfrey's Talent Scouts*, but subsequent attempts hosted by Steve Allen, Garry Moore, and Jack Paar brought out his true genius. He has had his own show. In 1968 the *Jonathan Winters Show* arrived for two seasons on CBS. Another of his programs was *The Wacky World of Jonathan Winters*.

Winters usually shuns political humor and caustic comedy. "I always take the sting out of the monologue," he once said. This is not to say that his humor is devoid of strong social commentary. Al-

Jonathan Winters

of his popular characters, including Chester Honeyhugger and King Kwasi of Kwasiland, have a purpose. Even Maudie Frickert, the eighty-four-year-old grandma-swinger. "We shelve our old people," he says. "We tell them they've got to sit in chairs in Fort Lauderdale. People don't automatically stop being hip because they grow older."

Jonathan Winters' routines always included evocative sounds that he did himself with his mouth, never using sound effect instruments. They were part and parcel of his comedy.

When I was young I worked at a filling station. So, for instance, this lady would drive up (*sound of car pulling up*). Madam, would you move the car just a little bit forward? The reason I say it, one of your tires is on my foot. . . . Thank you. Would you please lower the window? (*sss-t*) Oh, electric, eh? How does that work? (*sss-t*) Ouch! Madam, would you lower that window just once more? (*sss-t*) Thank you. Oh, boy, those fingers will be blue in the morning! All right now, I'll open the hood, let's see now—oh, you say you have to push a release from the inside? (*whack!*) Oops, and I just had that tooth filled, too. Madam, would you mind just getting out of the car and standing over there? Only please don't smoke there, because some gas spilled there a while ago (*whoosh!*). Madam, will you come down off that tree and pay for your gas?

ROBERT WOOLSEY

see WHEELER and WOOLSEY

ED WYNN Ed Wynn was a true innovator among comedians. Just one of his many inventions was a pair of eyeglasses with small mechanical windshield wipers, a must for grapefruit eaters. Wynn is also credited with encouraging and ultimately convincing such talented pantomime performers as W. C. Fields and Will Rogers to add spoken comedy to their acts.

Isaiah Edwin (thus, Ed-Wynn) Leopold was born in Philadelphia on November 9, 1886; his father was a hat manufacturer, which may account for Wynn's comic use of hats as stage props. By age nineteen he was headlining at top vaudeville theaters for $450 a week.

In 1915 Wynn was costarring with W. C. Fields in the *Ziegfeld Follies*. But hostility developed between them when the bewildered Fields began hearing laughs at the wrong moments of his immortal pool table routine. Finally he got wise and looked under the pool table, where he found Wynn engaged in a hilarious bout of catching flies.

Barred by the Shuberts from stage appearances due to his participation in the 1919 actors' strike, Wynn tried writing plays. He turned out a succession of hit comedies, including *Ed Wynn's Carnival* (more than two years on Broadway), *The Perfect Fool* (his national nickname), and *The Grab Bag*.

As the letter-answering Texaco Fire Chief, Wynn was a favorite of radio listeners in the 1930s, and he became a television star in the next decade. But fate is fickle in show business; Wynn won the very first TV Emmy Award in 1949, and couldn't find work in 1950. With the encouragement of his son, actor Keenan Wynn, he made a comeback as a dramatic actor. Dramatic roles in such films as *The Great Man* (1957), *Marjorie Morningstar* (1958), and *The Diary of Ann Frank* (1959) reestablished Wynn as an acclaimed artist.

He fully savored his comeback before his death in 1966. In all that time Wynn never lost his preference for comedy: "Of the two, the greater art is by far comedy. For me, making people laugh is the greatest of achievements."

And here's how he made people laugh:

I went to the circus. A man in front of me said to the usher, "I'm so fat I bought two seats so I could be comfortable." The usher said, "I'd like to see that, they are on opposite sides of the aisle."

The rubber man was happy; he just was told his wife had a bouncing baby boy. She used to be a lion tamer—boy, what a puss she had! He told her, "I can feed a family of eight on twenty-five cents." She said, "How can you do that?" "I'll buy 25 cents worth of apples, feed it to a horse, the horse will follow me home and we'll eat the horse."

She told him, "I'm an old-fashioned girl who will cook for you, an old-fashioned girl who will sew for you, an old-fashioned girl who will clean the house for you." He said, "After three old-fashioned, I don't care how you look."

I have so many jokes like this, my son will eventually have to support me.

When they were getting married, the justice of the peace said, "Do you take this woman for your wife?" He said, "I do." And the justice said, "That's funny, I took her for your mother."

Ed Wynn

343

ALAN YOUNG A generation of TV addicts knows him only as straight man for talking horse *Mister Ed* in the feeble-minded series that started in 1961 but seemed to go on forever in reruns. This is too bad, for he is a talented, likable comedian whose specialty is the portrayal of a well-meaning bumbler.

Between 1944 and 1950, Young played in the highest-rated comedy shows on radio. When he went to television that year, his show was chosen the best variety show of 1950, and stayed on for three seasons. Then he tried a situation comedy that failed, and alternated with Ben Blue as guest star on the *Saturday Night Revue* in 1954. Then he had to bide his time until the horse rescued him.

He had roles in a number of Hollywood comedies, and created the definitive Androcles for George Bernard Shaw's comedy *Androcles and the Lion*, which was filmed in 1953.

Alan Young's first name is actually Angus, and he was born to Scotch parents in North Shields, Northumberland, England, on November 19, 1919. When he was four, his family moved to Vancouver, Canada. By the time he graduated from high school there, he had his own radio program, *Stag Party*, on the CBC network.

After discharge from the Canadian Navy, Young came to New York, where ABC gave him his own program in October 1944. In 1945 he was named the top funnyman in the Crossley ratings, and won a popularity poll in *Radio Daily*, a trade paper of the industry. In 1946 he switched to NBC. A year later they dropped his contract, but an appearance on Jimmy Durante's show on radio in

1948 renewed audience interest in him, and NBC gave him another try during the following season.

Alan Young has warmth and can create audience sympathy. His biggest problem seems to have been inferior material. It was reported in several interviews that he was among the friendliest stars, and writers thought dealing with him was a pleasure. Perhaps this lack of aggressiveness caused them to give him only their second-best efforts.

HENNY YOUNGMAN "I haven't spoken to my wife in three weeks—I didn't want to interrupt her. . . . Zsa Zsa Gabor's been married six times now, she's got rice marks on her face. . . . Wanna drive a friend nuts? Send him a telegram saying 'Ignore the first wire.' . . . She wasn't a Lana Turner—more of a stomach turner." The one-liners come as rapidly and plentifully as raindrops in a tempest whenever Henny Youngman is nigh. He is universally acclaimed as "King of the One-Liners," and woe to the heckler who tries to match wits with him.

Born in Liverpool, England, in 1906, Youngman grew up in Brooklyn taking violin lessons by edict of his mother. The violin was his entree to show business, "but I was such a lousy fiddler people laughed at me. So I became a comedian." Afraid of failure, he compressed as many laughs as possible into each minute on stage, and that became his style.

Youngman came to national attention in the 1930s as a regular comedian on Kate Smith's radio program. It wasn't then (and still isn't) his method to polish his routines endlessly or to delete jests that were less than gems. It is the endless onslaught of punchlines that gets the laughter snowballing. Although he most regularly uses jokes of ancient vintage

Henny Youngman

(he still never fails to say, "Take my wife—*please*!), Youngman also keeps up with the times. "The reason the postal authorities haven't issued a Nixon stamp," he explains, "is that everyone would spit on the wrong side."

The times also enjoy keeping up with Henny Youngman. When the New York Telephone Company hired him as one of the comedians for their "Dial-a-Joke" service in 1974, Youngman drew a record 300,000 calls daily.

One reason for his popularity is his regard for the audience's sensibilities. He doesn't push them to laugh. Youngman is a real professional who earns his laughs, maintaining a deadpan face while he goes from joke to joke. Like this:

Man asks another, "Have you seen a cop around here?"

"No."

"Good, then stick 'em up."

"Stick what up?"

"Don't confuse me, this is my first job."

The lady is in the shower. The doorbell rings.

"Who is it?"

"The blind man."

So she opens the door, and he says, "Okay, lady, now where do you want me to put these blinds?"

Z

ZACHERLEY In 1958, WABC-TV in New York presented a series of horror films. The host was something new in the interlocutor line: a creepy creature of the crypt who looked like death warmed over, ate spider soup, discoursed on his collection of human heads, and gave the latest news from Transylvania, lessons on how to wrap a mummy, and recipes for fried batwings.

The format caught on; soon there were Zacherley groupies and fan clubs; a rival station started a similar fad with a female hostess, Vampira; and for a while no horror film was properly introduced on TV unless the emcee rose out of a coffin or an open grave.

The cause of all this was a perfectly normal looking, mild-mannered announcer turned actor, John Zacherle, born in Philadelphia in 1919. After serving in World War II as an officer, he became a radio announcer, and by 1954 had a small part in a soap opera on television. Then the station (WCAU-TV) needed someone to announce their upcoming *Shock Theater* program; Zacherle, assigned to the job, thought the only way to make the creaky old horrors suitable for revival was to kid the pants off of them, and this approach was more successful than he had ever dreamed. He got an offer to repeat his macabre bit on the ABC network's anchor station in New York. Eventually, he recorded it: the LP sold a quarter-million copies.